LATVIAN DREAMS
Knitting From Weaving Charts

Joyce Williams

Schoolhouse
Press

Technical Editor, Lizbeth Upitis
Cover Design, Juli Martin
Color Photography, Alvis Upitis
Cornfields Color Photography, Meg Swansen
Black and White Photography, Meg Swansen
Illustrations, Joyce Williams

Published by:
Schoolhouse Press
6899 Cary Bluff
Pittsville, WI 54466
(715)884-2799

Library of Congress Control Number 00-131539

Williams, Joyce, 1935 –
    Latvian Dreams: Knitting From Weaving Charts
    ISBN 0-942018-19-2 (Hardbound)
    1. Knitting patterns 2. Knitting techniques 3. Knitting/Weaving charts I. Title

Printed in the United States by Signature Press Inc., Amherst Junction, WI

Table of Contents

Comments by Meg Swansen

Introduction—Author   1

Techniques   3

Digression   25

Techniques—Basic Patterns   26

Garments   33
    What A Difference A Gauge Makes   34
    Highland Jacket   40
        Highland Socks   46
    Tay's Sweater   48
    Bountiful Harvest   56
        Bountiful Harvest Socks and Gloves   59
    Circles   64
        Circles Socks and Gloves   68
    Cornfields   70
        Cornfield Socks   73
    Don's Vest   80
    Joyous Jacket   84
    Morocco   90
    Park High Pullover   96
        Park High Socks   99
    Snowflake Cardigan   104
        Snowflake Socks   109
    The Star   114

Design—E.P.S.   121

Charts   124

Final Digression—Acknowledgments   163

Bibliography   164

Comments by Meg Swansen

Joyce Williams and her husband Don live in a magical part of Wisconsin. Their farm is tucked away in a coulee (in the "driftless" or unglaciated section of the state) and includes the landmark sandstone cliff called Face Rock, which is in plain view from their living room window. Joyce draws both color and design inspiration from her surroundings ... not that she and Don spend that much time at home. They are tireless travelers and have visited every continent (including Antarctica) and most countries of the world. Her knowledge, skill, inventiveness, experiences and love of knitting are all visible through the garments in this book.

For the past decade or so Joyce Williams' inventive knitting brain has been turning out a steady stream of unique ideas, imaginative techniques and spectacular designs. For insiders, Joyce's low-key, unadvertised videos and booklets have disseminated her ideas to a relatively small group of knitters. But now, through the extraordinary book you hold in your hands, we all can share in the excitement. After you have caught your breath from gazing at the staggeringly beautiful garments, check out the details of, for instance, the built-in-mitered-facing-corners on her cardigans (pages 48, 90, 104 and 114), or the singular "Joyce's Heel" on her socks (page 28).

After several years of work by Joyce, this book was put together by a group of enthusiastic but amateur book-producers, with one "ringer": Alvis Upitis is the world class photographer responsible for the dazzling color shots. The rest of us: editor Lizbeth Upitis, graphic artist Juli Martin, proof reader Mary Anderson, original designer Katherine Misegades and publisher me, were all smitten by Joyce's talents and wanted to play a part in getting this book to the light of day. At times, the project had the feel of, "C'mon kids, let's put together a show in the garage!"

Well, here it is at last. Which sweater are you going to knit first?

Meg Swansen, Cary Bluff, July '00

Introduction—Or All About Me, The Author

At an early age I asked my mother to teach me how to knit. She told me because she was left handed and I was right handed she could not teach me. When I was seven, World War II was in progress and my grade school class in Sheboygan, Wisconsin learned to knit. We spent one half hour each day knitting on khaki squares which were later sewn together by Red Cross volunteers and made into blankets for the British Army. Why they went to the British rather than the American military I do not know, but we referred to our knitting time as "knittin for Brittin." I know some knitting for Britain took place before the United States became involved in the war, but at the time I started knitting the United States was at war

Upon learning how to knit in school, I announced to my mother that I could now knit and wanted to make a pair of mittens. She gave me a booklet on two needle mittens and told me to pick out which pair I wanted to knit. I chose a pair with a cable running down the back. My mother tried to encourage me to knit a plain pair rather than those with the cable, as she had never knit a cable. However, I was adamant about knitting that pair. (My personality has not changed much over the years.) With my mother reading the instructions to me, (after all, I was only seven) I knit my first pair of mittens, cable and all. I recall wearing them with great pride for several years.

Since that time I do not remember when I did not have a knitting project under way. Over the years there was not a pattern I would not tackle, but I was definitely a pattern follower and did not deviate from the design very much. Then in 1985 I bought the premier issue of *Knitter's* magazine. That was my introduction to Elizabeth Zimmermann and to a new knitting life for me.

Elizabeth's articles fascinated me and I followed up by ordering all three of the books she had written at that time. I started out by reading *Knitting Workshop*. On page 13 (the impact was so great the page number has been infused into my brain) the question is asked, "Which way is the stitch supposed to be on the needle?" Elizabeth explained "If the stitch is regarded as a loop, the right-hand side should be in front of the needle," etc. I immediately reached for my knitting and looked at it. For the first time in my life I was aware what a stitch was all about on a needle and mine had the left-hand side of the loop in front on the needle.

It was important that I finally understood what a stitch was all about. However, I feel I also learned the most important knitting lesson a person can learn— **look at your knitting**. You can then get an understanding of what is actually happening. Prior to this time I had been so busy reading and following patterns, I never really looked at my knitting. Of course, I was watching to see where the needle went into the loop, etc. But I was not really looking at what was happening as the stitches were formed, how the patterns were progressing, etc. As an example, when working cables, each time I came to the row where the cross over occurred and the pattern referred to a 3RC or 3LC, I would read the instructions to figure out whether the stitches on the cable needle were to go in front or behind my work. If I had been looking at my knitting, I would have been able to figure this out by seeing which way they were crossing!

WHY DID I TELL YOU ALL THIS?

My personal knitting background is the basis for the philosophy behind the instructional format in this book. I tell you what I did and why I did it. I hope this gives the "blind followers" a better understanding of their knitting and with this vision the ability to change something within a pattern if they are not totally enamored with it.

Introduction—Or All About Me, The Author

WHY LATVIAN WEAVINGS?

Some years ago I purchased the book, *A Joy Forever Latvian Weaving, Traditional and Modified Uses* by Jane A. Evans. I purchased the book, not because I had any idea of how to weave, but rather because looking at some of the charts in the book I felt they would make excellent knitted designs. I knit several of the designs from the book and thoroughly enjoyed doing so, as it was exciting to see what these weaving squares were producing in the knitting in my hands. The Latvian designs were calling me.

Meg Swansen's Knitting Camp time was approaching. I called Lizbeth Upitis and asked her if she would be so kind as to bring some of the Latvian books in her collection to Camp so I could see them. Lizbeth brought three books by Z. Ventaskrasts entitled *Izsuvumu, Adijumu un Audumu Raksti* (Sewn, Knitted and Woven Designs) which were published in the 1950s while Latvia was under the Soviet Union regime. I was enthralled with the charts in the books and Lizbeth allowed me to take the books home with me so I could copy some of the charts.

I sat down at the computer with my *Stitch Painter* program, my mouse in one hand and magnifying glass in the other, and started copying the charts. (The grid in the books is 25 stitches to 1 inch.) I was only going to copy those charts which were adaptable to knitting and which I would want to knit some day. Which is what I did. I actually would like to knit every single design in this book. I am seriously thinking of blindfolding myself, opening the book, pointing at a chart, and designing a garment using that chart. It would save time as I find it difficult to figure out which one I want to knit next.

Part way through my copying it became obvious that in my lifetime I would never be able to knit all the designs that I found so intriguing, and I felt strongly that they should be shared with others. I called Lizbeth and suggested she do a book with the charts. Fine friend that she is, she told me I should do the book. Lizbeth said that she had never looked at the charts as knitting designs since she is a weaver and she thus saw the designs as weaving patterns.

I followed up by showing Meg Swansen some of the charts to see if she found them as interesting as I did, and wondering if she thought other knitters would be interested in having access to them. Her response was very positive. In fact, it was so positive she said she would publish the book. But Meg also wanted to see some of my own designs and techniques included in the book. There went my days as a hobby knitter!

SO, WHAT IS THIS BOOK ALL ABOUT?

First, it is charts, even though they are at the end of the book. Every one of these charts I feel would be wonderful knitted up into something or other. The something or others are endless.

Second, techniques are covered. The techniques range from how to create your own design using Elizabeth Zimmermann's Percentage System©, to some techniques I have "unvented." "Unvention" is a word coined by Elizabeth Zimmermann. When she developed a technique, Elizabeth felt certain some knitter must have used the technique before, only unbeknownst to her. I feel the same. Thus the word "unvention" rather than invention. Technique titles are written in italics in the patterns with a referenced page number.

Last, but hopefully not least, are some of my designs using Latvian patterns. These are meant to be an inspiration to show knitters the results of using Latvian designs, although there are complete instructions for knitting the items.

WHAT! NO LATVIAN DESIGN BACKGROUND OR HISTORY?

The closest I have ever been to Latvia was to fly over it going from Moscow to Copenhagen. Fortunately it was a clear day and it appeared to be a beautiful country from the air. My small knowledge of Latvia comes from knowing Lizbeth Upitis and the information I have learned from her personally and from her book, *Latvian Mittens, Traditional Designs & Techniques*. I also gained some background information on Latvian textiles, etc. from Jane A. Evans in her book *A Joy Forever, Latvian Weaving*.

I have looked at the charts in this book with purely an artistic eye and not a scholarly one.

Techniques—Please Read This Section (or you will miss the fun)

There are numerous ways techniques such as casting on, increasing, decreasing, etc. may be performed. Only those I used on garments in this book are presented here. They were my preferred method for that garment at that time and the descriptions are how I interpret the technique. Please consider a technique used in a pattern a suggestion, but use one of your own choice if it differs from mine. We are knitting to please ourselves. Right?

Knit Stitch: The most important lesson I learned from Elizabeth Zimmermann is to look at and read my knitting, so let's start with an explanation of how I look at a stitch. A stitch is an open loop. To keep each stitch an open loop, with working yarn behind, place needle tip through **center** of loop **from the front**. This applies if you are right or left-handed and whether right leg or left leg of loop is over front of needle. The top of the loop of stitch knit into falls in back of the new stitch.

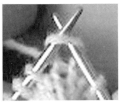 

Knitting into center of loop, right leg in front   *Knitting into center of loop, left leg in front*

When I teach children how to knit I tell them to pretend the tip of the needle is a horse. The horse runs through the hole in the fence (center of loop). You then wrap the rope around the horse's neck. Bring the horse back through the fence with the rope still around its neck. You then throw the fence away (after all, it did have a hole in it) and tighten up the rope. But, then the horse finds the next hole in the fence, runs through it, "etc., etc., etc!"

Purl Stitch: To keep stitch an open loop, with working yarn in front, place needle tip through **center** of open loop **from the back** whether right or left leg of loop is over front of needle. The working yarn is thrown away from your body over needle tip, then it is brought through the open loop and the open loop purled into is dropped from the needle. The top of the loop of stitch purled into falls in front of the new stitch.

Twisted or Crossed Legs—Right or Left Twists or Crosses? At times you intentionally wish to have one leg of a stitch cross the other. When I tried to determine which to call a right or left twisted or crossed

stitch, I realized it depends upon how you look at what happens in the crossing process. As an example; right leg of loop crosses in front of left leg. Since the right leg crosses over this is a right cross or twist, right? But, it crosses and points to the left. Are you sure you want to call it a right cross? But then again, you can take the loop off the needle, twist it clockwise so the right leg crosses the left, and put it back on needle. Clockwise is a right twist, right? Right or left cross—terminology knitters can debate for years to come!

If you wish the right leg to cross over the left leg, have the right leg of the loop over front of needle and with working yarn behind place tip of needle behind right leg from the right side (commonly called knitting into back of stitch) and proceed to finish knitting the stitch. The right leg of the stitch you knit into crosses over the left leg. Whatever direction twist you call it, it is seen in Austrian and Bavarian knitting.

If you want the left leg to cross over the right leg, have the left leg of the loop over front of needle and with working yarn behind insert tip of needle behind left leg from left side and proceed to finish knitting stitch. The left leg crosses over the right leg. Crosses in this direction (left or right?) are seen in Eastern European knitting.

You are in charge. Look at your knitting. Arrange and work into stitches from the appropriate side so legs cross or do not cross as you desire and call them what you please.

Right or Left Leg of Stitch Over Front of Needle: Many knitters who carry their yarn in their left hand (referred to as continental style knitting) wrap the yarn from back to front when they purl with the result that the left leg is forward. The stitch is not twisted if you knit into center of loop, which is what I did the majority of my knitting life. However, many knitters do not use as much yarn when throwing yarn from back to front while purling, so these purl stitches may be tighter. Some knitters find their purl tension looser than their knit tension when working stockinette stitch flat and throwing their yarn from front to back. A solution may be found by wrapping the yarn around the needle when purling from back to front. A knit stitch with a purl stitch to its left may be looser than the knit stitch to its right (as in ribbing or cables). This may be corrected if you wrap the last knit stitch and following purl stitch from back to front. Some knitters wrap only the first purl stitch from back to front to correct their problem.

Techniques

Knitting Stockinette Stitch Flat Without Turning Work: When I teach beginners how to knit (mostly children), I start them out immediately with stockinette stitch. However, not by learning to purl, but by knitting onto their right needle (KORN) and then knitting onto their left needle (KOLN). The reasons I have for doing this seem to me to be quite rational! Most non-knitters think of knitting as stockinette stitch and that is what they expect to achieve when they learn to knit. Have you ever noticed a disappointed look on a beginning knitter's face when learning to knit and the result is garter stitch? Often a first knit project (and sometimes only) is a long garter stitch scarf and the knitter dislikes garter stitch the rest of their life. I teach the knitter what they expect to knit: stockinette stitch. I later teach purling as a decorative, texture stitch.

I also see no reason why anyone would want to look at the inside of their knitting as they work. That is why I have students KORN and KOLN and they are always looking at the outside of their knitting. Knitting is a two-handed operation. Students that start out learning to knit onto both needles are adept with either hand as they progress with their knitting.

Why do I refer to it as KOLN rather than knitting back backwards as it is frequently referred to (even by myself)? I have students use 24 inch circular needles and have them start to knit using right needle tip. I figure by referring only to tips and not hands I am fooling them into not thinking about which hand they are using and they do not have any preconceived idea it is going to be clumsy. Then I have students knit with left tip. I feel if I told them to knit back backwards it would automatically trigger the idea more difficult as usually things are more difficult to do backwards. Probably no one is fooled by my vocabulary trickery, but I like to think they are.

Knitting Onto Left Needle (KOLN): 1. Insert tip of left needle into center of stitch on right needle going behind right needle. 2. Wrap working yarn from back to front to back around left needle. 3. Bring left needle tip and

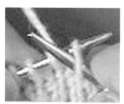

KOLN—Step 1

yarn wrap through stitch to front of work, and release stitch from right needle. Repeat steps 1 to 3.

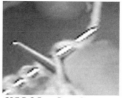
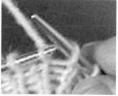

KOLN—Step 2 *KOLN—Step 3*

One Color Yarn Carry: There is a wide variety among knitters as to how and in which hand they carry their yarn. I carried my yarn in my right hand (British or American style) up to the time I was eighteen. Then a yarn shop owner suggested I switch and carry my yarn in my left hand (continental style) because she said left hand carriers had a more even tension. I switched, but my tension is not very even. I believe it is how an individual person knits that produces an even tension, and not which hand carries the yarn. I think speed is an individual thing as well and not a matter of where the yarn is carried.

The way yarn is held in either hand also varies greatly. In watching other knitters I have found only one other that carries their yarn in the left hand and wraps their yarn in the direction I do around the index finger. I have no idea when or how I came up with my wrap. It works very well for me as when I have a number of stitches to purl I have the yarn around my thumb. The way the yarn is around my index finger makes it easy to transfer the yarn between index finger and thumb.

Two Color Yarn Carry: Knitters have success with two color stranded knitting either carrying one color in each hand, or carrying both colors in the hand where they usually carry their yarn. With two color stranded knitting, the strands are not crossed as you knit and one color is maintained throughout the project as top carried color and the other as bottom carried color. When carrying a color in each hand, the yarn carried in right hand is the top carry and the left hand is the bottom carry. If you forget which color you have been carrying on top and which one on bottom, look at the **stranding** on the inside of your knitting not at the purl bumps at the base of the stitch. The top strand goes directly from the stitch where it was last used across to the stitch where it was again used. The bottom strand goes under the top strand,

Dark Yarn-top carry
Light Yarn-bottom carry

across and again under the top strand to where it was used again.

Techniques

Predominant Color: It is frequently reported that the yarn carried on the bottom is the predominant color. I (and many other knitters I know) am proof this is not true. My predominant color is that carried on the top. In a survey of knitters with their top carry their predominant color I found knitters that carry both yarns in right hand, both colors in left hand, and some that carry one color in each hand. Hence, another example why you cannot give absolute rules in knitting: there is too much variance in results due to knitting styles.

To determine which carry is predominant, knit a swatch of alternating colors; i.e., Row 1 Color A, Color B, Color A, Color B, etc. Row 2 Color B, Color A, Color B, Color A, etc. Alternate Rows 1 and 2 and knit for several inches with Color A on top and Color B on bottom. Then switch and have Color B on top and Color A on bottom and knit for several inches. Where do you carry your predominant color? With some knitters it may be even. As an interesting experiment, continue to swatch, but switch the carry every row. No, I am not going to tell you what results. You have to experiment for yourself.

ALPHABET & NUMBER CHART

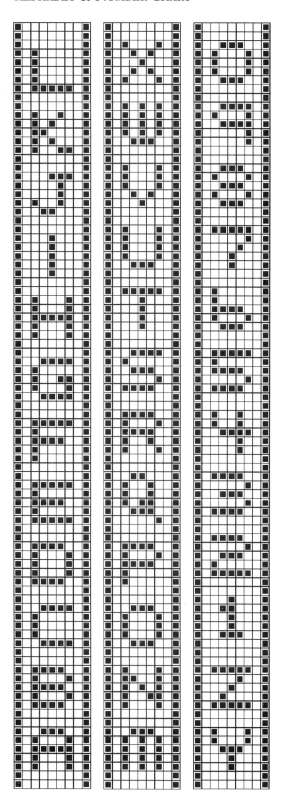

BIND-OFFS

I use a blunt yarn needle and work a sewn bind-off except for *Bind-Off: Three Needle*. A sewn bind-off, if not pulled too tightly, is very stretchable. I prefer the sewn bind-off as I have better control over tension and it may be adjusted after all stitches have been bound off before weaving in the ends.

For sewn bind-off, use a piece of working yarn approximately four times the length of what you plan to bind off. Thread a blunt yarn needle with yarn. Work from right to left. To maintain tension, **keep stitches on the flexible portion of the needle** until bind-off is complete.

Sewn I: I use this bind-off when I cast on with *Cast-On: Long Tail* (page 11) as their appearances are similar. I thought I used Elizabeth Zimmermann's sewn bind-off, but writing out these instructions I realize it is not the same. I have no idea where this came from, possibly one of my "unventions."

1. Bring blunt sewing needle (SN) tip through second stitch from right edge, under the flexible portion of the knitting needle (KN) from inside to outside of work. Pull SN and yarn through to outside leaving approximately a 6 inch tail on inside.

2. One stitch to the right (edge stitch), insert SN tip into stitch under the flexible portion of the KN from outside of work. Pull SN and yarn through to inside of work, being certain stitches on flexible portion of KN being bound off remain evenly spaced and not pulled in.

3. Two stitches to the left, bring SN and yarn through the stitch and under the flexible portion of the KN from inside to outside of work. Pull SN and yarn through to outside of work in same manner as on inside of work.

4. Insert blunt SN from outside into stitch one stitch to the right under the flexible portion of the KN, but above the yarn strand on inside of work. Pull SN and yarn through to inside of work as established.

Bind-Off: Sewn I Step 4

Repeat 3 and 4. When all stitches are bound off you may wish to adjust tension either before or after the KN is removed.

Sewn II: This bind-off is used when I have cast on using *Cast-On: My Method of Long Tail* (page 12) as their

Techniques

appearances are similar.

1. Bring threaded blunt sewing needle (SN) through right edge stitch and under flexible portion of knitting needle (KN) from inside to outside of work. Leave approximately a 6 inch tail on inside of work.

2. Two stitches to the left insert SN through stitch and under flexible portion of KN from outside of work. Pull SN and yarn through to inside being certain stitches on flexible portion of KN being bound off remain evenly spaced and not pulled in.

3. One stitch to the right, insert SN through stitch and under flexible portion of KN and **under yarn strand** from inside to outside of work. Pull SN and yarn through to outside of work as established.

Bind-Off: Sewn II Step 3.

Repeat 2 and 3. When all stitches are bound off, you may wish to adjust tension either before of after the KN is removed.

Latvian: When done properly, this bind-off is very stretchable and also decorative. Instructions are for working the bind-off with a double yarn to match the *Cast-On: Latvian* (page 13) also used in this book. (However, single strands may be used both for the cast-on and bind-off.) Use two strands of yarn, following length instructions above.

1. Bring tip of blunt sewing needle (SN) through right edge stitch and under flexible portion of knitting needle (KN) from inside to outside of work. Leave approximately a 6 inch tail on inside of work.

2. Two stitches to the left insert SN through stitch and under flexible portion of KN from outside of work. Pull SN and yarn through to inside of work being certain stitches on flexible portion of KN being bound off remain evenly spaced and not pulled in.

3. One stitch to the right, insert SN through stitch and under flexible portion of KN **and under yarn strand** from inside to outside. Pull SN and yarn through to outside of work as established.

Bind-Off: Latvian Step 3.

4. Two stitches to the left insert needle through stitch and under flexible portion of needle from outside of work. Pull needle and yarn through to inside of work as established.

5. One stitch to the right insert SN through stitch and

under flexible portion of KN **and above yarn strand** from inside to outside of work. Pull SN and yarn through to outside of work as established.

Repeat 2 through 5. When all stitches are bound off you may wish to adjust tension either before of after the KN is removed.

Bind-Off: Latvian Step 5.

Note that on *Bountiful Harvest Sweater, Socks and Gloves* (pages 56 & 59) this bind-off was used as a decorative trim. The bind-off was worked, but stitches were not removed from the knitting needles. Later in the pattern the bind-off was again worked and knitting needles were removed. The other *Bind-Offs: Sewn I & II* could also be used in this manner

Three Needle: As the name implies, this bind-off involves the use of three needles. This technique may be used with insides of work together for a decorative bind-off. However, where it is used in this book, the outsides of work are together. When the outsides are together, use a needle one or two sizes larger for the bind-off. This somewhat alleviates the dimple on the outside of the garment when the bind-off is complete. On stranded knit garments, bind off in pattern as instructed.

Hold the two needles with stitches to be bound off together parallel with outsides facing.

1. With a third needle one or two sizes larger than used for project, knit together one stitch from the front and one stitch from the back needle. (Do this twice for first bind-off.)

Bind-Off: Three Needle Step 1.

2. On right needle pass stitch on right over stitch on left. (One stitch remains on right needle.)

Repeat 1 and 2, being certain knitting is not too tight, until all stitches are bound off. Break yarn and pull tail through last loop on right needle.

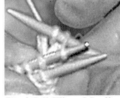

Bind-Off: Three Needle Step 2.

BLOCKING

With my knitting, blocking is an extremely important step in the production of a garment. I use the same method for blocking garments as I do for washing them, as most have been through some severe

Techniques

punishment while they were being worked on. If they have managed to stay out of trouble while I worked on them and are clean, I soak them as described in the rinse instructions.

Fill wash machine starting with hot water to dissolve the washing agent, then switch to cold water with tepid water the end result. For very dirty items I use Orvus which is used to wash show animals and sold in farm supply stores. I assume city dwellers would have to go to a rural area to purchase Orvus. For less soiled garments I use a scented wool wash that contains moth repellents.

After the wash machine has filled, immerse the garment by gently pushing it into the water. Soak the garment for at least 20 minutes so the fibers are totally soaked. Then with both hands gently gather up the garment and place into a waterproof container. Empty washer of water.

To rinse, refill washer with clear water the same temperature as garment was removed from. Immerse the garment as before and let it soak an additional 20 minutes. Turn the machine to spin cycle. When spin cycle is complete, remove garment. If water appears soapy after first rinse, I repeat rinse procedure.

If garment is a drop or semi-drop shoulder design, I dry on a woolly board sized to garment measurements. Other garments I lay flat on a large terry towel or atop framed plastic mesh. After approximately four hours I flip the garment to finish drying. If I use blocking wires and pins, I use foam insulation board.

Buttonholes

An easy to knit, nice looking buttonhole is **One Row Buttonhole by Elizabeth Zimmermann©**: Knit to buttonhole position. Slip 1 stitch as if to purl. Bring yarn forward and **leave** it there. Slip 1 stitch as if to purl.

Pass 1st slipped stitch over 2nd. Slip 1 stitch as if to purl. **Pass** 2nd slipped stitch over 3rd. Slip 1 stitch as if to purl. **Pass** 3rd slipped stitch over 4th. **Put** 4th slipped stitch on left-hand needle, **reversing it.**

Reverse, twist, or turn the last stitch on right-hand needle. Pull wool tightly, lay it over the right-hand needle from front to back and pull the turned stitch over the wool.

Make 4 firm backward loop cast on stitches on the right hand needle. **Knit 2 together, knit on.** On the next row work into the back of the four cast on stitches.

Sally Wall's Rambling Ridge Design Buttonhole© adapts Elizabeth Zimmermann's buttonhole to firm the corners and make the top and bottom of the buttonhole look more uniform. The adaptation includes turning your work (which Elizabeth avoided), but the results are a very neat buttonhole.

1. Work pattern to spot for buttonhole.
2. Yarn forward, slip 1 as if to knit, yarn to back, *slip 1 as if to purl, pass first slipped stitch over second slipped stitch*. Repeat between asterisks for required number of stitches. (I usually bind off three stitches.)
3. Pass remaining slipped stitch back to left needle.
4. Turn work. Put yarn to back of work.
5. Make a stitch by inserting the right needle between 1st and 2nd stitches of left needle. Place the new loop onto left needle. (*Cast-On: Cable*) Cast on in this manner the same number of stitches that were bound off.
6. Cast on an extra stitch, but before placing it on the left needle bring the yarn forward, then place the loop onto the left needle.
7. Slip 1 stitch from right needle to left needle and bind off 1 stitch on left needle (a backwards bind-off).
8. Turn work and finish row.

Buttonhole With Facing—a la Roberta Centers© which I learned from **Charlie Hada:** I debated about whether or not to include the following buttonhole in the book because it is difficult to explain. The technique may be confusing until you have done it several times, but I like it better than other buttonholes with a facing. I did not know about it when I knit the *Snowflake Cardigan*, but I used it in *Tay's Sweater* and unless I find something I like better I plan to use it in the future for all buttonholes with a facing. Hopefully I have described it so many knitters will find it no challenge at all. **Please knit some samples of this buttonhole before incorporating it into a garment.** Once understood, this technique works like a charm.

Instructions—Sample Faced Buttonholes: Use a light colored worsted weight yarn as the main color and a darker one of the same weight yarn for the scrap yarn.
Cast on 19 stitches.

Row 1: Knit 9, purl 1, knit 9. (Right Side)

Row 2: Purl 9, knit 1, purl 9. (Wrong Side)

(**Note:** All garments in this book are knit in the round so when working buttonhole on a garment repeat Row

Techniques

1 and eliminate Row 2. Band, facing and buttonhole widths may vary, but 19 stitches (9 stitch bands) give a nicely balanced 3 stitch buttonhole.)

**Repeat rows 1 and 2 for approximately 1-1/2 inches, ending with row 2.

Buttonhole Row: *Knit 3 with main color, knit 3 with scrap yarn, break scrap yarn leaving a 2–4 inch tail at each end. Place 3 scrap yarn stitches just knit back on left needle. With main color, knit the 3 scrap yarn stitches (tighten up the scrap yarn if it pulls loose), knit 3,* purl 1. Repeat between single asterisks. Work Row 2.**

Repeat between ** at least one more time (2 practice buttonhole rows). Work rows 1 and 2 for 1-1/2 inches above last buttonhole (row with scrap yarn).

To finish buttonholes: (This may be done an inch or so after inserting the scrap yarn or you may wait to do all when finishing the cardigan.) Hold knitting upside down with wrong side facing you. The "tails" (dark color scrap yarn) should be going up (Figure A). Think of the stitches as "frowns" and "smiles" as shown in Figure B. Insert a crochet hook through the main color frown (light yarn) that the last smile of scrap yarn goes into on the lower right. Continue up with the crochet hook through the main color frown to the right of the last scrap color frown on the right, as shown by Arrow 1 in Figure C. With the crochet hook catch the scrap yarn tail and pull through. The result should look like 1 in Figure D.

Do the same type thing on the left side. Insert a crochet hook through the main color frown that the last smile of scrap

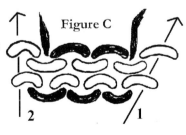

Figure A

Figure B

← Frowns

← Smiles

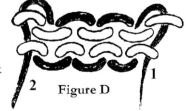

Figure C

2 /1

Figure D

2

yarn goes into on the lower left. Continue up with the crochet hook going through the main color frown to the left of the last scrap frown, as shown by Arrow 2 in Figure C. With the crochet hook catch the scrap yarn tail and pull through the frowns. The result looks like 2 in Figure D. Repeat with other buttonhole.

Figure E: Fold the knitting along the line of two buttonholes with the right sides together. Fold the piece again at the front edge line (purled stitches) so that the tails of the scrap yarn are on the outside of the fold.

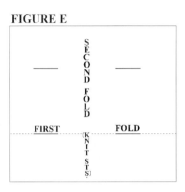

FIGURE E

SECOND FOLD

———   ———

FIRST   FOLD

(KNITS TS)

Ignore the smiles and frowns that you see related to the scrap yarn on the inside of the fold, and pay attention only to the smiles and frowns related to the scrap yarn on the outside of the fold. With a crochet hook go through the frown on the lower right with the scrap yarn tail coming through it, then go through the smile on the opposite outside edge of the fold that has the other scrap yarn tail. (Arrow 1, Figure F). With main color and a 4–6 inch tail, form a loop over the crochet hook and pull it through the smile and frown. With

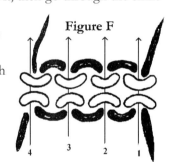

Figure F

4   3   2   1

the loop still on the crochet hook, go through the next frown on the left, across and through the smile on the opposite side, (Arrow 2, Figure F). (Yes, you will see frowns and smiles with the scrap yarn on the inside of the fold while you do this. Be certain you go through the frowns and smiles of the scrap yarn on the outside of the fold as shown in Figure F.) Hook the working yarn, pull it through the smile and frown, then through the loop on the crochet hook. Only one loop is on the crochet hook. Repeat the procedure you did for Arrow 2 for Arrows 3 & 4 in Figure F

Break the working yarn, leaving approximately a 12 inch tail. Pull the tail of the working yarn through the last loop formed. Place the crochet hook under the portion of the buttonhole you have just crocheted together and have the tip pop up through the hole between the buttonhole and the front edge of the garment. Grab the tail and pull it to the inside. Refold the work to expose the underneath side of the buttonhole. The tail of your working yarn is exposed. (Figure G)

With the crochet hook, go through the frown on the lower right at the outside of the

Figure G

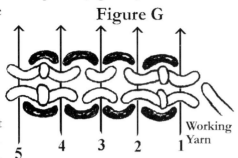

Working Yarn

5   4   3   2   1

fold, then through the smile on the opposite outside edge of the fold. (Arrow 1, Figure G) With the crochet hook, pull the working yarn through the smile and frown. Keep the loop that is formed on the crochet hook. Go through the next frown on the left (just to the left of the vertical yarn) and through the smile on the opposite side, (also just to the left of the vertical yarn—Arrow 2, Figure G). Hook the working yarn, pull it through the smile and frown, then through the loop on the crochet hook. One loop remains on the crochet hook. Repeat this procedure as shown by Arrows 3, 4, & 5 in Figure G. (Note: On this side you must go through frowns and smiles 5 times, but only 4 times on the opposite side.)

When the last crochet slip stitch is complete, pull the tail through the loop. Find the main color tail where you started crocheting, and tie the two tails in a square knot. Cut, leaving approximately 1" tails. Turn your knitting right side out and remove scrap yarns.

Voila, a beautiful buttonhole!

I find it easy to use the above crochet method, but you get the same appearance for a buttonhole by grafting the open buttonhole stitches together. To accomplish this remove scrap yarn and proceed as described in *Kitchener Stitch* (page 17). To avoid the necessity of going back and forth through the buttonhole with needle and yarn when grafting, bring the open loops from back to working side on a double pointed needle.

CAST-ONS

Cable: Cast on two stitches with *Cast-On: Long Tail* (page 11). Put needle with two cast-on stitches in left hand.
1. Insert tip of right needle

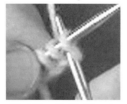
Cast-On: Cable Step 1

under left needle between the first two stitches at tip of needle.
2. Wrap yarn around right needle and bring yarn through to front.
3. Place loop onto end of left needle and adjust. Repeat Steps 1–3 for desired number of stitches, but before placing last stitch onto left needle, bring yarn forward under left needle.

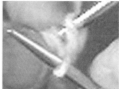
Cast-On: Cable Step 2

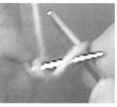
Cast-On: Cable Step 3

Eastern European—Variation:
The Eastern European Cast-On produces a closed end for your knitting and is used in such places as sock toes, glove fingers, purses, or centers of circular shawls. Because I had problems of stitches unraveling, could not knit between the two stiff needles, and needles dropped out when trying to accomplish the cast-on using the customary two double pointed needles, I came up with this technique.

Use 2 same size circular needles. I prefer to use 24" lengths which give a long stiff portion to hold, and the tips of needle not in use hang down out of the way.
1. With working yarn make a slip knot on stiff portion of needle #2. With both needles in left hand, hold tip of needle #1 above and horizontal to the tip of needle #2. Bring working yarn from slip knot up **behind** needle #1 and

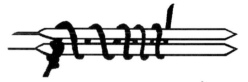
Cast-On: Eastern European—Variation Step 1

around the front of needles #1 and #2. Wrap the needles in this direction as many times as desired number of stitches on each needle: one-half total number of stitches.
2. After wrapping lightly hold working yarn next to needles with thumb and index finger and slide needle #2 (the bottom needle) so wraps are on the flexible portion of needle. With opposite end of needle #1, knit wraps off needle #1. When all stitches are knit on a needle, slide them to the flexible portion of needle. Turn work, slide wraps on needle #2 to tip of needle, remove slip knot and knit wraps from

Knit Wraps Off Needle #1

needle #2 with opposite end of needle #2. The yarn for the **first** stitch comes directly from the opposite needle. When wraps have been knit from needle #2 it is the end of the first round. Continue to knit with alternate needles bringing the first stitch knit with each needle up next to the stitch on the flexible portion of opposite needle. The tail lies **opposite** the beginning of the round.

Invisible or Provisional: The result of this cast-on is open stitches on an auxiliary yarn as well as on the needle.

If you turn the drawing on right upside down, you see stitches also around the auxiliary yarn. The auxiliary yarn stitches have the left leg of every other loop forward. When you work the cast-on stitches with left side forward be certain to knit into the center of open loop (back of stitch).

This is my most frequently used cast-on for I can start a garment and determine what treatment I want at the bottom as I progress. I also use this cast-on when I know I want a hem. Then the stitches on the auxiliary yarn are knit together with body stitches at the appropriate hem length. It is also my fastest method of casting on. An inexpensive cotton yarn (such as Lily's Sugar 'n Cream) works very well as an auxiliary yarn. It is strong, does not fuzz off onto working yarn, its size works with most yarns (I double it when working yarn is bulky) and is readily available. I have tried various methods for invisible or provisional casting on, but always go back to the first method I learned from Elizabeth Zimmermann in *Knitting Without Tears*, described below.

1. Have auxiliary yarn one to two feet longer than circumference or length of project. Knot together working yarn and auxiliary yarn, leaving at least a 6 inch tail.

2. Hold knot securely against needle in right hand. With auxiliary yarn away and working yarn toward your body, place left hand thumb and index finger between the two yarns, secure them against palm with little finger, and spread thumb and index finger apart. Auxiliary yarn is around index finger and working yarn that becomes stitches on needle is around thumb, which is opposite *Cast-On: Long Tail* yarn positions.

(Figure 1.)

3. Rotate left wrist back. Take tip of right needle down **between** the two yarns, and scoop tip toward yourself catching working yarn and raise the tip. There is a stitch on needle **in front** of the auxiliary yarn, Figure 2

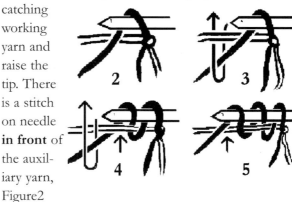

4. Rotate your left wrist forward. Take tip of needle down **behind both** the auxiliary and working yarns, scoop tip toward yourself catching working yarn, and raise tip, (Arrow, in Figure 3). Stitch formed on needle is **behind** auxiliary yarn, (Small arrow, Figure 4). Raise needle tip high enough to form a full loop with right leg forward over the needle and auxiliary yarn horizontal under needle.

5. Rotate left wrist back. Take tip of right needle down **between** the two yarns, and scoop tip toward yourself catching working yarn and raise the tip, (Large arrow, Figure 4). Stitch formed on needle is **in front** of auxiliary yarn, (Arrow, Figure 5).

Alternate **Step 4** and **Step 5** above for desired number of stitches. To prevent stitches from unraveling as you count, make a backward loop over needle tip with both yarns. Remove backward loop when count is complete.

With an even number of stitches cast on, working yarn is in position to start to knit (Figure 6). With an uneven number of stitches cast on, be certain working yarn comes under auxiliary yarn as you start to knit (Figure 7).

To keep tension even and stitches on auxiliary yarn uniform, have stitches on left needle bunched up near tip and do not allow them to be stretched out along needle when knitting first row.

Long Tail or German: A simple and fast method to cast on is to make backward loops onto a needle. However, if you are not careful with tension as you

Techniques

knit loops off the needle, the length of yarn between loops will get longer and longer and you end up with a large loop below the knitting at the end of row. A remedy is to knit into the loop instead of placing it on the needle directly and thus have a row knit when you finish your cast-on. This is called long tail or German cast-on.

Usually to perform long tail cast-on, you fold the yarn in half. The long tail around your thumb forms the loop to knit into and the working yarn around your index finger is used to form the stitch on the needle. But if you do not judge the right length for the tail, you may run out of yarn before you have the required number of stitches cast on. Conversely, after you cast on, you are left with a very long tail. If you do not break it off you may end up knitting with the tail rather than working yarn. (Some people will tie a long end into a small ball and use it later to sew up seams, but since I have no unnecessary seams in my garments that is not an option for me.) I have had both problems too many times in my life, so I now use a different method. I tie both ends of the ball of yarn together or use two balls of yarn. After the cast-on I break one off. It takes far less time to weave in the extra tails than it does to have to repeat the cast-on or to rip out stitches knit with a long tail.

1. Using both yarns, make a slip knot approximately 6 inches from the ends to hold yarn on the needle. (I find it much easier to weave in with a tail at least this long.) **Or**, when casting on a small number of stitches where it is easier to determine length of tail required (approximately one inch per stitch), fold yarn at distance established for tail. Follow #2 below, but eliminate the left hand swivel. Do secure yarn against palm and spread thumb and index finger slightly apart. Then with needle in right hand place tip of needle tightly up against left side of yarn. Swivel left hand to the left so palm is facing up. As you swivel your hand the yarn will encircle the needle to form your first stitch.

2. With tail end toward you and working yarn end away from you, insert your left hand index finger and thumb between the two strands. Swivel left hand to the left so palm is up and secure both yarns against palm with little finger. Spread thumb and index finger apart.

3. Move needle tip in direction from wrist to thumb tip under thumb yarn strand closest to wrist. Keep thumb strand taut as you raise the needle up to form a loop. Continue to move needle tip beyond and over top of

yarn strand on thumb side of index finger.

4. Bring needle tip back under strand on index finger (catching it) traveling in direction of finger tip to wrist (scooping toward yourself)

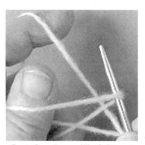 

Cast-On: Long Tail Step 3　　　*Cast-On: Long Tail Step 5*

5. Bring tip of needle with yarn back through the taut thumb strand loop.

6. Remove thumb from loop, re-insert thumb back between two strands, spread thumb and index finger apart to adjust loop.

Repeat steps 3 to 6 until desired number of stitches are cast on. Adjust loops so stitches are at even intervals and equivalent to desired gauge for project. Remove, do **not** knit slip knot.

My Method of Long Tail: On above long tail cast on, if you tighten thumb loop directly onto needle without bringing the index finger strand through loop, the working yarn strand at base of stitches comes out in front of strand from previous loop and the left leg of loop is over front of needle. This base is the same as an *Increase: Loop—Right Slanted* (page 16). Somewhere along in my knitting days I decided I wanted the base of my cast on to slant to the left (but I have no idea why). To achieve this, the thumb loop is formed in a different way.

1. Follow #1, *Cast-Ons: Long Tail* above (either method).

2. With tail end toward you and working yarn end away from you, insert your left hand index finger between the two strands. Move thumb away from body under tail strand and lift up with thumb. Turn left hand so palm is up and secure both yarns against palm with little finger. Spread thumb and index finger apart.

3. With needle tip go down into center of two strands. From front to back, go under and up thumb strand closest to palm, catching it

Cast-On: My Long Tail Step 3

Techniques

to form a loop. (This is the loop you knit into.). Continue to move needle tip up and over yarn strand on index finger.

4. Bring needle tip back under strand on index finger (catching it) traveling in direction of finger tips to wrist (scooping toward yourself).

5. Bring tip of needle with yarn back through thumb loop.

Cast-On: My Long Tail Step 5

6. Remove thumb from loop, move thumb away from body under tail strand and up, catching strand and spread thumb and index finger apart to adjust loop.

Repeat steps 3 to 6 until desired number of stitches are cast on. Adjust loops so stitches are at even intervals and equivalent to desired gauge for project.

Latvian or Combined Two-Strand: I first saw this cast-on used on a pair of Latvian mittens in the collection of Lizbeth Upitis, so I refer to it as Latvian Cast-On, even though Lizbeth and Latvian knitters she knew in the Twin Cities area were unfamiliar with how it was done. Because of my uncommon method of performing *Cast-Ons: Long Tail*, for me it was not difficult to determine how to work the cast-on. I have "unvented" a method to work a matching bind-off, which may also be used as a decorative trim.

Since then I have seen Estonian knitting samples in Nancy Bush's collection where this cast-on was used. This is not surprising as Baltic Countries have many common knitting techniques. Nancy said she found the cast-on documented in Estonia. When doing research on cast-on techniques for this book, I discovered this technique documented by Montse Stanley in *The Handknitter's Handbook* under "Combined Two-Strand Cast-On."

(See photographs for *Cast-Ons: Long Tail* and *My Method of Long Tail*, but have two strands of yarn around thumb.)

1. Follow #1 and #2, *Cast-On: Long Tail*, but tie 3 strands of yarn together. Have 2 strands around thumb and 1 strand around index finger.

2. Work *Cast-Ons: Long Tail*, but after thumb is removed from loop move thumb away from body under two tail strands and up, catching strands, and spread thumb and index finger apart to tighten up loop.

3. Work *Cast-Ons: My Method of Long Tail*, but after thumb is removed from loop place thumb back between index finger strand and the two thumb strands as for regular *Cast-Ons: Long Tail*. Spread thumb and index finger apart to tighten up loop.

Repeat #2 and 3 for desired number of stitches.

Purl: I like to knit a row before joining to knit in the round as I find I am less likely to twist the knitting. However, when using *Cast-Ons: Long-Tail or Cable*, this results in the purl bumps being on the outside of the garment. Many times I prefer the bumps on the outside, but not always. When I want the purl bumps on the inside I use *Cast-Ons: Purl*.

Because a purl stitch has the top of loop worked in front of the newly formed stitch, for purl cast-on a loop of yarn should end up in front of stitch formed on needle. So direction of cast-on is reversed, the loop is formed with index finger strand, and thumb strand is brought through loop to form stitch on the needle.

1 & 2. Follow #1 and #2 *Cast-Ons: My Long Tail*, but have tail around index finger.

3. Tail yarn goes from needle to index finger thumb side, around to back and comes out between index and middle finger. Insert needle tip under yarn along right side of finger, bring needle tip up toward finger tip, catching strand to form loop. (This is the loop you knit into.)

Cast-On: Purl Step 3

4. Hold tip taut against index finger loop and continue to move needle tip toward yourself, go under strand that is around thumb and catch yarn.

Cast-On: Purl Step 4

5. Bring needle tip and yarn up then back through index finger loop.

6. Remove index finger from loop, but re-insert index finger back between both strands. Spread index finger and thumb apart to tighten up loop.

Repeat steps 3 to 6 until

Cast-On: Purl Step 5

desired number of stitches are cast on. Adjust loops so stitches are at even intervals equivalent to desired gauge for project.

Techniques

DECREASES:

Notice I eliminated the word "slanting" on decreases? I prefer to think of a decrease as what stitch is eliminated rather than direction it slants. When working with very fine yarns, direction of the slant is barely discernible.

Right: Place tip of right needle into center of second stitch on left needle and then into center of first stitch on left needle, and knit the two stitches together. The stitch on right will be eliminated.

Left: Place tip of right needle into center of stitch on left needle and slip stitch off left needle. Place tip of left needle into stitch slipped onto right needle from the left and in front of right needle to transfer stitch back to left needle. Leave right tip in transferred stitch, insert it also under right leg (back of stitch) of second stitch on left needle, and knit the two stitches together. The stitch on left will be eliminated, but twisted.

The above method is my fastest way for a left decrease. As it is eliminated, the twisted stitch does not show. However, if working on something reversible such as lace, you may not wish to have the eliminated stitch twisted. Place tip of right needle into center of first stitch on left needle and transfer to right needle. Repeat with second stitch. Insert tip of left needle from left into both stitches, with left needle tip in front of right needle tip. Knit the two together onto right needle. The left stitch will be eliminated, but not twisted.

Double: Place tip of right needle into center of second and then first stitch on left needle and transfer together to right needle. Place tip of right needle into center of next stitch on left needle and transfer it to right needle. From left place tip of left needle into all three stitches on right needle in front of right needle and knit the three stitches together. A stitch is eliminated on right and left of remaining center stitch and no stitches are twisted.

Tip of left needle in three stitches on right needle.

GAUGE—DETERMINING

Gauge is stitches per inch, usually measured over four inches. Divide the desired circumference into the total number of stitches in the garment to determine required gauge for that size. A workable gauge may not be possible for all sizes and all patterns. (See *Swatches*, page 22 and *Design*, page 121.)

HEMS—KNIT-IN

If a garment is designed with a hem, *Cast On: Invisible*, (page 11) the number of body stitches there will be when hem depth is reached. The hem is knit with a smaller needle size and, when practical, with a finer yarn. A purl round is knit at completion of hem for a turning ridge. Change to needle for the body gauge and knit to depth of hem. Turn hem at purl round to inside of garment (insides facing).

The invisibly cast on stitches may either be placed on a separate needle, or knit directly off auxiliary yarn. With a needle one or two sizes larger, knit start of round stitch together with first invisibly cast on stitch. Continue around knitting together a body stitch with an invisibly cast on stitch. A larger needle is used for the join of body to hem to eliminate a dimple in the knitting at join. This larger needle technique is used by machine knitters and I learned it from Mary Anderson. Remember to change back to needle for the body after the join.

An alternative to *Cast-On: Invisible* is the *Cast-On: Eastern European—Variation* (page 10). Take two smaller needles for the hem and wrap for total number of hem stitches. Join and knit around with Needle #1 only for hem and turn. Change to needle for the body gauge and knit to depth of hem. When body reaches depth of hem, knit stitches on Needle #2 together with body stitches as above. This technique works well when working with fine yarns.

I-CORD

As you leaf through this book you may notice I used I-cord on the majority of garments. I often wonder how I would finish a project if Elizabeth Zimmermann's "unventions" had not taken I-cord off a spool! Of course I could use cord made on a spool, but to apply it would involve the use of a needle with an eye, which I avoid. My love for idiot cord, as it was then called, started as a child. (Elizabeth Zimmermann coined the more polite name of I-cord.) I made miles of it, so it seems, using a spool. I-cord's more conventional use was to attach it to mittens and thread it through the sleeves of a coat to maintain mittens as a pair. However, I recollect one time using a very long I-cord attached to two tin cans for a phone line with a neighbor. Needless to say, I-cord does not carry sound!

Techniques

Elizabeth's Built In I-Cord is used in the *Joyous Jacket* (page 84) and instructions for the technique are included in that pattern.

In many items Elizabeth's Applied I-Cord was used on open stitches, *Knit Up*, or *Picked Up Stitches* (page 18). Usually I pick up approximately 4 to 6 inches of stitches at a time where I want to apply I-cord.

Normally when an I-cord of contrasting color is applied, a glitch of the color the I-cord is applied to will peek through the I-cord. Before I "unvented" glitchless I-cord (see *Applied to Contrasting Color*), I knit up stitches using the contrasting color of the applied I-cord, and worked the I-cord on the knit up stitches. But that is more time consuming, and you commit in advance the application ratio (although that may be adjusted as you work).

Instructions are for a 3 stitch I-cord, but 2 or 4 stitch I-cords may be used.

Applied to Same Color: Cast on 3 stitches. *With yarn behind, transfer stitches to left needle. (If working with a double point needle, slide stitches to opposite end of needle.) Yarn for the first stitch comes behind work from third stitch on the needle. Knit 2 stitches, knit 2 together through back loops (the third I-cord stitch and a picked up stitch).* Repeat between asterisks. Or, rather than knit 2 together, slip third I-cord stitch, knit picked up or open stitch, pass slipped stitch over.

Because I knit I-cord loosely, I use a needle one or two sizes smaller than used for garment. As I-cord is applied, every few inches examine it to assure it is neither too tight or too loose. If I-cord appears to be too tight and pulling up on the garment, a larger needle may be used or a round of *I-Cord: Free* inserted at intervals (see below). Rounds of *I-Cord: Free* should also be used at corners. For a sharply turned corner, work one round *I-Cord: Free*, apply one round to corner stitch, and work one round free. For a more curved corner, do not apply to corner stitch, but instead work a round of *I-Cord: Free*.

If I-cord appears too loose, a smaller needle may be used or an occasional picked up stitch may be dropped from needle and skipped. If I-cord is being applied to open or knit up stitches, knit the third I-cord stitch together with **two** stitches.

Applied to Contrasting Color: Cast on 3 stitches. *With yarn behind, transfer stitches to left needle.

Working yarn for the first stitch comes behind work from third stitch on the needle. Knit 2 cord stitches, slip 1 cord stitch, yarn over, knit picked up stitch, pass 2 stitches over (the yarn over and the slipped stitch).* Repeat between asterisks. (The yarn over becomes a little shield covering the picked up stitch.)

Bind-Off: I-cord bind-off is worked the same as *I-Cord: Applied*, except you apply it to open stitches.

Buttonholes: Work *I-Cord: Applied* around edges but at appropriate space for buttonhole, work several rows *I-Cord: Free*. For an almost hidden buttonhole, skip the same number of rows on the garment as *I-Cord: Free* was knit and again work *I-Cord: Applied*. For a larger loop buttonhole, work more free rows and attach on row next to last *I-Cord: Applied*.

Free: *With yarn behind, transfer stitches to left needle or if working with a double point needle, slide stitches to opposite end of needle. Knit 3 stitches.* Repeat between asterisks. *I-Cord: Free* is used for adjusting tension and turning corners as mentioned above, but it is also used for *I-Cord: Twisted*, or *Buttonholes*.

Twisted: Use a circular needle and pick up stitches where you wish to apply *I-Cord: Twisted*. With yarn A, cast 3 stitches onto a double point needle. (Bamboo or wood are preferable.) *With yarn A behind needle transfer 3 stitches to circular needle. Follow *I-Cord: Applied* instructions above and apply 5 rounds of I-cord. (Use a double point to knit the stitches and transfer them to the circular at end of each round.) After fifth round has been applied, do not transfer stitches but slide them to opposite end of double point. With double points, knit 6 rounds of *I-Cord: Free*. Leave *I-Cord: Free* on double point **with working yarn** in front of work.* With a double point needle and yarn B, cast on 3 stitches. Knit 1 round *I-Cord: Applied*, applying it to a stitch next to the **first row of first I-cord**. Knit 5 rounds *I-Cord: Free*. Repeat between asterisks above but with yarn B. When complete, repeat between asterisks above with the first I-cord and yarn A.

Ready to Knit B I-cord with A I-cord and working yarn in front.

Continue to repeat between asterisks alternating I-cords and yarns A and B. As you progress ascertain

Techniques

whether they are pulling up or too loose and make adjustments as needed to *I-Cord: Applied* and *Free*. *I-Cord: Applied* and corners may be adjusted as mentioned in *I-Cord: Applied* techniques, and *I-Cords: Free* adjusted by additional or fewer rounds. Five *I-Cord: Applied* and six *Free* are sample numbers and may be adjusted for the best visual appearance for a gauge.

When I use *I-Cord: Twisted* around the circumference of a cardigan, I prefer to have the twists a mirror image at center front. To accomplish this, direction of the twists must be switched somewhere on their way around. In *Joyous Jacket* (page 84) the I-cords were separated as they went around the collar and the twist was reversed when they again joined. To accomplish the change of direction in the twist, the I-cord and working yarn on hold is behind the work.

INCREASES

Loop—Left Slanted: With left hand and yarn coming from right needle, make a loop so yarn as it continues on is behind yarn that comes from the needle. From behind, place tip of right needle through center of loop and adjust

Loop—Left Slanted

loop on needle. Notice stitch on needle has **right leg of loop over front** of needle and **base slants** up and to the **left**.

Loop—Right Slanted: With left hand and yarn coming from right needle make a loop so yarn as it continues on is in front of yarn that comes from the needle. From front, place tip of right needle through center of loop and tighten

Loop—Right Slanted

loop on needle. Notice stitch on needle has **left leg of loop over front** of needle and **base slants** up and to the **right**.

The above two increases leave a slight hole at their base so may not be as invisible as some other increases. However, they work well if you want an increase directly above another increase, for they are formed using the working yarn and not yarn from a previous row. I am aware that some people think an increase should never be above an increase in the row below. I do not believe in the word "never" when it comes to knitting. For example, I feel increases above each other work well for a sock gusset.

These increases are sometimes referred to as a make

one, but be aware that at times a yarn over will also be referred to as a make one. A yarn over is as the name implies; the yarn goes over top of needle. In the row that follows knit the yarn over, forming a hole in the row below. A yarn over is used when knitting lace and it does not appear in this book, but I want to point out the duplication of names.

To remember which increase will slant in which direction I think of the word "opposites." Note the loop with the **right leg forward** on needle is **left slanted**, and the loop with **left leg forward** is **right slanted**. When making paired increases (usually separated by one or more stitches), I prefer to have them slant toward each other; i.e., as you look at your knitting the increase on right slants left, and increase on left slants right. Again opposites!

Raised Bar or Running Yarn—Left Slanted: Yarn as it travels between two stitches is referred to as a bar or running yarn. From the front go under bar with tip of **left** needle and catch bar. Insert **right** needle tip from the right behind right and in front of left legs of bar to back of left needle, forming a loop. Knit loop off left needle. Note bar forms a left slanted loop at base of stitch. Again, opposites with right leg of bar forward on needle, and left slanted base.

Left needle under bar from the front

Raised Bar or Running Yarn—Right Slanted: Yarn as it travels between two stitches is referred to as a bar or running yarn. From the back, go under bar with tip of **left** needle and catch bar. Insert **right** needle tip from the left under left leg of bar at front of left needle, forming a loop. Knit loop off left needle. Note bar forms a right slanted loop at base of stitch. Again, opposites with left leg of bar forward on needle, and right slanted base.

Left needle under bar from the back

Raised bar increases are very similar to loop increases as same type loops are formed for the increased stitch and leave the same small hole at the base. With raised bar increase, the increase occurs in the row below your knitting and you borrow yarn from the adjoining stitches in that row to form the increased stitch so it is a tighter increase. With *Increase: Loop*, the increase occurs in the row you are knitting and the increase has its own working yarn to form the stitch.

Knit in the Row Below—Right: Insert right needle tip from the right under right leg of stitch in row below. Place stitch onto left needle by inserting tip of left needle through center of stitch and in front of right needle. Knit stitch onto right needle. (It is a twisted stitch.) Knit stitch above stitch just knit.

Right needle in row below stitch

Knit in the Row Below—Left: Catch left side of second stitch down from stitch just knit on right needle (third stitch down on right needle) by inserting left needle tip under left leg of stitch and out through center of stitch. With right needle knit into stitch from left side of stitch (twisting it).

Left needle in second stitch down

These increases are the least visible and my preferred technique. However, the others have advantages in some circumstances. It is so nice to have choices.

KANGAROO POUCH

When knitting in the round, sometimes stitches are put on hold before you start a steek for an armhole or neck. New stitches are cast on for a steek above those on hold. The stitches on hold look like a pouch so Elizabeth Zimmermann coined the phrase "kangaroo pouch."

KITCHENER STITCH: GRAFTING

Kitchener Stitch (named for the "unventor") is a method of **grafting** or **weaving** open loops together to form an invisible seam. A blunt yarn sewing needle and project yarn are used in this procedure which is simple once learned but can seem befuddling at first. I explain how I look at the procedure before the step by step instructions.

With working yarn (coming from Side 1) Side 2 stitches 1 and 2 are connected. Then Side 1 stitches 1 and 2 are connected. Back to Side 2 and connect stitches 2 and 3. Back to Side 1 and connect stitches 2 and 3. Continue to alternate sides and connect two adjoining stitches until all stitches have been linked together. The "connection" is the same as the running yarn between two stitches as you knit in stockinette stitch. Just as the running yarn is on the back side of

your knitting, so too must the sewn connection be on the back side. To accomplish this the tip of the blunt needle goes into a stitch from the outside of work and comes back out through the adjoining stitch on the outside of work. Yarn travels under left leg of first stitch and right leg of adjoining stitch.

When doing Kitchener stitch I find it easier to take the stitches off the needle so the two stitches are connected in one step. When working at a fine gauge or with slippery fiber, I thread a strand of contrasting color Perle cotton through the loops before removing them from the needles to prevent the stitches from dropping down. If a stitch starts to slip down, pull up on the Perle cotton each side of the stitch to raise it. Perle cotton slides out easily when grafting is completed, and does not leave contrasting colored fibers behind as yarn might do.

Procedure: Side 1 is side closest to you. Side 2 is away from you. As you cross from one side to the other, go back into the same stitch you came out of before crossing over.

1. Thread a blunt yarn needle with new working yarn of a length three to four times the width you want to join.

2. Have outsides of work facing you and open loops headed towards each other. (It is not always possible to have the outside facing in places like sock toes or buttonholes. As I work those situations I still think of going in and coming out on the outside of work and peek over the top to see it.)

3. On Side 1, insert blunt needle through first stitch at right edge from inside to outside of work. Pull yarn through, leaving approximately a 6 inch tail.

4. On Side 2, insert needle tip into first stitch at right edge from outside of work and then insert tip into adjoining stitch on left from inside and bring it to outside of work. Pull needle and yarn through. It is not necessary to tighten to match gauge as it is easier to match gauge by adjusting after all stitches have been grafted.

5. On **Side 1**, insert needle tip from outside of work into the stitch the yarn came out of before it crossed over to Side 2. Then insert tip into adjoining stitch on left from inside to outside of work. Pull needle and yarn through

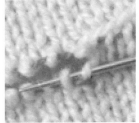

Kitchener Stitch Step 5

as established.

6. On **Side 2** insert needle tip from outside of work into the stitch the yarn came out of before it crossed over to Side 1. Then insert tip into adjoining stitch on left from inside to outside of work. Pull needle and yarn through as established.

Kitchener Stitch Step 6

Repeat steps 5 and 6 until all stitches on each side have been linked together. To help see the stitches, Perle cotton stays in as you tighten grafting to match gauge of project. Start adjusting at center and work toward edges, then remove Perle cotton.

Half Graft: I refer to this as half graft even though you are weaving two pieces of fabric together. However, in this case only one side has open loops and you weave them to a selvage or possibly a cast on edge as when encircling a garment with I-cord.

Side 1 has open loops which you weave exactly as in *Kitchener Stitch: Grafting*. If Side 2 is a selvage, I prefer to go under two running yarns between the first and second stitch, but you may go under the top loops at center of edge stitches. As with *Kitchener Stitch*, on Side 1 go back into same stitch yarn came out of before it crossed to Side 2. There may be a variance in stitch/row relationship so on Side 2 it may be necessary to skip up a running yarn or two to make the join lay flat.

If joining to a cast on edge, Side 1 is worked as *Kitchener Stitch*, and on Side 2 the needle and yarn are brought under both legs of the stitch just above the cast on.

KNITTING SMALL CIRCUMFERENCES WITH TWO CIRCULAR NEEDLES

Although it was my mother's favorite method of knitting, I am not fond of double pointed needles so "unvented" this method to avoid their use. Originally I used two 16 inch circulars, but now use 24 inch because I like the longer stiff portion and the longer flexible portion allows the stiff portions to hang out of the way when knitting with the opposite needle.

1. On Needle #1, cast on total required number of stitches.
2. With Needle #1, knit one-half

of stitches and slide them to flexible portion of needle. With Needle #2 knit second half of stitches and slide to flexible portion of needle.

3. Slide Needle #1 all the way to the left in preparation to knit. Bring stitches on flexible portion of Needle #2 behind and parallel to stitches on Needle #1, being certain not to twist. *With right tip of **Needle #1**, knit the stitches from left tip of **Needle #1**. Your working yarn for first stitch will be coming from last stitch knit on Needle #2. When stitches have been knit off Needle #1, slide them to flexible portion of needle.

4. With right tip of **Needle #2**, knit the stitches from left tip of **Needle #2**. Your working yarn for first stitch will be coming from last stitch knit on Needle #1. When stitches have been knit off Needle #2, slide them to flexible portion of needle.*

5. Repeat between asterisks.

When working stranded knitting with double points prior to this "unvention", I would turn my work inside out and knit with needles on far side. This prevented the strands from "cutting corners", but I was able to see the right side of my knitting as I worked. I continue to knit stranded knitting with my work inside out as I like the slight additional length of the strands going around the outer circumference.

KNIT UP/PICK UP STITCHES

Following is a description of how I use the terms knit up and pick up stitches in this book.

Knit Up Stitches: Stitches are knit up along selvages for things such as sleeves knit from the top down, borders, necklines, etc. With working yarn coming from inside of garment, new stitches are formed on outside with the use of either running strand(s) or the top of stitch loop(s) as a divider between the knit up loops. My preference is to knit up between two stitches so a complete stitch is at the edge.

A knitting needle may be used to catch the yarn from the inside of garment, but I prefer a crochet hook, especially when working with fine yarns.

1. *Insert tip of crochet hook between two running strands between two stitches. Catch working yarn on inside of garment and pull through to right side of work.

Knit Up Step 1

2. Place stitch onto needle and adjust tension.* (After several stitches are placed on the needle it is stable.) Repeat between asterisks, being

Techniques

certain to work along a straight column of running strands.

To maintain proper stitch/row ratio in some designs, it is necessary to skip more than one running strand. Many of the designs in the book have the sleeves repeat the body pattern. When you work these, insert the hook between every running strand and knit up in pattern.

Knit Up - Step 2

Pick Up Stitches: Insert a needle either under a running yarn, into the top loop, or under right or left leg of a stitch. Choose method most appropriate to the application.

MITERED CORNERS KNIT IN THE ROUND

Several cardigans in this book have the hem and facing knit while knitting the cardigan. A mitered corner was incorporated while knitting the cardigan in the round so hem and facing will lay flat when folded to the inside of the garment.

A mitered corner is best explained using a sheet of paper. To create a miter, one corner is cut-off and the paper is folded along lines to the inside. As you look at A on the left it becomes clear increases

are required. So take A, add a steek, mirror image A, and you have a mitered corner knit in the round.

For *The Star* (page 114) and *Morocco* (page 90) increases are made on each side of the steek on the solid color hem. At end of hem, front corner has been reached, and a turning row is knit. Pattern design is then started. A purl or garter stitch is knit as a fold line at center front. Continue to knit and increase until width of the facing is obtained. Facing is knit in solid color. Therefore, a long carry results from body to steek, but since facing is folded to inside and tacked down, the carries are not in danger of being caught.

For *Tay's Sweater* (page 48) and *Snowflake Cardigan* (page 104) there is a solid border on the sweater as well as a mitered corner hem and facing. This allows for a nice straight column of knit border stitches to the bottom of the jacket. The solid color along the front is quite wide because it is both border and facing. Because the facing is folded to inside and tacked down, the yarn carry need only be as wide as the facing. This

causes a pucker in your knitting. However, if the carries are only as wide as the facing, once the steek is cut and the facing tacked down, the front will lay flat.

A few words of warning. I machine stitched the steek when knitting the *Snowflake Cardigan*, and when I cut the steek the long carried red yarns pulled out from the machine stitching. To prevent further pulling out, I machine stitched over the running yarns between the border and start of pattern. When using a dark color and working with matching thread, the machine stitching is not visible. From my previous experience, I expected the long carries to pull out when I cut the steek for *Tay's Sweater*. Therefore, before cutting the machine stitched steek, I hand backstitched with the border yarn over the running yarns between the last border and first pattern stitches.

I now crochet my *Steeks* (page 21) and with this method my long carries hold without pulling out.

Knitting in Mitered Hems: Due to the steek and increases for the miter corner, the entire hem cannot be knit together with body stitches. When you knit in a mitered corner hem, knit across the body to a point several stitches beyond where the first increase was made for the miter. Follow the next body stitch down to the invisibly cast on stitch in line with the body stitch, fold the hem up at fold line, and start to join hem and body stitches. Work around to opposite side several stitches before first increases. The remaining hem stitches are tacked down after the steek is cut. (*Hems: Knit-In*, page 14.)

NEEDLES

Sizes: Unlike other knitting books, you will not see needle sizes with each individual pattern. This is intentional. Sizes for several of the garments with overall designs are determined by changing gauge and/or yarn rather than the number of stitches. Therefore you decide what size garment you want, then what gauge is necessary to attain that size. Once gauge is decided, you determine needle size for that gauge. **Approximate** needle sizes for specific yarns and gauges may be found under *Yarn Suggestions and Amounts* (page 24). Also see *Swatches* (page 22).

Knitters using the same yarn and needle size will end up with a wide variety of gauges, yet I find far too many knitters work a project with the size needle called for and ignore the instruction "or size to give gauge." Then they are unhappy when the finished size is not what they expected. You may think this is a case

Techniques

of "the pot calling the kettle black" since I do not knit gauge swatches, but I always know the circumference of my knitting after I have knit several inches and make adjustments if necessary. My swatch becomes the number of stitches required for the project. Since a needle size is not listed with a pattern, I hope each knitter will give more consideration to correct gauge and thus obtain the desired garment size.

Circular: I prefer knitting to sewing so go to extremes to avoid the use of a needle with an eye to finish a garment. Therefore I use circular needles and instructions in this book are given for circular needles. As far back as my teen years I converted patterns and knit in the round to the underarms. I have yet to be convinced there is any advantage to knitting with straight needles nor a need for side seams on knitted garments. But it is your knitting and if you prefer to knit on straight needles and have unnecessary seams in your garments, you have the right to do so. I promise to try not to cringe if I ever see a design of mine knit with side seams.

Lengths and Quantity: I cannot think of a project that cannot be knit if you own two 24 inch circulars of every size. In recent years my needle use has narrowed down to using two 24 inch circulars for everything from glove fingers to sleeves, etc. and a 40 inch circular for larger garment bodies. (See *Knitting Small Circumferences With Two Circular Needles*, page 18) On occasion I will use double points when working I-cord, but find more and more I use 24 inch circulars even when knitting I-cord and transferring the stitches rather than sliding them to the opposite end of the needle.

Materials: What material or brand of knitting needles a knitter uses is very personal. Some knitters like very slippery needles, others want them less slippery, some like sharp points, others like duller points, etc. Knitting is an individual technique and it is not true for everyone that one needle material will make your knitting looser or another will make your tension more even. You must decide what gives you the best results and what feels best in your hands.

Row Markers

A tip learned from Lizbeth Upitis to keep track of rows for such purposes as cable crosses, increases, decreases, etc. is to take a length of non-fuzz yarn and fold it in half. Tie knots equivalent to the number of

desired rows for spacing with proper distance between knots so knitting needle may be easily inserted. Example: Decreases desired every 5 rows equal five knots. At first decrease round, insert needle through top loop. When reaching knotted yarn on each following round, insert needle one loop down. After the bottom loop, return to top loop and decrease again.

Transferring Marker

Knotted yarns may be placed at the start of each pattern section when working on an item with more than one pattern (such as cables) and pattern repeat rows vary. And, it is useful when setting a project aside for a time. The knotted yarn is right there when you resume to let you know where you are in the sequence.

Short Rows—Yarn Over Or Wrap

Additional length may be added to a specific area by knitting short rows. They are worked by reversing direction of knitting where additional length is desired such as on sock heels, back of garment, neckline shaping, darts, etc. Short rows may be worked by either increasing or decreasing the number of stitches between each reverse of direction, dependent on the desired shaping. With the use of a yarn over or a wrap, a hole does not appear at the reversing point. I use the yarn over method as the result is identical (the yarn over is in the same position as wrap when worked together) and I find it faster to work.

Yarn Over: For a yarn over, knit to reverse point. Wrap yarn around left needle from back to front to back. Either knit onto left needle (KOLN) or turn and purl back to desired reverse position. If purling, turn. Wrap yarn around right needle from back to front to back and knit onto right needle. When met, the yarn over on the left is eliminated by working it together with the stitch on its left (right decrease). The yarn over on the right is eliminated by working it together with the stitch on its right (left decrease).

Sleeve Gauge and Size

My gauge is usually tighter when I knit a small circumference than when I knit a larger circumference. To obtain equal gauges I usually use a needle **one size larger** when knitting sleeves than used on the body.

Techniques

Some designs in this book have the sleeve pattern a continuation of the body pattern. In these sweaters I want to have the sleeve **stitch gauge** the same as the body **row gauge**. Therefore, for these garments needles **one size smaller** are used for the sleeves.

SPACING DECREASES AND INCREASES

I attended the Oft Timers session my second year at Elizabeth Zimmermann's Knitting Camp. Charlie Hada, a wonderful knitter and technician, explained a mathematical formula to determine spacing for increases or decreases. I thought, "Boy, am I in over my head with this group," but took notes. When I returned home I studied the notes and it all made sense. I have been thankful to Charlie ever since as she certainly made my knitting life easier.

Example: Use 20 as a base number, which may be either stitches or rows. We will use 6 as the number we want to insert into 20. This 6 may be increases or decreases or number of rows between. Divide 20 by 6. If the divisor does not go evenly into the dividend, add 1 to the quotient. Draw Arrow 1 from the remainder to the answer after adding one. Subtract the remainder from the divisor. Draw Arrow 2 from this answer to the original quotient. The arrows **point to** the number of spaces between increases or decreases or rows and **start at** the number of times that spacing is used.

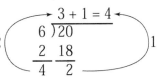

In the example above, when increasing around Arrow 1 shows to [knit **4**, increase 1] 2 times. Then Arrow 2 shows to [knit **3**, increase 1] 4 times. If decreasing [knit 2, knit stitches 3 & **4** together] 2 times, then [knit 1, knit stitches 2 and **3** together] 4 times. If used to determine rows to increase or decrease on [knit 3 rows, increase or decrease on **4**th row] 2 times, [knit 2 rows, increase or decrease on **3**rd row] 4 times.

SPLICING YARNS

When joining a new ball of yarn or new color I splice the yarns together.

1. Un-ply the working yarn into two strands approximately 6 inches before end of ball. Example: Separation of 5 ply yarn is one 3 ply strand and one 2 ply strand, 3 ply is one 2 ply and one 1 ply, and 2 ply is 1 ply each.

2. Un-ply approximately 5 inches of new ball yarn into two strands as established.

3. At separation point of working yarn, half hitch new ball larger strand to working yarn smaller strand leaving approximately a 1 inch tail of new yarn.

4. Wrap smaller strand tail of working yarn around larger strand of new ball until you reach separation point of new ball. Half hitch old working yarn around small strand of new yarn ball.

5. "Knit on" working with wrapped yarns and when they end, with new ball of yarn. Later ends are broken or cut off.

STEEKS—CROCHETED

A steek is a group of stitches added to create a field for cutting a garment that is knit in the round. They are often used at the center front for a cardigan, at sleeves, and necklines. Steeks are not included when measuring a garment.

Steek stitches are usually secured with a sewing machine before cutting. I am not a fan of that method, and have knit many garments *KORN* and *KOLN* (page 4) to avoid steeks. However, in *Knitter's* magazine, Fall 1996, Eleanor-Elizabeth Bernard described a method of using single crochet to secure the steek stitches. Katherine Misegades adapted Ms. Bernard's method to a slip-stitch crochet for two color knitting and I adapted my method from Katherine's. A lot of adaptations!

My steek consists of 10 stitches and has been tested with extremely slippery yarns and they held. However, Meg Swansen has successfully worked this slip stitch crochet method with three steek stitches when working with wool and a single color. Knit a test swatch if you question the holding ability of a given yarn.

Cast on a 10 stitch steek with *Cast-On: Long Tail*, one color over index finger and second color around thumb. The use of long tail cast on and both colors is important in securing the yarn.

Work steek in following pattern (from right to left):

1. Background color.

2. Pattern color. (I like to have pattern color secured close to cut. Even with machine stitching a yarn is more likely to pull out if there is a long carry between last stitch and where it was secured.)

3 and 4. One background color and one pattern color alternated every row.

5. Background color.

6. Pattern color. (I cut between 5 and 6 so have a clear visual line where to cut. This relieves my fear of cutting the crochet stitch.)

7, 8, 9 10. Repeat 4, 3, 2, 1.

For center front, necks and vest armholes, knit all steek stitches. When steeks are crocheted and cut they automatically fold back on themselves ready to be tacked down. If you wish a sleeve steek to lay flat under the sleeve instead of under the body, knit the background color on each edge, but purl remaining steek stitches. When you slip stitch crochet the armhole stitches, turn work to inside and work on the knit side of the steek.

Bind off steeks in alternating colors. Katherine Misegades also grafts the steeks at top of shoulders so the slip stitch crochet goes over the top of sleeve uninterrupted.

Slip stitch crochet: Use project yarn or finer yarn. Start on left side of steek looking from bottom to top. Make a slip knot and place it on crochet hook. *Catch the working yarn and pull it through the loop.* Repeat between asterisks. Start with a few of these crochet slip stitches. Then slip stitch together the two bottom loops of Stitches 8 and 7 formed by the strand around thumb when casting on. To do this, insert tip of crochet hook through the two loops, hook the working yarn, and pull it through all three loops, ending with one loop on hook. Next slip stitch crochet together cast-on Stitches 8 and 7 (the stitches formed with index finger strand when casting on). *Insert tip of crochet hook under right leg of Stitch 8 and left leg of Stitch 7, hook working yarn, and pull through three loops, ending with one loop on hook.* Repeat between asterisks.

Hook working yarn and pull through three loops

When working with stranded knitting it is quite easy to see adjoining stitches as they are opposite colors both horizontally and vertically. With solid colors be sure to connect adjoining stitches horizontally and do not skip a row as you go up vertically. At top, work bound-off stitches as you did the cast-on stitches. Break yarn and bring tail through loop, pull on tail to tighten and weave in end. Work right side of steek as left, except from top to bottom and insert crochet hook under left leg of Stitch 3 and right leg of Stitch 4.

SWATCHES

To be able to determine gauge, a swatch is usually knit. It is recommended **at least** 4 inches of stitches and rows be measured for gauge. Because of possible differences in tension at selvages, a six inch square will allow an accurate measurement at center of swatch. The larger the swatch you measure, the more accurate your gauge measurement

Use project yarn for swatch, not something similar. The same type yarn may vary in size with color or even dye lots. Knit swatch with same stitch pattern as project, and use needles of same brand and material you intend to use for project. Be aware that stranded knit gauge may differ from single color knit gauge.

For an accurate gauge, swatch should be knit the same as project. If project is knit in the round, swatch should be knit in the round. But, you may attain a different gauge on a small circumference (such as a sleeve) than on a large circumference (body). My small circumference gauge is tighter than on a larger circumference and I know many other knitters with the same tendency. I usually knit sleeves with a needle one size larger than I use for body to attain the same gauge for both. In some garments in the book, to have visual consistency in pattern flow, I want sleeve stitch gauge to match body row gauge and go down in needle size for sleeves.

Because of this discrepancy in gauge, the use of a sleeve or a hat is not always an accurate gauge swatch. However, there is a method that may be used to knit a swatch without the necessity of knitting a large circumference. Using the circular needle to be used for project, cast on an adequate number of stitches to give you proper width for your gauge measurement, plus at least an extra inch of stitches on each side. *Knit across row. Slide stitches to other end of needle. Leave a more than ample length of working yarn(s) behind stitches so swatch may be laid flat to measure.* Repeat between asterisks for wanted length of swatch. To maintain a relatively tight selvage, when you work the first and last stitches, hold the strand(s) of working yarn from the previous row taut with middle finger of left hand. This gives a swatch knit in the same manner as knit in the round, and without cut ends. A swatch knit with the carries across back may be ripped out and yarn used if additional yarn is needed to finish project.

Determine gauge after you have knit swatch, but **before** blocking. A swatch is not a guarantee you will knit the project at the same gauge as swatch. You must measure your knitting (the total width) as you progress to be sure you are knitting at desired gauge.

To determine gauge, lay swatch flat on a flat surface. Place a straight pin alongside edge of a stitch approximately one inch from selvage. With a stiff ruler, measure across 4 or more inches and place a second straight pin **exactly** where your measurement ends, although it may be just partially into a stitch. Count number of stitches between pins. If you had a partial stitch at end, decide the size of the partial stitch; i.e., 1/2, 1/3, 1/4. Divide number of stitches by distance measured to determine number of stitches per inch. Repeat procedure for row gauge.

Make note of answers for pre-blocked measurement.

Now block swatch. You may block with steam, but if project will at some time be washed it is best to wash swatch. It is not necessary to wash the swatch with soap, but I soak wool at least 20 minutes so fibers are totally saturated. After soaking, swatch may be rolled in a towel (and stomped on as Meg Swansen sometimes does) or spun in spin cycle of washer. Lay damp swatch onto towel on flat surface and pat flat to dry.

When swatch is dry, measure again for post-blocked gauge. If concerned about stretch, hang dry swatch overnight and then measure gauge. This post-blocked or post hung gauge is used for garment planning. When following a written pattern, gauge needs to be attained exactly to have project the desired size. If a pattern calls for 20 stitches/4 inches (5 sts/inch), 21 stitches/4 inches (5.25sts/inch) will not work. As an example, a 42-inch circumference times 5 sts/inch would need 210 stitches. But 210 stitches divided by 5.25 sts/inch would result in a 40 inch garment.

If required gauge was not attained, knit another swatch with different needle size. If your gauge is a **higher** number than required such as 5.25 sts/inch and you need 5 sts/inch go **up** in needle size. Conversely, if your gauge is a **lower** number than required such as 4.50 sts/inch and you need 5 sts/inch go **down** in needle size. *Design,* page 121, explains use of gauge in designing.

I prefer to block as close to the natural fall of the knitted stitches as possible, so I change needle sizes to obtain proper gauge rather than stretch or squash the knitting to do so. If desired gauge falls between needle sizes and cannot be attained, garment may be blocked to wanted size (especially when working with wool).

As you knit, always measure gauge with pre-blocked gauge. If your pre-blocked gauge was 22 sts/4 inches, but blocked gauge was 21 sts/4 inches (the desired gauge), measure garment as you knit to be sure you are getting 22 sts/4 inches. If garment at desired gauge is 42 inches in circumference, the circumference while knitting will be 40 inches. To determine desired working circumference, divide your blocked gauge by your pre-blocked gauge; i.e., 21 divided by 22 equals .955. Multiply your desired circumference of 42 inches by .955 and you get 40 inches, your working circumference.

I Do Not Knit Gauge Swatches. After that explanation on how to swatch, I now confess and admit I do not knit gauge swatches. I am basically a self-taught knitter. When learning, if I knitted something that was not the desired size I ripped out and started over. I still follow that practice today. But now, through experience, I am aware I usually need to use a needle three sizes smaller than recommended for gauge. After I knit several inches, I check the total circumference. On a garment for myself I simply eyeball the size, which I do quite successfully. When I want an exact measurement, I knit a round onto two or more circular needles so the garment may be laid flat to measure.

To start a project, I use the needle size I think will attain my desired gauge. If I err in attaining gauge, I prefer to have it on the too tight side as there are more options for my adjustments. If gauge is too tight I go up one needle size, knit several rounds and go up a second needle size if needed. This gradual change in gauge is not noticeable except by close examination. I have intentionally used the technique as a means of tapering. If a taper is not desired, the narrower portion of circumference may be stretched during blocking.

Change of design is another option. On a vest I made gradual increases at underarms to form a long underarm gusset. I once changed what was planned as an Aran coat to a pullover Aran dress. That dress is one of the top receivers of compliments in my lifetime of knitting. When gauge was too loose, I have redesigned for a flared bottom or scrunched in the bottom while blocking. As in life, the problem may be seen as an opportunity for a new approach. However, most of the time that gauge is too loose I rip out and start over. We cannot do that with life!

Elizabeth Zimmermann in *Knitting Without Tears* explains the importance of gauge and says you *must* (her italics) make a swatch. Being a dutiful Elizabethan,

Techniques

I started a hat for a swatch shortly after I read the book. I then proceeded to knit the garment and after several inches measured the full garment and discovered I was not knitting to my swatch gauge, so had to rip and start over. I have not knit a gauge swatch since. (Sorry Elizabeth.) I figure if I had to rip when I knit a swatch, why waste my time with the swatch? Approximately 95 percent of the time I attain desired gauge from the start.

I knit a swatch before I knit the *Highland Jacket* for the book to see how a stranded knit design would look at a large gauge. I knit a 24 inch wide and 9 inch high swatch in the round with a steek. When cut and measured I had attained my desired 16 stitches/4 inch gauge. So I cast on the required number of stitches for the design and I merrily knit away carefully measuring my gauge over four inches as I went along. My gauge appeared to be always right on. When jacket was finished and cut, it appeared smaller than the expected 47 inches. It measured 44 inches, or a gauge of 17 stitches/4 inches. I always measure entire width as I knit, but probably because I had a false confidence due to the swatch, I just measured over four inches as I worked on this jacket. But I also must have subconsciously stretched the knitting when I measured because now when I measure over four inches I definitely get 17 stitches. It would have been possible to stretch the jacket when it was blocked to 47 inches, but because I prefer to see stitches in their natural shape it remains a 44 inch jacket. I rationalize that a 47 inch jacket probably would have looked way too big on me!

YARNS AND YARDAGE REQUIREMENTS

All yarns used in garments for the book are available from Schoolhouse Press. I admit to being uninformed about a wide variety of yarns as I prefer to knit and wear wool. I think of yarns as what gauge they ideally knit up at (their recommended gauge) rather than what needle size is used or their name such as bulky, worsted, etc. I purchase yarn using a ballpark yardage requirement based on the recommended gauge.

I am listing the yarns by gauge and estimated yardage required for garments. My motto is to always buy at least three extra skeins, although I think it is recommended to buy one extra. I have to admit I do not run out of yarn. Unused balls or skeins may be returned to Schoolhouse Press without a time limit, but I tend to use it to knit matching socks, gloves, eyeglass cases, etc.

Yarn requirements are estimated for average adult long sleeved garments (40–42" garment circumference, 27–28 inches in length). For different sizes, add or subtract 10% for each difference in size bracket from the average size yardage requirement. For vests, deduct approximately one third off the total yardage. For stranded knitting, add between 50% to 75% of total yardage for second color. The main color yardage may be reduced in relation to amount of second color in the pattern.

Gauge: 7 to 10 stitches per inch stranded knit/**8 to 10 stitches per inch** single ply
Yarn: Icelandic Laceweight (Spun) 50 gram (1.75 oz.) balls = 250 yards
Approximate Needle Sizes: US 000–4, 1.5–3.5 mm
Yarn Requirements: 10–12 skeins, 2500–3000 yards

Gauge: 6 to 9 stitches per inch
Yarn: Shetland Jumper Weight 1 oz. skein = 150 yards
Approximate Needle Sizes: US 0–5, 2.0–3.75 mm
Yarn Requirements: 12–14 skeins, 1800–2100 yards

Gauge: 6 to 9 stitches per inch for sweaters, up to 10 stitches per inch for mittens
Yarn: Helmi Vuorelma Oy Satakieli 3.5 oz. Skein = 360 yards
Approximate Needle Sizes: US 0–5, 2.0–3.75 mm
Yarn Requirements: 5–7 skeins, 1800–2520 yards

Gauge: 6 to 8 stitches per inch
Yarn: Guernsey Wool 3.5 oz. balls = 245 yards
Approximate Needle Sizes: US 0–5, 2.0–3.75 mm
Yarn Requirements: 8–10 balls, 1960–2450 yards

Gauge: 5 to 6 stitches per inch
Yarn: Quebecoise 3.5 oz. skein = 210 yards
Approximate Needle Sizes: US 3–7, 3.25–4.5 mm
Yarn Requirements: 8–10 balls, 1680–2100 yards

Gauge: 4 to 4.5 stitches per inch
Yarn: Highland Wool 4 oz. skein = 175 yards
Approximate Needle Sizes: US 6–10, 4–6 mm
Yarn Requirements: 9–11 skeins, 1575–1925 yards

DIGRESSION

Since Elizabeth Zimmermann digressed in *Knitting Around*, I hope I too will be allowed some digressions by the same publisher. As I work on this book I have a big problem: I am distracted by the beauty of nature outside my window.

I live in what is referred to as the Coulee Region of southwestern Wisconsin. Coulees are gullies formed through the centuries by the many streams in the area. This results in a very hilly area. We have several springs on our property that form a stream which joins up with other streams further along. These combined streams become the La Crosse River, which pours into the Mississippi River. I am always in awe, especially when I visit one spring on our land that bubbles out of the side of a hill, that part of the mighty Mississippi River starts right here. I was raised on the shores of Lake Michigan in eastern Wisconsin and as a child I loved to read stories that related to the Mississippi River. I still recall the great thrill it was to see the Mississippi for the first time in my late teens. I am amazed when I think we actually own land where part of "The Mighty Mississippi" begins.

But, I digress from my digression about my distraction today. I tend to do this as I talk and Meg Swansen refers to it as "Joycieism." We designed and built a log home and perched it part way up one of the hills. The front of the house looks out across a valley to more hills including a rock outcropping called Face Rock. You can find Face Rock on topographical maps of the area. The room where I sit at the computer is located at the back of the house which faces up the hill. There is a much smaller rock outcropping atop this hill.

We had a mild winter and early spring and I do not recall any previous years that were as bountiful with blooms as this year. Today the hillside is covered with a huge variety of flowers and it is absolutely breathtaking. Other than several peony bushes we have planted on the hillside, all the blooms are totally natural. It is a virtual carpet of color with shades of violet from Spider Worts with their graceful slender stemmed foliage and Lobelias. Various shades of pinks are represented by clover and wild roses. The wild roses were several individual bushes last year but this year have spread out into a massive bush absolutely loaded with roses, some almost red in the small bud stage, a darker shade of pink in the mid bud stage, and beautiful pale pink in their open stage. There are both pink and white peonies which also are in various stages of bloom and color tones. White is also represented by Field Pussytoes and Daisy Fleabane. The early Spring carpet of Birdfoot Violets has been replaced by a vast ground cover of Orange Hawkweed with Dandelion type blooms in beautiful shades of orange. They are sometimes referred to as Indian Paintbrush as they are a similar color, but I have never seen true Indian Paintbrush in this part of the Country. Needless to say, all this color is amidst what seems like millions of shades of green. Beautiful! If I could only begin to capture its beauty with yarn…

Techniques—Basic Patterns

BASIC GLOVE PATTERN

As I designed gloves my goals were that they should "fit like a glove," no double points used to knit fingers, and a needle with an eye would only be used for bind-off. So, thumb shaping contours the glove to the palm of the hand. Fingers are cast on with a variation of *Cast-On: Eastern European—Variation*, and knit with 2 circular needles. A palm stitch is crossed to the back and a back stitch is crossed to palm side at finger joins. Two cuff variations are given in the book, but cuff variations are endless.

To allow for various sizes and gauges, instructions are for either a 56 or [64] stitch circumference around the hand. Measure the circumference of glove wearer's hand. Divide 56 [64], the number of stitches around hand, by the measured circumference to find required gauge for desired size.

Important: A round consists of knitting the stitches on needle #1 and needle #2. Needle numbers are noted where a complete round is not knit or there is a variation of stitches on each needle.

Fingers: Index, middle and ring fingers have the same number of stitches. I prefer to knit all 10 digits first before starting to join fingers, etc. Place an identification tag on each digit as it is completed.

Use *Cast-On: Eastern European—Variation* (page 10) and wrap needles 4 [5] times.

Rounds 1, 2, 4, and 5: Knit.

Rounds 3 and 6: *Knit 1, increase 1, knit to last stitch on needle, increase 1, knit 1.* Repeat between asterisks. (My preference here is *Increase: Knit in the Row Below*, page 17.) 8 [9] stitches each needle, total 16 [18] stitches.

Following Rounds: Knit around on 16 [18] stitches to appropriate length for each finger. To measure finger length, try on. When length is achieved, knit across needle #1 only: finger length on back of hand is one row longer than palm side. Break yarn and place stitches from each needle on separate large coilless pins or pieces of yarn.

Little Finger: Use *Cast-On: Eastern European—Variation* and wrap needles 3 [4] times. Follow finger instructions above, but increase to 7 [8] stitches each needle, total 14 [16] stitches.

Thumb: Use *Cast-On: Eastern European—Variation* and wrap needles 5 [6] times. Follow finger instructions above, but increase to 9 [10] stitches each needle, total 18 [20] stitches, but do not break yarns when length reaches web between thumb and index finger.

Thumb Gusset Increase Rounds: Needle #1, knit even 9 [10] stitches.

Needle #2–Left Hand: Knit 1, *Increase: Right* 1, knit to end of needle. (My preferred increase here is *Increase: Raised Bar*, page 16.)

Needle #2–Right Hand: Knit up to last stitch, *Increase: Left* 1, knit to end of needle.

Both Thumbs: Increase every round as established for a total of 5 [6] rounds.
9 [10] stitches needle #1, 14 [16] stitches needle #2, 23 [26] stitches total.
Break yarn, place stitches on hold, etc. as with fingers.

Join Index, Middle, and Ring Fingers: Needle #1 is palm side of glove. Place onto needle #1 in proper order the stitches that were on needle #2 when knitting fingers (one row shorter).

Left Hand: Right to Left—Index finger, middle finger, ring finger.

Right Hand: Right to Left—Ring finger, middle finger, index finger. Place opposite side stitches of each finger onto needle #2. With needle #1 in front, the yarn ends will be at the right edge of each finger on needle #2. See sketch below. 24 [27] stitches each needle, 48 [54] stitches total.

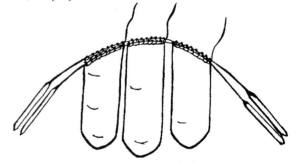

Round 1: Knit 7 [8], *Decrease: Right*, knit 6 [7], *Decrease: Left*, knit 7, [8]. 22 [25] stitches each needle, 44 [50] stitches total.

Round 2: Needle #1. Knit 7 [8], place next stitch on hold on a coilless safety pin and place pin behind needles. Knit 6 [7] and be certain as you knit the first stitch the working yarn is **behind** the stitch on hold. Place next stitch on hold as established, knit 7 [8], knitting first stitch as established. Needle #2. Knit 7 [8], *place stitch on hold from needle #1 onto left needle and knit it, place next stitch on hold as established*, knit 6 [7], repeat between asterisks, knit 7 [8].

Round 3: Needle #1: Knit 7 [8], *place stitch on hold from needle #2 onto left needle and knit it,*, knit 6 [7], repeat between asterisks, knit 7 [8]. Needle #2: Knit.

Join Little Finger–Left Hand: Round 4: Knit 44 [50] stitches. Then, with needle #1 in front (palm) place little finger stitches worked on needle #2 onto the left end of needle #1. Place the back side stitches onto needle #2. With needle #1 in front, yarn end will be at right edge of little finger on needle #2.

Round 5: Needle #1. Knit 21 [24], *Decrease: Right*, knit 6 [7]. Needle #2. Knit 6 [7], *Decrease: Left*, knit 21 [24]. 28 [32] stitches each needle.

Round 6: Needle #1. Knit 21 [24], place next stitch on hold as established, knit 6 [7]. Needle #2. Knit 6 [7], place stitch on hold from needle #1 onto left needle and knit it, place next stitch on hold as established, knit 21 [24].

Round 7: Needle #1. Knit 21 [24], place stitch on hold from needle #2 onto left needle and knit it, knit 6. Needle #2. Knit.

Join Little Finger–Right Hand: Round 4: Needle #1. Knit. Needle #2. With needle #2 in front, place little finger stitches that were knit on needle #1 onto the left end of needle #2. Yarn end will be at left edge of little finger. Place stitches from opposite side onto needle #1. Knit 21, [24], *Decrease: Right*, knit 6 [7].

Round 5: Needle #1. Knit 6 [7], *Decrease: Left*, knit 21 [24]. Needle #2. Knit 21 [24], place next stitch on hold as established, knit 6 [7].

Round 6: Needle #1. Knit 6 [7], place stitch on hold from needle #2 onto left needle and knit it, place next stitch on hold as established, knit 21 [24]. Needle #2. Knit 21 [24], place stitch on hold from needle #1 onto left needle and knit it, knit 6 [7]. 28 [32] stitches each needle.

Following Rounds–Both Hands: Knit around on 56 [64] stitches until piece measures 2 inches from first finger joins (or desired length to thumb join).

Join Thumb–Left Hand: Round 1: Needle #1. Knit.

Needle #2. With needle #2 in front (back of hand) place thumb stitches knit on needle #2 (14 [16] stitches) onto left end of needle #2. The edge with the 5 increased stitches will abut back of hand. Place 9 [10] thumb stitches from opposite side onto needle #1 (palm side). Knit 27 [31], *Decrease: Right*, knit 13 [15].

Round 2: Needle #1. Knit 8 [9] thumb stitches, *Decrease: Left*, knit 27 [31]. Needle #2. Knit 27 [31], place next stitch on hold as established, knit 13 [15] thumb stitches.

Round 3: Needle #1. Knit 8 [9], place stitch on hold from needle #2 onto left needle and knit it, place next stitch on hold as established, knit 27 [31]. Needle #2. Knit 27 [31], place stitch on hold from needle #1 onto left needle and knit it, knit 13 [15].

Round 4: Needle #1. Knit 8 [9], place marker, *Decrease: Left,* knit to end of needle. Needle #2: Knit 28 [32], place marker, knit 13 [15].

Join Thumb–Right Hand: With needle #1 in front (palm) place the 9 [10] thumb stitches knit on needle #1 onto left end of needle #1. Place 14 [16] knit on needle #2 onto needle #2. The edge with 5 increased stitches will abut back of hand.

Round 1: Needle #1. Knit 27 [31], *Decrease: Right*, knit 8 [9] thumb stitches. Needle #2. Knit 13 [15], *Decrease: Left*, knit 27 [31].

Round 2: Needle #1. Knit 27 [31], place next stitch on hold as established, knit 8 [9]. Needle #2. Knit 13 [15] place stitch on hold from needle #1 onto left needle and knit it, place next stitch on hold as established, knit 27 [31].

Round 3: Needle #1. Knit 27 [31], place stitch on hold from needle #2 onto left needle and knit it, knit 8 [9]. Needle #2. Knit.

Round 4: Needle #1. Knit 26 [30], *Decrease: Right*, place marker, knit 8 [9]. Needle #2. Knit 13 [15], place marker, knit to end of needle.

Thumb Shaping–Both Hands: Determine desired number of stitches for cuff. (*Bountiful Harvest Glove*, page 59 and *Circles Glove*, page 68.) Decrease to desired number as follows:

Left Hand: Needle #1. Knit 8 [9], slip marker, *Decrease: Left*, knit to end of needle. Work decrease every round until you reach 28 [32] stitches on needle

#1, then decrease as established but every other round. Needle #2. Knit to 2 stitches of marker, *Decrease: Right*, slip marker, knit to end of needle. Work the decrease every other round. Non-decrease rounds, knit.

Right Hand: Needle #1. Knit to 2 stitches of marker, *Decrease: Right*, slip marker, knit 8 [9]. Work decrease every round until you reach 28 [32] stitches on needle #1, then decrease as established but every other round. Needle #2. Knit 13, [15], slip marker, *Decrease: Left*, knit to end of needle. Work decrease every other round. Non-decrease rounds, knit.

Both Hands: When you reach desired number of stitches for cuffs, continue to knit around even to desired length for start of cuff. Cuff lengths in book are approximately 2-1/2 inches.

GENERAL SOCK INFORMATION

Over many years I have experimented with both the method I use to knit socks and their fit and feel I am honing in on what works for me. I went through the gambit: taking all sorts of foot measurements, doing all sorts of shaping, knitting right and left foot socks, etc. My conclusion; socks that I use ankle circumference for the base number fit just as well as those that make adjustments for various foot measurements. I was once convinced that right and left toe shaping was more comfortable so knit socks for right and left feet. However, after wearing a pair of knee socks all day I noticed the cable which should be going up the outside of my leg was going up the inside. I had those beautifully contoured right and left socks on the wrong feet all day and had not known the difference. I have not knit right and left feet since. The conforming feature of knit fabric is marvelous!

I knit my socks with two 24 inch circular needles. (*Knitting Small Circumferences With Two Circular Needles*, page 18.) To ascertain required number of stitches for socks, I multiply ankle measurement by gauge. For knee highs, I subtract 1 to 2 inches from actual calf measurement (larger number for non stranded knitting) and multiply the answer by gauge for required number of stitches at top of sock. Knee highs are knit even from knee to widest part of calf, and then evenly decreased to number of stitches required at ankle.

Socks knit at a tight gauge wear better than those knit loosely. If you do not like the sock leg knit at the tighter gauge, you may knit the top at one gauge and the foot at a finer gauge. Or, you may knit just the heel

and sole at a tighter gauge. My method of using two circulars makes this very easy to do. Use a smaller needle for the sole of the sock. Keep in mind you may have to increase the number of stitches on the sole, but I prefer the tighter fit and do not add stitches. Add short rows to the sole to make it longer than top of foot.

Wooly Nylon used for surge sewing machines may be carried along with working yarn when knitting the foot. Although nylon is more expensive than polyester which is also available, the nylon abrasion strength is better. I am not convinced this makes socks wear better, but I frequently use it.

For stranded knitted socks I start at the top and work to toe. I increase one eighth the total number of stitches at each side of instep to form a gusset, which is decreased away as you work down the foot. Heels are turned with short rows. Toes are decreased every row or every other row, depending on design, to approximately a 2 inch circumference and then grafted shut. I think because of the double thickness of stranded knit socks, they wear very well.

For socks of one color, striped, textured, or with a stranded pattern on the leg only I usually start at toe and work to top. Toes are increased every other row, soles are short rowed for shaping and heels are turned with short rows. A gusset is not added except for an extremely high instep as there is more stretch to a solid color knit fabric than stranded knitting. Tops have a sewn bind-off.

BASIC PATTERN FOR STRANDED KNIT SOCKS

Follow these written instructions for several of the stranded knit socks in the book (pages 46 and 73) or enlarge and copy chart (page 32) to design your own socks using my technique of a gusset formed by increases and a short row heel turn. The chart has a total of 64 stitches. Leg length (to top of foot) is 48 rows and foot length is 62 rows. Divide ankle circumference into 64 to determine gauge required to knit a desired size sock. When gauge is established, divide row gauge into 48 and 62 to determine length of leg and foot. Change chart size if required for pattern or further size adjustments.

The number of stitches increased for the gusset (Rounds 49 to 56) equals one-eighth the total number of stitches. Adjust gusset size accordingly if you change total number of stitches. If you lengthen foot, gusset decreases (Rounds 64 to 82) may be changed from every three to every four rounds.

Short row heel turn is indicated on chart by arrows. Short rows are made over approximately one-third of the outer edge stitches of the heel

I prefer a hem when knitting stranded knit socks, but you may start with ribbing.

As with all charts in book, Color A is background and Color B is pattern.

Hem: With needle 1 to 2 sizes smaller than stranded knitting needle and **Color B**, *Cast On: Invisible* required number of stitches.

With needle used to cast on (Needle #1), knit one-half of stitches. With second same size needle (Needle #2), knit last half of stitches. (*Knitting Small Circumferences With Two Circular Needles*, page 18.)

Join, being certain not to twist, and start to knit in the round. Continue to knit around to total of 8 rows including cast-on.

Purl one round.

Sock Body–Pattern Round 1: Use **stranded knitting needle** and join Color A. Follow Row 1 on appropriate chart and work with Needle #1 from Point A to B, and with Needle #2 from Point C to D.

Rounds 2–8: Follow chart as established in Round 1.

Round 9: Join Hem to Sock Body. Fold hem to inside on purl ridge. Use **one size larger needles** and join leg stitches in pattern together with invisibly cast on hem stitches. (*Hems: Knit In*, page 14.)

Rounds 10–48: Use **stranded knitting needles** and work around in established pattern.

Round 49: Start Gusset Increases. Work Needle #1 as established. On Needle #2 with Color B make 1 *Increase: Loop—Left Slanted*. Tighten increase up to last stitch knit with Needle #1. Knit in pattern across Needle #2, with Color B make 1 *Increase: Loop—Right Slanted*.

Rounds 50–56: Needle #1, work in pattern. Needle #2, with Color B increase at each end of needle as in Round 49 and work in pattern.

Round 57: Work around.

Rounds 58–59: Short Row Heel Turn. Needle #1 only–half of total stitches.

Follow **Short Row Heel Turn**, Numbers 1 to 7 in *Top to Toe Socks*, page 31. Work in pattern and wrap

both Color A and Color B over the needle for the yarn overs. When knitting stitch with yarn over you will be working three together, the stitch and both yarn over strands. Number 7 of short row heel turn is Round 59.

Round 60: Rearrange Stitches. Work as established, but to prepare for gusset decreases, place last stitch on each end of Needle #1 onto each end of Needle #2

Round 61: Begin Gusset Decreases. Work Needle #1. Needle #2, with Color B *Decrease: Left*, work across to last 2 stitches, with Color B *Decrease: Right*.

Rounds 62 to 82: Work as established on Needle #1. On Needle #2 decrease every 3 rounds as indicated on chart.

Round 83: Rearrange Stitches. Place last stitch on each edge of Needle #2 back onto sides of Needle #1. Work around as established.

Rounds 84–108: Knit around in pattern.

Rounds 109–120: Both needles. *Decrease: Left*, knit to last 2 stitches, *Decrease: Right*.

With Color B, *Kitchener Stitch: Graft* (page 17) sole stitches to top stitches. To help eliminate squared toes, *Decrease: Left* the first two stitches on each needle and *Decrease: Right* the last two stitches on each needle when grafting. Weave in ends.

Knit second sock. If you want the end of round jog on each sock on the inside of your leg, work second sock from Point C to D and then Point A to B. Then when you wear the socks make sure you put each on the proper foot.

Wear with a pair of sandals and wiggle your toes to show off your achievement.

TOE TO TOP SOCKS

This is for socks of one color, striped, textured, or with stranded pattern on leg only.

One advantage of knitting a sock from the toe up is that increases have less bulk than decreases, resulting in a very smooth knit toe. If you are unsure of the amount of yarn you have for the socks, you may knit each foot and then divide the yarn evenly for the tops and knit until you run out of yarn. Of course, if you knit from the top down you can always make toes from different yarns and if you do not wear sandals no one knows the difference. Or, if you wear sandals, the toes become a design feature.

Toe to Top Sock General Instructions: *Cast On: Eastern European—Variation* (page 10), approximately 8 stitches. This is width of tip of sock toe so may vary with size and gauge. **Knit one round.** Choose one of the following toe increases or your favorite toe shaping for next rounds.

Toe Increase I: This toe increase produces a single line of increases on each side.

Toe Increase Round 1: Needle #1. *Increase: Loop—Left Slanted* 1, knit across, *Increase: Loop—Right Slanted* 1. (*Increases*, page 16.) Needle #2. Knit across, *Increase: Loop—Right Slanted* 1.

Round 2: Needle #1. Knit. Needle #2. *Increase: Loop—Left Slanted* 1, knit across.

Toe Increase II: This increase has two stitches between the increases at each side of sock.

Toe Increase Round 1: Needle #1 and Needle #2. Knit 1, *Increase: Left* 1 (your choice of *Increases*). Knit to last stitch, *Increase: Right* 1, knit 1.

Round 2: Knit around.

Either Toe Increases: Repeat Rounds 1 and 2 until you have attained required number of stitches (ankle measurement times gauge). The number of stitches required may be adjusted to accommodate pattern repeats if a design is to be used in leg of sock.

Knit even to mid-foot length.

Sole Short Row Shaping Row 1: (Sole short rows add additional length to the sole and aid in elimination of wrinkles across instep.) **Needle #1** (Sole). **Knit 1** wrapping the yarn from back to front over right needle (left side of loop will be over front of needle). Knit to last stitch on Needle #1. Reverse, yarn over left needle. *Knit Onto Left Needle* (KOLN), page 4, or purl to last stitch on Needle #1. (*Short Rows*, page 20) Reverse, yarn over right needle, knit to yarn over, *Decrease: Right* (last stitch on needle eliminates yarn over). Needle #2 (Instep). Knit.

Sole Short Row Shaping Row 2: Needle #1. *Decrease: Left* (stitch with left side forward eliminates yarn over). Knit across. Needle #2. Knit.

Following Rounds: Knit around and insert short rows in the sole approximately every 1/2 to 1 inch (finer gauges require more short rows than larger gauges). Work to sole length (Needle #1) of approximately 1/2 inch short of total foot length.

Short Row Heel Turn: (Worked on Needle #1.) To determine number of stitches for the short rows, divide the number of sole stitches by three; i.e., the short rows will be worked on one-third the stitches on each side of the center third. However, if you have a high instep work more short rows on each side and have fewer stitches in the center back, but have at least one inch of stitches at center back.

1. Knit across one-third the stitches wrapping yarn from back to front over right needle so left side of loop is over front of needle. (By doing this now, you may later knit or purl the stitch together with a yarn over without having to replace it on the needle to avoid a twisted stitch.)

2. Knit across next one-third stitches in normal manner. Reverse.

3. Yarn over left needle. KOLN or purl one-third center back stitches. Reverse.

4. *Yarn over right needle. Knit onto right needle (KORN) across to yarn over, *Decrease: Right.* Reverse.

5. Yarn over left needle. KOLN or purl to yarn over, *Decrease: Left* so the yarn over is the eliminated stitch and ends up on wrong side of knitting.* (If KOLN insert needle tip from right to left first into stitch and then yarn over and knit the 2 together. If purling, yarn forward, with right needle behind left needle insert tip first into stitch and then into yarn over and purl the two together.

Repeat 4 and 5 until you knit the last stitch on Needle #1 together with its adjacent yarn over. Knit across Needle #2. When you start next round, Needle #1, *Decrease: Left* (eliminating the yarn over), finish round. Knit one more round.

Following Round–Short Row Heel Shaping: (The sole has now become the back of heel.) Follow as earlier in directions **Sole Short Row Shaping** Rows 1 and 2.

Continue to knit around to desired length for start of pattern or ribbing. If working a knit two, purl two rib, decrease if necessary to a number of stitches divisible by four.

Work pattern or rib. Bind off with *Bind–Off: Sewn* (page 6).

TOP TO TOE SOCKS

This is for socks of one color, striped, textured, or with stranded pattern on leg only.

Ankle measurement times gauge determines the number of required stitches. Adjust figure if necessary for pattern repeats. If knitting a knit two, purl two rib for sock top use a number divisible by four.

With a stretchable cast-on of your choice (I usually use *Cast-On: Long Tail*, page 11), cast on desired number of stitches onto a circular needle. Knit around using *Knitting Small Circumferences With Two Circular Needles* (page 18) in desired rib or pattern. Short row heel turns begin when desired leg length reaches bottom of ankle bone. I prefer to stop my pattern or rib somewhere between one to three inches above this point.

Short Row Heel Turn: Needle #1 only–half of total stitches.
1. Knit to last stitch on Needle #1. Reverse.
2. Yarn over left needle. *Knit Onto Left Needle* (KOLN), page 4, or purl to last stitch on Needle #1. Reverse.
3. Yarn over right needle. Knit onto right needle (KORN) to stitch prior to previous reverse (one stitch before yarn over). Reverse.
4. Yarn over left needle. KOLN or purl to stitch prior to previous reverse. Reverse.
Repeat 3 and 4 until you have approximately one-third

total heel stitches between reverses. (About 1-1/2 to 1 inch. For a high instep knit to 1 inch between reverses.)
5. Knit to yarn over, *Decrease: Right* (page 14) to end of Needle #1. (Each stitch will be eliminating its adjacent yarn over.)
6. Knit across Needle #2.
7. Needle #1, *Decrease: Left* (page 14) across until last yarn over has been eliminated. (Each stitch will be eliminating its adjacent yarn over.) Finish round.

Continue to knit around. See **Sole Short Row Shaping** Rows 1 and Row 2 in *Toe to Top Socks*, previous page. If desired, add this shaping every 1/2 to 1 inch until reaching mid-length of foot.

At approximately 2 inches shy of total length begin toe decreases of your choice. My preferred method is:

Row 1: Needles #1 and #2. Knit 1, *Decrease: Left*, knit across to last 3 stitches, *Decrease: Right*, knit 1.

Row 2: Knit around.

Repeat Rows 1 and 2 until desired width for tip of toe. *Kitchener Stitch: Graft* (page 17) toe stitches together. When grafting *Decrease: Left* the first two stitches on each needle and *Decrease: Right* the last two stitches on each needle to help eliminate squared toes.

32

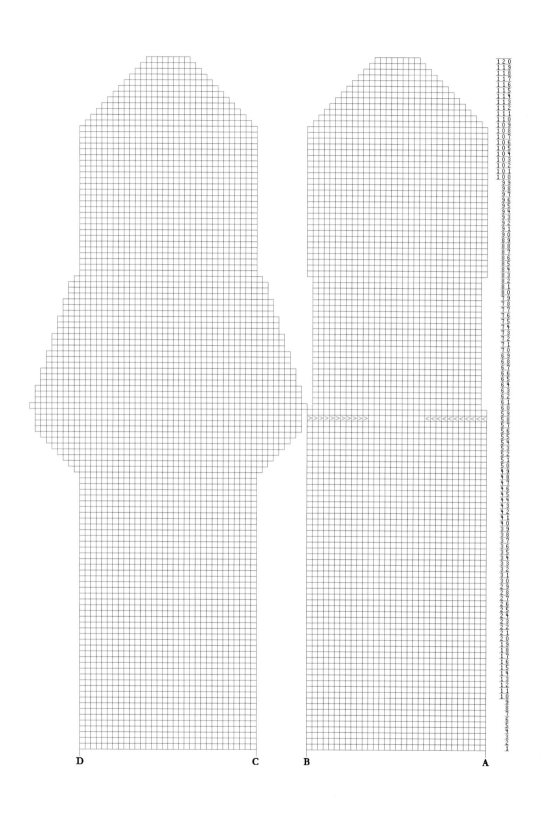

D C   B   A

Latvian Dreams

GARMENTS

READING CHARTS

Every garment in the book has accompanying charts. Read charts from bottom to top. Instructions for repeats of a chart row for a given round are given in each pattern.

CHART SYMBOLS:

□	Knit - Color A
■	Knit - Color B or C
⊟	Purl - Color A
⊟	Purl - Color B
B	Buttonhole
⋔	Stitch On Hold
⊳	Short Row
⊲	Short Row

Steeks: Center Front Chart

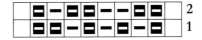

← Start of Round

Steeks: Armhole Chart

What A Difference A Gauge Makes

This design incorporates a large square motif found in Z. Ventaskrasts' book. (*Bibliography,* page 164.) The front and back of the body are the same; each one motif wide, and one and a half motifs in length. The pattern is an example of "what a difference a gauge makes." The number of stitches is the same for all sizes and gauge determines the size of the finished garment.

The model sweater was knit with a basic drop shoulder and a straight boat neck, but there is an optional V-neck. Another option is the sleeve color; one of each as in the model, or both the same color.

Body Gauge—Stranded Knitting	Circumference	*Body Length	*Sleeve Circumference
32 sts/36 rows = 4" (10 cm)	26"	17"	13"
30 sts/34 rows = 4" (10 cm)	28"	18"	14"
28 sts/32 rows = 4" (10 cm)	30"	20"	15"
26 sts/29 rows = 4" (10 cm)	32"	22"	16"
24 sts/27 rows = 4" (10 cm)	35"	24"	17"
22 sts/25 rows = 4" (10 cm)	38"	26"	19"
20 sts/23 rows = 4" (10 cm)	42"	28"	21"
18 sts/20 rows = 4" (10 cm)	46"	32"	23"
16 sts/18 rows = 4" (10 cm)	52"	36"	26"

*May be adjusted. (*Design, E.P.S.,* page 121, *Yarn Suggestions and Amounts,* page 24, and *Needles,* page 19.)

Model Measurements and Gauge:

28" circumference, 18" long
30 sts/34 rows = 4" (10 cm) stranded knitting

Model Materials:

Color A—#96 Pale Yellow Jamieson & Smith Shetland Jumper Weight, Five – 1 oz. skeins
Color B—#30 Lovat Jamieson & Smith Shetland Jumper Weight, Five – 1 oz. skeins
1 Button

BODY

Hem: Use needle 2 or 3 sizes smaller than stranded knitting needle and Color B, *Cast On: Invisible* (page 11) 208 stitches.

Hem Row 1: Knit.

Hem Round 2: Place marker. Join, being certain not to twist, and start to knit in the round.

Hem Rounds 3–10: Knit around.

Hem Round 11: (11 rows of knitting including invisibly cast-on row.) Purl.

Body Round 1: Knit.

Round 2: Begin stranded knitting. Use stranded knitting needle and join Color A. Slip marker, *knit Row 2 of **Body Chart** (page 38) from Point A to B, Point C to D*, place marker. Repeat between asterisks. (Stitches A/D are side stitches and Stitches C/B are center back and center front stitches. You may also wish to place a marker at Points B.)

Rounds 3–11: Knit around as established.

Round 12: Join Hem to Body. Use needle one size larger than stranded knitting needle. In pattern knit body stitches together with invisibly cast-on stitches. (*Hems: Knit In,* page 14.)

Knit In Hem

Rounds 13–92: Use stranded knitting needle, knit around and follow **Body Chart** as established. (See below, **Optional Arm Opening Depths**)

Round 93: Arm Openings. *Slip marker, place next stitch on hold. With Color A around thumb and Color B around index finger, *Cast-On: Long Tail* (page 11) a 10 stitch steek, **place marker**. Knit from Point D to B, Point C to D.* Repeat between asterisks. (*Steeks,* page 21.)

<u>**Optional Arm Opening Depths:**</u> If you want a sleeve circumference different than that given for your size in the chart above, follow instructions for Round 93 in the round of your desired depth. (*Design, E.P.S.* page 121.)

Rounds 94–106: Work **Body Chart** from Point D to B, Point C to D twice each round. Repeat Rows 1 and 2, *Steeks: Armhole Chart,* page 33.

Repeat Rounds 3–53 of Body Chart: Knit around

What A Difference A Gauge Makes

etc. (See below, **Optional V-Neck Shaping**)

Repeat Round 54: In alternating colors, bind off steek stitches. Knit from Point D to B, Point C to D (Back). In alternating colors, bind off steek stitches. **Do not repeat** (Front). Break yarns.

Optional V-Neck Shaping: The above instructions create a high stand-up boat neckline after the neck ribbing has been knit (as on model and similar to those found on some traditional Fisherman sweaters). If you object to this high neckline, you may insert a V-neck in line with the design. (Similar V-neck shaping is found in *Highland Jacket* and *Cornfields*, pages 40 and 70.)

You have several V-neck options. If you want a narrow V-neck with an I-cord edge, start on Repeat Round 34. If you want a wider V-neck with either an I-cord or ribbed edge, start on Repeat Round 23. Knit from Point D to B, Point C to D. Knit from Point D to C, place center front stitch C/B on hold, place marker, cast on a 10 stitch steek as you did for arm openings, place marker and knit from Point C to D. Decrease on each side of the center front steek every round and repeat Rows 1 and 2 of *Steeks: Center Front Chart*, page 33. (*Decreases*, page 14.) In alternating colors, bind off center front steek in Repeat Round 53.

Steek: *Slip Stitch Crochet* (page 21) armhole steeks. (Slip stitch crochet and cut center front steek if you have one.) Place front stitches on same size or smaller needle(s).

Join Shoulders: *Use needle one size larger and have outsides facing each other. Begin at armhole edge and *Bind Off: Three Needle* (page 7) 31 stitches **in pattern** following Row 54 of **Body Chart**. Break yarns.* Turn and repeat between asterisks for opposite shoulder. Leave center stitches on needles. Weave in ends.

Optional V-Neck: Same as above, but bind off to center front steek.

Row 1–Neck Ribbing (Boat Neck): Use hem needle size and Color B. Start at the left shoulder and knit across the front and back neck stitches **and** also knit up 1 stitch at each shoulder. (88 stitches). **Turn**.

Row 2: Make buttonhole tab. Start with purl 2, knit 2 and work in ribbing. At end of row, **turn**, (*Cast-On: Cable*, page 10) to left needle 6 stitches, and bring yarn forward before placing the sixth stitch on needle.

Row 3: Start with knit 2, purl 2 and work in ribbing to

end of row. **Turn**.

Row 4: Start with purl 2, knit 2, and work in ribbing to end of row. **Turn**.

Row 5: Knit 2, purl 2 together, yarn over, (buttonhole), knit 2, purl 2 across. **Turn**.

Rows 6–10: Work back and forth in ribbing as established.

Optional Raised Back Neckline (Boat Neck): On the model, I inserted a short row across the back. This short row was inserted approximately half way up the ribbing and 4 stitches in from each shoulder on the back. (*Short Rows*, page 20.)

Bind Off: Latvian (page 7) neck ribbing.

Neck Finish For Optional V-Neck: Starting at left shoulder, *knit up 1 stitch for every row along center front steek*, knit stitch on hold at center front, repeat between asterisks and knit across back stitches. Use one of the options below to finish neckline.

I-Cord Edge: *Cast On: Cable 2* stitches on left needle, and bring yarn forward before placing second stitch on needle. *Bind Off: I-Cord* (page 15) around. *Kitchener Stitch: Half Graft* (page 18) 2 stitches to cable cast on.

Ribbed Edge: Knit up as above but mark the center front stitch and decrease across the back if necessary so your final stitch count is divisible by 4 plus 3 (A number divisible by 4 is required for knit 2, purl 2 ribbing, and the 3 extra stitches allow a balanced center front decrease.) Work the following rounds in knit 2, purl 2 rib up to 1 stitch prior to the marked center front stitch, *Decrease: Double* (page 14). Mirror image the stitch(es) before and after the double decrease, and continue to knit around in knit 2, purl 2 rib. When the ribbing is approximately 1 inch, *Bind Off: Latvian* (page 7).

What A Difference A Gauge Makes

SLEEVES

Sleeve Gauge	Body Circumference	*Sleeve Length
32 sts/44 rows = 4"	26"	13.5"
30 sts/42 rows = 4"	28"	14"
28 sts/40 rows = 4"	30"	15"
26 sts/36 rows = 4"	32"	17"
24 sts/34 rows = 4"	35"	18"
22 sts/30 rows = 4"	38"	20"
20 sts/28 rows = 4"	42"	21"
18 sts/24 rows = 4"	46"	21"
16 sts/22 rows = 4"	52"	21"

*Sleeve lengths are easily adjusted.

The armhole steek may be cut before of after stitches have been knit up. The model was knit with one sleeve Color A and the second sleeve Color B. Use stockinette needle and color of your choice to knit the stitch on hold at the underarm. *Knit Up* (page 18) 52 stitches on the front and 52 stitches on the back of the sleeve opening—105 stitches which includes the underarm stitch. (Approximately *knit up 1 stitch every row 3 times, skip 1 row,* repeat between asterisks.)

Place marker, knit around and decrease every fourth round at the underarm; i.e., slip marker, knit 2, *Decrease: Left*, knit around to 3 stitches prior to marker, *Decrease: Right*, knit 1. (*Decreases*, page 14.) Knit around as established to approximately 3 inches prior to start of ribbed cuff. (*Design*, page 121.) Use **stranded knitting needle** and attach contrasting color. Knit from **Sleeve Chart** with the design centered at top of sleeve **and** knit the center underarm stitch with main sleeve color. Decrease as established as you knit from the **Sleeve Chart**. When design is complete, break contrasting color yarn. Use **stockinette needle** and continue to knit around sleeve as established to desired length prior to ribbing.

Twenty-five percent of the total body stitches (52 stitches) will give the cuff a loose fit, whereas twenty percent (44 stitches) will give the cuff a tight fit. Or, you may go half way between and use 48 stitches. Your choice. If you have more than the desired number of stitches for the cuff when you reach the appropriate length, decrease evenly around to attain the correct number of stitches. (*Spacing Decreases/Increases Evenly*, page 21.) With hem needles, work around in knit 2, purl 2 ribbing to desired length. Knit a long ribbing for a child's sweater and fold it up while the child grows.

Bind off the ribbing with *Bind Off: Latvian*.
Knit second sleeve.

I-Cord: Apply a 2 stitch I-cord around the join between the body and the sleeve and the lower edge. On the model the color of the sleeve was used at the body-sleeve join and Color B at the bottom edge. (*I-Cord: Applied* , page 15.)

Weave in ends, sew small button to neck and block. May the recipient wear it with pride and pleasure.

Body and Sleeve Join with I-Cord Trim

Body Chart

Sleeve Chart

BC

DA

Highland Jacket

I made this jacket using Highland wool to demonstrate that Latvian designs may be knitted at larger gauges and still be very attractive (and warm). It also shows how important gauge is. The model *Highland Jacket* has a 44 inch circumference, but has 19 stitches less than the model of *What A Difference A Gauge Makes* which has a circumference of 28 inches. Both *What A Difference A Gauge Makes* and this jacket use large square motifs from A. Ventaskrasts' books that are repeated on the front and the back for the circumference. Size variations are made by change of gauge, not stitch numbers.

The model was made with a set-in sleeve, but the chart allows for an optional drop shoulder. After the body was knitted, a facing and hem were added of Shetland jumper weight yarn to give less bulk. If you use a finer yarn for your jacket, you may wish to knit the facing and hem concurrent with the jacket as in *The Star* and *Morocco*, pages 114 and 90.

Sizes: Divide 189 (the total number of body stitches) by the circumference you desire and you will have the stitch gauge required to obtain that circumference. The length will vary by gauge, but the length may also be adjusted by knitting fewer or more row repeats. Because there are fewer stitches in the motif, you do not have the wide variety of sizes available with this motif as with *What a Difference a Gauge Makes*. However, that chart certainly may be substituted for this jacket. There are additional motifs of this type with various stitch counts in the Chart Section of this book.

Model Measurements and Gauges:
44" circumference, 28" long, 24" sleeve length
17 stitches/18 rows = 4" (10 cm) in stranded knitting
17 stitches/24 rows = 4" (10 cm) in stockinette stitch

Model Materials:
Color A—Cream Highland Wool, Five – 4 oz. skeins
Color B—Bressay Blue Highland Wool, Eight – 4 oz. skeins
Color C—#FC47 Bressay Blue Jamieson & Smith Shetland Jumper Weight, Two – 1 oz. skeins (Hem and Facing)
5 Pewter Buttons

For yarn requirements, size variations and needle sizes, see *Yarn Suggestions and Amounts*, page 24 and *Needles*, page 19.

Steek: For Body Row 1 and Round 2, work steek with Color B. Following rounds work *Steeks: Center Front Chart* (page 33) and alternate Rows 1 and 2.

BODY

Use stockinette stitch needle and Color B, *Cast-On: Invisible* (page 11) 199 stitches. This figure includes 10 steek stitches.

Row 1: With Color B, knit.

Round 2: Join, being certain not to twist. With Color B, start to knit in the round. Knit 5 steek stitches, place marker, knit to 10 stitches prior to marker, place marker, knit 5 steek stitches.

Body Chart Round 1: Begin stranded knitting. Use stranded knitting needle and join Color A. Knit the 5 steek stitches, slip marker, *knit Round 1 of **Body Chart** (page 44) from Point A to B (side) , Point C to D* (center back). Repeat between asterisks, but end knit to Point A (center front) , slip marker, and knit 5 steek stitches. If you wish, place markers at the sides and center back.

Rounds 2–75: Knit in pattern as established above.

Body Side

Set-In Sleeve–Round 76: Arm Openings. (As in **Model.** See next page for **Optional Drop Shoulder.**) Knit steek, slip marker, *knit 38 stitches from Point A, place next 19 stitches on hold, place marker. With Color A around thumb and Color B around index finger: *Cast On: Long Tail* (page 11) a 10 stitch steek, place marker, knit to Point D.* Repeat between asterisks, but end at Point A, knit steek.

Highland Jacket

Rounds 77–95: Knit center front steek as established and repeat Rows 1 and 2, *Steeks: Armhole Chart*, (page 33). As indicated by dark line on **Body Chart**, decrease at arm openings on even numbered rounds 7 times; i.e., knit steek, slip marker, *from Point A knit to 2 stitches prior to armhole steek, *Decrease: Left*, slip marker, work steek, slip marker, *Decrease: Right*, knit to Point D.* (*Decreases*, page 14.) Repeat between asterisks, ending at Point A, knit steek. After decreases there are 31 stitches between Point A and *Steeks: Armhole* (Point E) and 61 stitches on back between *Steeks: Armhole*.

Repeat Rounds 2–16 (or Round 6 if a wider neck opening is desired): Knit steek, slip marker, *knit from Point A to E, slip marker, work steek, slip marker, knit from Point E to D*. Repeat between asterisks, but end knit to Point A, knit steek.

<u>Optional Drop Shoulder</u> – Round 76: Arm Openings. Knit steek, slip marker, *knit from Point A to C, place next stitch on hold, place marker. With Color A around thumb and Color B around index finger *Cast On: Long Tail* (page 11) a 10 stitch steek, place marker, knit from Point C to D.* Repeat between asterisks, but end at Point A, knit steek.

Rounds 77–95: Knit center front steek as established and repeat Rows 1 and 2 *Steeks: Armhole Chart* for armhole steeks, (page 33). Knit steek, slip marker, *knit from Point A to C, slip marker, work armhole steek, slip marker, knit from Point C to D*. Repeat between asterisks, but end knit to Point A, knit steek.

Repeat Rounds 2–16 (or Round 6 if a wider neck opening is desired.): Knit steek, slip marker, *knit from Point A to C, slip marker, work steek, slip marker, knit from Point C to D*. Repeat between asterisks, but end knit to Point A, knit steek.

Both Shoulder Treatments – Repeat Round 17 (or Round 7): **Neck Shaping.** (See below **Optional Additional Length**) Knit steek, slip marker, *Decrease: Right* , *knit to arm opening as established, slip marker, work steek, slip marker* knit to Point D. Repeat between asterisks except end knit to 2 stitches prior to Point A, *Decrease: Left*, slip marker, knit steek.

Repeat Rounds 18–31: Knit as established in Repeat Round 17 (or Round 7) and decrease at the front edges every round. Start to read the chart one stitch to the left every round to maintain pattern. Your center front will begin to look deformed, but it will fall into a nice V-neck once the steek is cut.

Repeat Round 32: Knit as established, and bind off all steeks in alternating colors.

<u>Optional Additional Length</u>: The model jacket ends at Repeat Round 32, but you may knit to Repeat Round 48 for additional length. If you lengthen your jacket, start your neck shaping at Repeat Rounds 25 or 32, following instructions for Repeat Round 17 above. On the following rounds decrease at center front every round as established in Repeat Round 17.

Steeks: *Slip Stitch Crochet* (page 21) all steeks. Cut center front steek.

Join Shoulders: Place front stitches on same size or smaller needle(s). *Have outsides facing each other. Use needle one size larger. Begin at armhole edge and *Bind Off: Three Needle* (page 7) in pattern a repeat of Row 32 (or the last row knit). Break yarns.* Turn and repeat between asterisks for opposite shoulder. Place center back stitches on hold. Weave in ends.

Facing and Hem: Use Shetland jumper weight wool to match or blend with jacket yarn (Color C) and 40" stockinette stitch needle (or several shorter needles). You will be knitting around the entire jacket perimeter. Start at lower center back and knit the invisibly cast-on stitches to the front edge, knit up 1 stitch for every row along front edge to shoulder seam, knit across back stitches that were on hold, knit up 1 stitch for every row to bottom front, knit invisibly cast-on stitches to center back, place marker for start of round. (*Knit Up*, page 18.)

Facing and Hem

Round 1: Slip marker, knit around and place a coilless safety pin on the stitch at each of the lower front edge

Highland Jacket

corners, and place a marker at each shoulder seam.

Round 2: Knit to one stitch from front corner stitch marked with a pin, *Decrease: Double*. *Knit to the shoulder marker, *Increase: Right* 1, slip marker, knit 1, *Increase: Left* 1.* Repeat between asterisks. Knit to one stitch from front corner stitch marked with a pin, *Decrease Double*, knit to end of round. (*Decrease Double*, page 14 and *Increases*, page 16.)

Rounds 3–16: Continue to knit around on this huge number of stitches **and** decrease and increase **every round** as established in Round 2. I am a little strange (ed. note – "but lovable") and I chose to work the last 6 rounds in garter stitch for a decorative touch although it is not visible when wearing the jacket. Maybe I want to prove to people I do not mind purling! For the garter stitch edge, repeat *purl 1 round, knit 1 round,* 3 times and increase and decrease as established.

   Bind off and tack down facing and hem. (*Bind-Offs*, page 7)

SLEEVES

Knit Up Sleeves: Armhole steeks may be cut before or after sleeve stitches are knitted up. Transfer the 19 underarm stitches on hold to stockinette needle and with same needle and Color B, knit up 89 stitches evenly spaced around arm opening. Approximately *knit up 1 stitch every row 4 times, skip 1 row,* repeat between asterisks. (*Knit Up*, page 18.) Total 108 stitches. End, knit 9 underarm stitches, place marker for start of round (center underarm).

Following Rounds: Decrease every **5th round** by slip marker, knit 2, *Decrease: Left* , knit to 3 stitches from start of round marker, *Decrease: Right*, knit 1. Continue to knit in the round to desired wrist length. (*Knitting With Two Circular Needles*, page 18 and *Row Marker*, page 20.) For a more bloused look, knit an inch or 2 beyond actual wrist length (as in model).

Cuffs: It is decision time. Use 36 stitches for a tight fit, 42 or 48 stitches for a looser fit. To aid your decision, mark off the number of stitches along bottom of the jacket and wrap that portion around your wrist. After you determine the number of stitches desired, subtract the number from the total number of stitches now on your needles. Decrease around evenly the number of stitches in your answer.

Cuff

Cuff Round 1: With Color B, knit around.

Round 2: With Color A, knit around.

Rounds 3–11: Use stranded knitting needles and repeat **Cuff Chart** 6 [7, 8] times each round.

Round 12: With stockinette needles and Color A, knit. Break Color A yarn.

Round 13: With Color B, knit.

Round 14: With Color B, purl.

Cuff Hem Round 1: With Color B and stockinette needles, knit. Break yarn.

Following Cuff Rounds: Use Shetland jumper weight yarn (Color C) and stockinette needles. Knit around until depth of cuff. Bind off, turn hem to inside, and tack down.

Knit second sleeve.

I-Cord Trim: Apply 3-stitch I- cord around entire jacket, and make 5 I-cord buttonholes approximately 3 inches apart on the appropriate front edge of jacket. (*I-Cord: Applied* , page 15 and *I-Cord: Buttonholes*, page 15.) Also apply 3-stitch I-cord to the purl turning row of cuffs, around the top of cuffs, and around the sleeve and body joins. *Cast On: Invisible* 3 I-cord stitches for each application and *Kitchener Stitch: Graft* (page 17) the 3 I-cord stitches to the 3 *Cast-On: Invisible* stitches at the end of each application.

   Weave in ends, sew on buttons, and block.

   Wear or share proudly.

Body Chart

**Cuff
Chart**

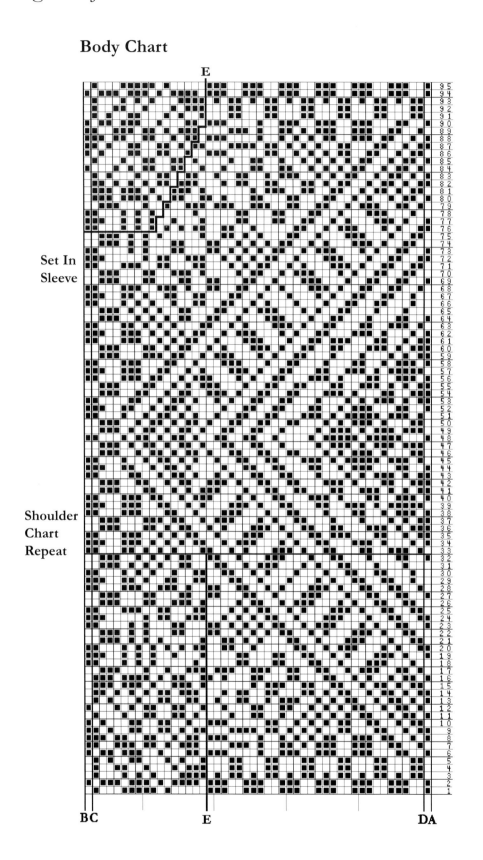

Set In
Sleeve

Shoulder
Chart
Repeat

Highland Socks

HIGHLAND SOCKS

For written details, see *Basic Pattern for Stranded Knit Socks* (page 28). Sock leg has 66 stitches. Divide your ankle measurement into 66 to determine required gauge for your sock size.

Model Gauge and Materials:
28 stitches/30 rows = 4" (10 cm) stranded knitting
Color A—#1A Cream Jamieson and Smith Shetland Jumper Weight, Two – 1 oz. skeins
Color B—#FC47 Bressay Blue Jamieson and Smith Shetland Jumper Weight, Two – 1 oz. skeins

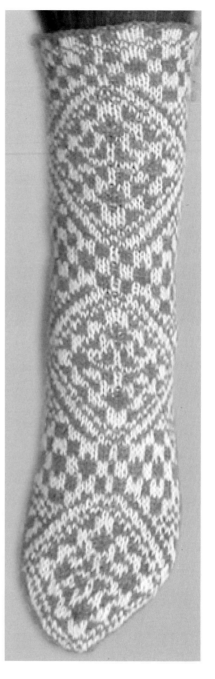

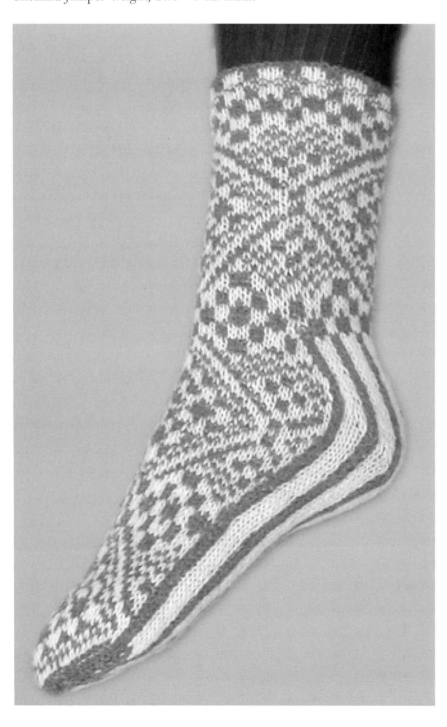

Needle #2

Needle #1

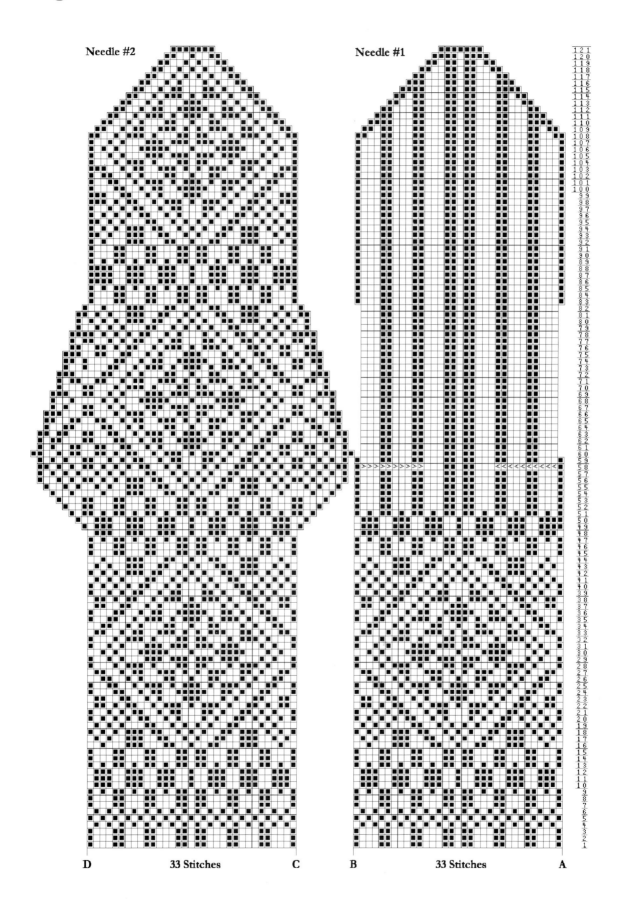

D   33 Stitches   C   B   33 Stitches   A

Tay's Sweater

The sweater on page 104 is called *Snowflake Cardigan* because of the border design; this one could be called *Snowflake II*. However, I named this sweater for its recipient, my niece. The longer Latvian designs are examined, the more variations you will see in the pattern. Examine this design and you will see it contains a version of the eight-point star or snowflake design.

This overall design is an adaptation of a woven blanket found in *A Joy Forever, Latvian Weaving* by Jane A. Evans. The stars are smaller (to eliminate long carries) and I reversed the light and dark colors to make the snowflakes off-white. The border is my design, which also goes across the shoulders and down the top of the sleeves. As in the *Snowflake Cardigan*, the solid border is knit at the same time as the sweater. (*Mitered Corners Knit In The Round*, page 19.) This sweater has a classic drop shoulder. The sleeves are started at the cuff and half-grafted to the armhole edge. In the underarm panels I knit my niece's name into one sleeve and "Xmas 1995" into the second sleeve.

Measurements and Gauges:

41" [45", 49", 53", 57"] circumference at underarm (buttoned), 27" [27", 27", 30", 30"] long
24 stitches/34 rows = 4" (10 cm) stockinette stitch
24 stitches/28 rows = 4" (10 cm) stranded knitting

Materials:

Color A—#40 Light Aqua Quebecoise, 7 [7, 7, 8, 8] – 3.5 oz. skeins
Color B—#92 Cream Quebecoise, 6 [6, 6, 7, 7] – 3.5 oz. skeins
Color C—#55 Burgundy Quebecoise, Approximately 5 yards for optional border trim.
Buttons: 7 [7, 7, 8, 8]

BODY

Hem: Use needle 1 or 2 sizes smaller than stockinette needle and Color A, *Cast On: Invisible* (page 11) 239 [263, 287, 311, 335] stitches. These figures include 10 steek stitches. (*Needles*, page 19)

Steek: (page 21) Use Color A through Round 24.

Row 1: Knit, and increase 1 stitch each side of the steek. (i.e, Knit 5 steek stitches, place marker, *Increase: Right*, knit to the last 5 stitches, *Increase: Left*, place marker, knit 5 steek stitches.) The increases at each side of the steek form a mitered corner inside the hem. (*Increases*, page 16)

Round 2: Join, being certain not to twist, and start to knit in the round. Knit 5 steek stitches, slip marker, *Increase: Right*, knit to the next marker, *Increase: Left*, slip marker, and knit 5 steek stitches.

Rounds 3–11: Knit, increase 1 each side of steek, as established.

Round 12: You have 12 rows of knitting, including invisibly cast-on row. (The center front looks bulky and funny, possibly different than anything you have seen before. Just wait, it gets funnier looking.) **Purl all stitches** (except steek), increasing 1 each side of steek as established. 263 [287, 311, 335, 359] stitches.

Round 13: Change to stockinette needle. Knit, increasing as established.

Round 14: Knit steek stitches, slip marker, increase 1, purl 1, knit to last stitch before steek marker, purl 1, increase 1, slip marker, knit steek stitches. (The 2 purl stitches are turning stitches for the facing of the cardigan. These stitches are purled every round (**Body Chart**, page 53).

Rounds 15–22: Knit around. Increase and purl as established. Increases are complete with Round 22. 283 [307, 331, 355, 379] stitches. Ten steek stitches included in count.

Round 23: Knit around without increases, but maintain purl stitches at the front.

Round 24: (There are 11 knit rounds after the purled round.) Fold hem on purl round and knit the body stitches to the invisibly cast-on stitches where possible. Use needle one size larger than stockinette needle for this joining round. (*Knitting in Mitered Hems*, page 19). See photograph below.

Tay's Sweater

Round 25: Begin stranded knitting. Use stranded knitting needle and join Color B. (**Steek:** Repeat Rows 1 and 2, *Steeks: Center Front Chart*, page 33, for subsequent rounds.) Knit the steek stitches, slip marker, knit Point A to Point B on the **Body Chart.** Knit from B to C 16 [18, 20, 22, 24] times. Knit remaining 47 stitches reading left to right Round 25 of **Body Chart**, Point D to Point A. Knit the 5 steek stitches.

Rounds 26–39: Knit as established in Round 25, following **Body Chart.**

Round 40: Knit a buttonhole of your choice on both the facing and the border as indicated on the **Body Chart.** (*Buttonholes*, page 8.) Buttonholes are placed on one front border only. For women they are placed on the border at the beginning of the round. For men, the buttonholes are placed on the border at the end of the round (when reading the chart back from left to right).

Rounds 41–63: Follow **Body Chart.**

Repeat Rounds 40–63 – 3 [3, 3, 4, 4] more times. (See below, **Arm Openings**) There are 23 rounds between each pair of buttonholes. Notice on the **Body Chart** the buttonhole is lined up with the widest point of every other diamond on the border design. No need to count rows, just look at your knitting. (Note this is not the same button placement as in garment photographs.)

Arm Openings: After knitting a total of 4 [4, 4, 5, 5] buttonhole pairs, knit through rounds 63 [61, 60, 60, 60] of the Rounds 40 to 63 repeat. Work steek and follow **Body Chart** as established on 76 [82, 88, 94, 100] stitches. (The next stitch for sizes 41, 45 and 53 will be the start of a pattern repeat and the next stitch for sizes 49 and 57 will be the center of a pattern repeat.) ***Place next stitch on hold**, place marker, with Color A around thumb and Color B around index finger, *Cast On: Long Tail*, (page 11) a 10 stitch steek, place marker.* Knit 119 [131, 143, 155, 167] stitches in pattern. Repeat between asterisks above. Finish round as established.

Continue to repeat Rounds 40 to 63 until total number of buttonhole pairs is 7 [7, 7, 8, 8] ending with Round 40. Knit *Steeks: Center Front* as established and repeat rows 1 and 2, *Steeks: Armhole Chart* (page 33) for armhole steeks.

Neck Shaping: Break yarns. Place 5 steek and the next 35 stitches on hold on a piece of yarn—total 40

stitches on hold. The stitches on hold will form a *Kangaroo Pouch* (page 17).

New Steek–Center Front: With Color A around thumb and Color B around index finger, *Cast On: Long Tail*, 5 steek stitches. Place marker, follow **Shoulder Chart** and knit Round 1 between Point A and C 16 [18, 20, 22, 24] times, make the necessary adjustments in the design at armholes, and knit armhole steeks as established. Knit from A to B, place marker. Cast on 5 steek stitches as before. Place the next 35 stitches, plus 5 steek stitches on hold on a piece of yarn. (You have a total of 80 stitches on hold—35 neck stitches and 5 steek stitches on each side.)

Shoulder Chart Rounds 2-17: Knit the rounds in pattern as established.

Round 18: In alternating colors bind off 5 front steek stitches, knit in pattern to first armhole steek, in alternating colors bind off armhole steek, knit in pattern to second armhole steek, in alternating colors bind off armhole steek, knit in pattern to front steek, in alternating colors bind off 5 steek stitches. (See *Steeks*, page 22, for Katherine Misegades' improved armhole steek treatment.)

Finishing: *Steeks: Slip Stitch Crochet* (page 21) the armhole steeks and the **top** center front steek. Cut these steeks. **Do not** slip stitch crochet or cut the body length center front steek at this time.

The shoulders are grafted to enable you to duplicate stitch Color A and C in pattern across the shoulders. *Use Color B, begin at the armhole edge and *Kitchener Stitch: Graft* (page 17) the front and back of the shoulder together until you reach the steek. Break yarn.* Turn and repeat between asterisks for opposite shoulder. Keep center back stitches on needle.

With Color A, duplicate stitch the pattern design between Points A and B of **Row 19** of **Shoulder Chart** over the grafted stitches. As you work, catch the working yarn under the strands on the inside to eliminate long carries. You will later duplicate stitch the Point B/C stitch with Color C.

Neck Border & Facing: Transfer the 40 right front stitches on hold to stockinette needle. (Neck border, facing, and steek are worked with Color A.) Knit 5 steek stitches, place marker, work 35 stitches, (the established purl turning stitches will be continued in neck border.) Place a safety pin on the last stitch knit (to become the center stitch of a *Decrease: Double*, page 14). *Knit Up* (page 18) 1 in row below first shoulder stitch, *Knit Up* along the "**New Steek: Center Front**" by [*Knit Up* 1, skip 1, *Knit Up* 2, skip 1] 4 times ending with knit 2—total 13 knit up stitches. Knit back neck stitches by knitting first and last stitches together with the stitch from the row below, and decreasing across the back by knit 2, knit 2 together. *Knit Up* 13 stitches as you did on the other side. Transfer the 40 left front stitches on hold to left needle. Knit first stitch from the left front, place a safety pin on this stitch, work 34, place marker, knit 5 steek stitches.

Neck Border

Neck Border Round 1: Knit 5 steek stitches, slip marker, *Decrease: Left*, *work to 1 stitch before stitch marked with pin, *Decrease: Double*. Repeat from*. Work to 2 stitches before steek marker, *Decrease: Right*, slip marker, knit 5 steek stitches. (*Decreases*, page 14)

Neck Border Round 2: Knit 5 steek stitches as established, slip marker, *Decrease: Left*, work to two stitches before steek marker, *Decrease: Right*, slip marker, knit steek stitches as established.

Repeat **Neck Border Rounds 1–2** – 5 more times. (Total of 13 rows, including the knit up row.) You are working a single decrease at each side of the steek every round and a double decrease at the neck corners every other round.

Turning Round: Purl all stitches (except steeks), decreasing at each side of steeks as established, but do not double decrease at the neck edge corners.

Neck Facing Round 1: Use needle 1 to 2 sizes smaller than stockinette needle and knit 5 steek stitches as

established, slip marker, *Decrease: Left*, *knit to 1 stitch before the center stitch of the double decrease, *Increase: Right* 1, knit 1 and mark stitch with safety pin, *Increase: Left* 1. Repeat from *. Knit to 2 stitches prior to the marker for the steek, *Decrease: Right*, slip marker, knit 5 steek stitches as established. (You are mirror imaging the double decrease by increasing on each side of the center stitch.)

Neck Facing Round 2: Knit 5 steek stitches as established, slip marker, *Decrease: Left*, knit to 2 stitches prior to the marker for the steek, *Decrease: Right*, slip marker, knit 5 steek stitches as previously established.

Repeat Rounds 1–2 – 5 more times. You are continuing to work a single decrease at each side of the steek every round, but making an **increase** on each side of the center stitch at the neck corners every other round. In the final round bind off the steek stitches. You have 12 rounds after the purl turn round.

Stitches may remain on the needle or be put onto a holder. *Steeks: Slip Stitch Crochet* (page 21) the center front steek. Cut center front steek. If using the *Roberta Center Buttonholes*, finish the buttonholes. Turn facings to the inside and tack down. When tacking down neck facing and remainder of bottom hem, use Color A and go through the open stitch loops with the yarn. If you use a buttonhole other than the *Roberta Center Buttonhole*, use a matching thread to tack down around the outer buttonhole to secure it to the inner facing buttonhole.

SLEEVES

Sleeve Gauge: (page 20)
28 stitches/39 rows to 4 inches (10 cm) stockinette stitch
28 stitches/32 rows to 4 inches (10 cm) stranded knitting

Sleeve Length: 16 [17, 17.5, 18, 17.5] inches

Use a needle 1 or 2 sizes smaller than sleeve stockinette needle and Color A, *Cast On: Invisible* 50 stitches.

Row 1: Prepare to knit in the round by knitting one half the stitches with the needle used to cast on and the second half with second circular needle of the same size. (*Knitting Small Circumferences With Two Circular Needles*, page 18)

Round 2: Begin knitting in the round Color A.

Rounds 3–12: Knit Color A

Tay's Sweater

Round 13: Purl Color A.

Rounds 14–25: Change to sleeve stockinette needles. Knit, using Color A.

Round 26: Join Hem. Use one size larger needles than sleeve stockinette needles. Knit the invisibly cast-on stitches together with the working stitches to form a hem. (*Hems: Knit In* , page 14.)

Round 27: Increase Round & Start of Sleeve Chart. Change back to sleeve stockinette needles and increase 20 stitches evenly around. (*Spacing Decreases/Increases Evenly*, page 21) Total 70 stitches. (I suggest using *Increases: Right* for the first half of the round and *Increases: Left* for the second half of the round.)

Round 28: Begin Stranded Knitting. Use sleeve stranded knitting needles. Move the start of the round 4 stitches to the right so there is no jog in the underarm panel, place marker. Join in Color B and with needle #1 knit from Point A to Point B on the **Sleeve Chart**, place marker, knit from Point B to C. With needle #2, knit from Point D to B (end of round). 40 stitches on needle #1 and 30 stitches on needle #2. Continue to have 10 more stitches on needle #1 than you have on needle #2 as you increase up the arm.

Underarm Panel Choices: Use the blank spaces in underarm panel of **Sleeve Chart** to write anything you wish. This is your sweater; your choice. (*Alphabet & Number Chart*, page 6.) Fill in spaces below and above your writing using the design (rows 28 to 30) in the underarm panel. If you do not wish to make a statement in the underarm, repeat rows 28 to 30 of the underarm panel.

Rounds 29–129 [135, 141, 147, 141]: Continue following **Sleeve Chart** as established. Note: You will increase 1 stitch every 3 rounds on each side of underarm panel, ending with 136 [140, 142, 142, 142] stitches. If more sleeve length is desired, continue to knit even for 12 additional rounds. (The top of the sleeves match up with the armhole edge pattern.) When sleeve is complete, place all stitches on a holder. Knit the second sleeve, changing the underarm message if desired.

Attach Sleeves: Use Color A and start at the underarm, *Kitchener Stitch: Graft* (page 17) the underarm stitch of the body to the center underarm stitch of the sleeve. *Kitchener Stitch: Half Graft* (page 18) each Sleeve

stitch to each Body stitch around the sleeve. Break yarn. Weave in ends. With Color B, duplicate stitch over the grafted stitches following **Sleeve Chart** Rows 130 [136, 142, 136, 142]. **Repeat for second sleeve.**

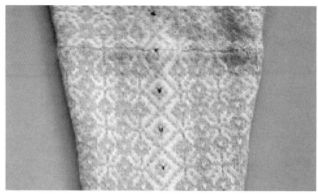

Top of Sleeve

Final Finishing: With Color C, duplicate stitch in the center of the large diamonds of the border, top of sleeves, and shoulders. Catch the yarn carried between diamonds under the stranded yarn.

Apply a 2 stitch I-cord around the entire perimeter of the cardigan and the cuffs to give the garment a nice crisp edge and to pull in the slight flair that may occur at the bottom edge. (*I-Cord: Applied*, page 15.)

Block, (page 7)

Sew on buttons.

Wear with pleasure.

Shoulder Chart

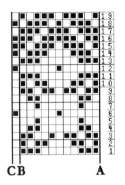

Body Chart

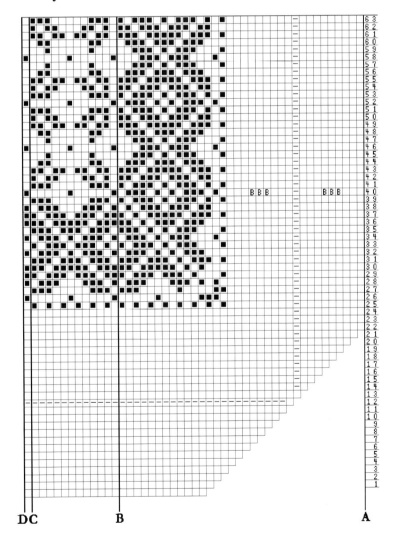

Tay's Sweater

Sleeve Chart

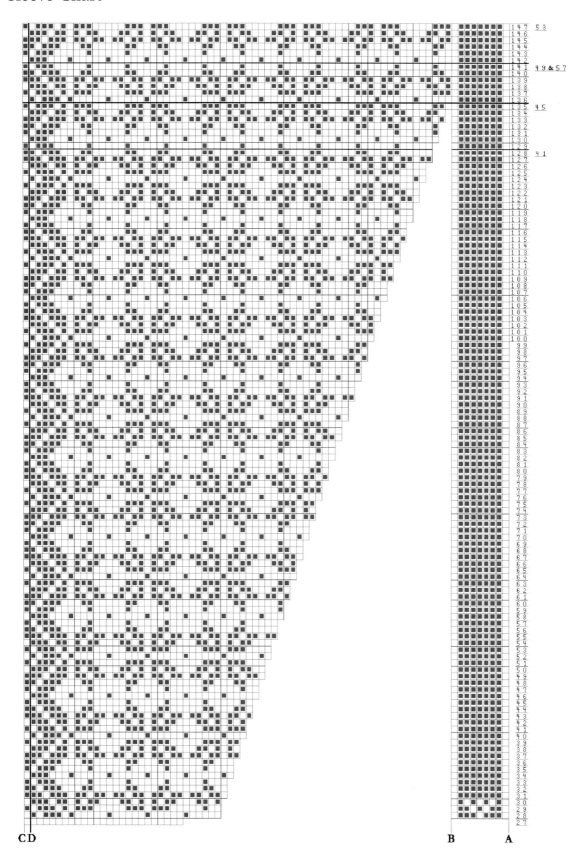

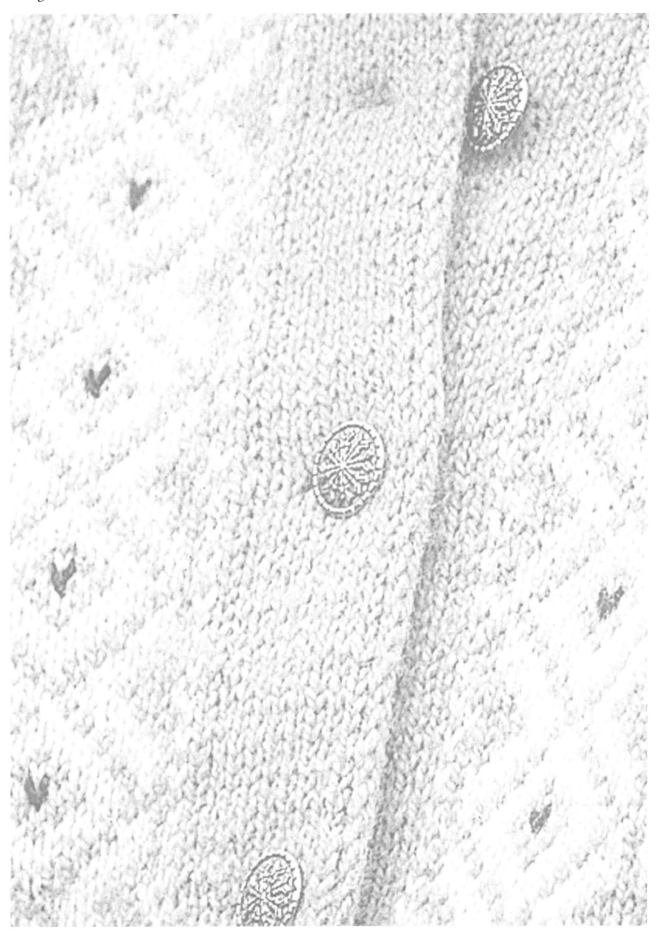

Bountiful Harvest

This design was taken from Z. Ventaskrasts' book. Grain, represented in the design, is a symbol of plenty in Latvia. The creature on the grain could be a bird or an insect; either of which would have a *Bountiful Harvest*, much to a farmer's chagrin.

The top portion of the design would require long carries if worked in stranded knitting, so I chose to work the design as texture. Many of the Latvian charts can be knit as attractive texture patterns.

This sweater is knit in the round to the underarms, then knit back and forth. It has drop shoulders, but they are shaped with short rows.

Sizes: Since this is a large overall pattern, the easiest way to adjust size is to change gauge. The total body has 328 stitches, and the length of the design is 404 rows. For your chosen size gauge and needle requirements, see *Gauge: Determining*, page 14, and *Needles*, page 19. Also note **Model Gauge** below.

Model Measurements and Gauges:
42" circumference, 29" long, 18" sleeve length
31 stitches/62 rows = 4" (10 cm) in pattern
31 stitches/43 rows = 4" (10 cm) in stockinette stitch

Model Materials:
#184 Gold Helmi Vuorelma Oy Satakieli, Nine – 3.5 oz. skeins

BODY

Cast On: Latvian (page 13) 328 stitches. Join, being certain not to twist, and knit one round.

Cast-on and Lower Body

Chart A Round 1: Begin pattern. The dark squares are purl, and the white squares are knit stitches. *Place marker, work Round 1 of Chart A from Point A to B, Point C to D*. Repeat between asterisks. Stitches A/D are side stitches, and stitches C/B are center back and center front stitches. You may wish to place markers at the center back and front. Note the side stitches are worked in garter stitch; i.e. purled every other round.

Rounds 2–32: Work around in pattern as established in Round 1. One pattern repeat completed.

Repeat Rounds 1–32 five more times. Total 6 pattern repeats, 192 rounds.

Then work **Rounds 1–73** as established. You will have 8 pattern repeats when you complete round 64.

Side View

Armhole Openings: Back and front of model sweater were worked individually by *Knitting Onto Right Needle–Knitting Onto Left Needle* (KORN–KOLN) from the arm openings up. (*Knitting Stockinette Stitch Flat Without Turning Work*, page 4) You have some options.
1. You may choose to KORN–KOLN. (A good chance to try the technique if it is new to you.)
2. You may turn your work. If you turn your work, on the uneven numbered rows you reverse the chart—you knit the dark squares, and purl the white squares. If you highlight the uneven rows it is easier to follow charts.
3. You may continue to knit in the round. You must then add steeks at the arm openings and at front and back neck opening.

The instructions assume back and front are knit separately.

Back Row 74: *Remove marker, **place next stitch on hold** (A/D), *Cast On: Cable* (page 10) 1 stitch, work to Point B, Point C to D*, work 1 *Increase: Loop—Left Slanted* (page 16). (The cable cast on and increase are new Stitches A/D. These extra stitches are added so the last body stitch at each side will be continuous

Bountiful Harvest

from the bottom of the sweater to the shoulder after the sleeves are knit in.)

Back Rows 75–186: Work from Point A to B, Point C to A and change to **Chart B** at end of Row 110.

Back Row 187: Short Row Shoulder Shaping. Work from Point A to B, Point C to 1 stitch before Point D, as shown by dark outline on chart. Yarn over or wrap the next stitch. (*Short Rows*, page 20.) You have a short row on the right back edge of your sweater.

Back Row 188: Work as Row 187 but you now have a short row on the left back edge of your sweater.

Back Rows 189–199: Work in pattern as established, but short row as indicated by dark outline on chart. You will short row 3 times each 2, 3, 4, and 5 stitches prior to the previous reverse.

Back Row 200: Back Neck Shaping. Work 45 stitches, place next 41 stitches on hold. Option time—you may join another ball of yarn and work the left side of the back neck shaping simultaneously with the right side or you may work the right side shaping until complete, then do the left side shaping. **Add one stitch at neck edge of each shoulder as worked at arm openings.**

Back Rows 201–212: Work short rows at edges as established. Decrease one stitch in from the neck edge (beside the cast on edge stitches) every row 6 times and every other row 2 times as indicated by bold lines. *Decrease: Left* (page 14) on the right edge of the neck, and *Decrease: Right* (page 14) on the left edge of the neck.

Back Row 213: If KORN–KOLN, **purl all shoulder stitches** (54) and if turning your work **knit all shoulder stitches**, and work the appropriate stitch together with the yarn overs or wraps. This gives the shoulder seam a decorative purled edge.

Front Rows 74–189: Work as back.

Front Row 190: Front Neck Shaping. Work 63 stitches and place next 31 stitches on hold. **Note "Option time" in Back/Row 200. Add one stitch at neck edge of each shoulder as worked at back neck shaping.**

Front Rows 191–212: Continue short rows at edges as established and decrease at the neck edge every row 7 times then every other row 6 times, as indicated by

bold lines. On the right side of the neck knit a *Decrease: Left* and on the left side of the neck knit a *Decrease: Right*.

Front Row 213: Work as Back Row 213.

Join Shoulders: *Have outsides facing each other and use needle one size larger than used to knit body. Beginning at armhole edge, *Bind Off: Three Needle* (page 7) 54 stitches. Break yarn.* Turn and repeat between asterisks for opposite shoulder.

Neck Band: Start at left shoulder and *Knit Up* (page 18) 17 stitches along left front neck edge, knit 31 front neck stitches on hold, *Knit Up* 17 stitches along right front neck edge. With second circular needle, *Knit Up* 11 stitches along right back neck edge, knit 41 back neck stitches on hold, and *Knit Up* 11 stitches along left back neck edge. 128 stitches. (*Knitting Small Circumference With Two Circular Needles*, page 18)

Thread a blunt needle with 2 lengths of working yarn approximately four times the circumference. *Bind Off: Latvian* (page 7) around neck stitches, but do **not** remove stitches from needles.

Neck Band

Work 12 rounds of knit 1, purl 1 ribbing. (The stitches for the first round will be tight on the needle because of the bind off yarns.)

Bind Off: Latvian around neck and remove needles. Weave in ends.

SLEEVES

Cast On: Use needle to attain gauge, and *Cast On: Latvian* 64 stitches. Start with the first stitch cast on and place 32 stitches onto a same size second needle.

Join, being certain not to twist, and knit one round with the 2 needles.

Chart C, Round 1: Work in the round from Point A to C with first needle, and from Point B to D with second needle.

Rounds 2–29: Work as established in Round 1.

Bountiful Harvest

Rounds 30–243: Work in pattern and increase every 5 rows as indicated on chart; i.e. increase rounds, work center underarm stitch (first stitch of round), *Increase: Right* 1 (page 16), work to Point C, work from Point B to D, *Increase: Left* 1 (page 16). Note the center underarm stitch will be worked in garter stitch as the body side stitches.

Round 244: Purl. Break yarn. Keep needles in sleeve.

Join Sleeve to Body: With another same size needle knit body side stitch on hold, *Knit Up* 148 stitches around body arm opening—74 stitches each front and back. (Approximately *knit up every row 2 times, skip 1 row,* repeat around.) Purl one round. With outsides facing, join sleeve and body with *Bind Off: Three Needle* (page 7) around.

Work second sleeve as first, and join.

    Weave in ends.

    Block.

    Wear or present to someone with Bountiful pleasure.

BOUNTIFUL HARVEST SOCKS

For written details see *Toe to Top Sock*, (page 29) or *Top to Toe Sock* (page 30). You choose which way you prefer to knit socks. Model was knit from toe to top. Sock has 64 stitches. Divide your ankle measurement into 64 to determine required gauge for your sock size.

Model Gauge and Material:

32 stitches/45 rows = 4" (10 cm) in stockinette stitch. #184 Gold Helmi Vuorelma Oy Satakieli, One – 3.5 oz. skein

Toe to Top: Follow written instructions and increase to 64 stitches. Work to approximately 2 inches short of total desired leg length. Work cuff.

Cuff: *Bind Off: Latvian* (page 7) around, but do **not** remove stitches from needles. Knit 1 round. Follow **Cuff Chart** and work from Point A to B two times each round. Knit 1 round. *Bind Off: Latvian*. Remove from needles.

Top to Toe: *Cast On: Latvian* (page 13) 64 stitches. Knit 1 round. Follow **Cuff Chart** and work from Point A to B two times every round. Knit 1 round. *Bind Off: Latvian* around, but do **not** remove stitches from needles. Follow written instructions and finish sock.

Cuff Chart

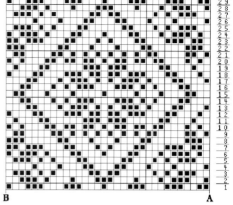

BOUNTIFUL HARVEST GLOVES

Model Gauge and Material:
32 stitches/45 rows = 4" (10 cm) in stockinette stitch #184 Gold Helmi Vuorelma Oy Satakieli, One – 3.5 oz. skein

Follow *Basic Glove Pattern* for 64 stitches, page 26.

Cuff: *Bind Off: Latvian* (page 7) around, but do **not** remove stitches from needle. Knit 1 round. Follow **Cuff Chart** above and work from Point A to B two times every round. Knit 1 round. *Bind Off: Latvian*. Remove from needles.

Wear and wave to friends with Bountiful joy.

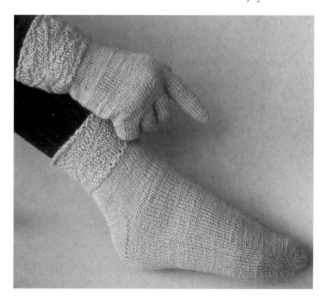

Chart A

Chart B

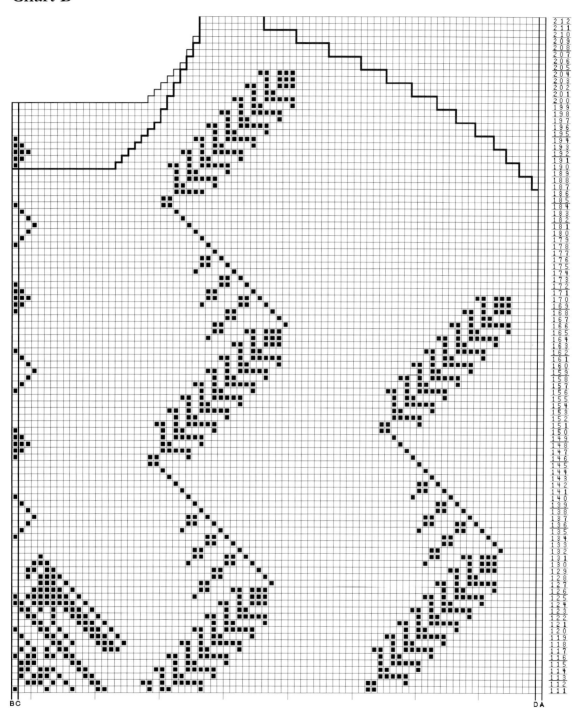

Chart C

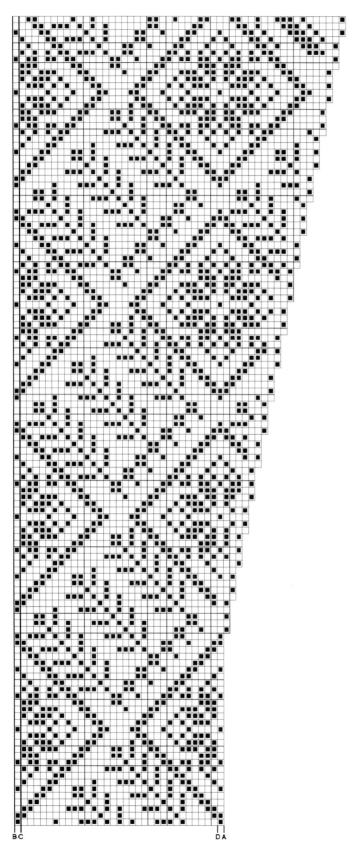

BC   DA

Chart D

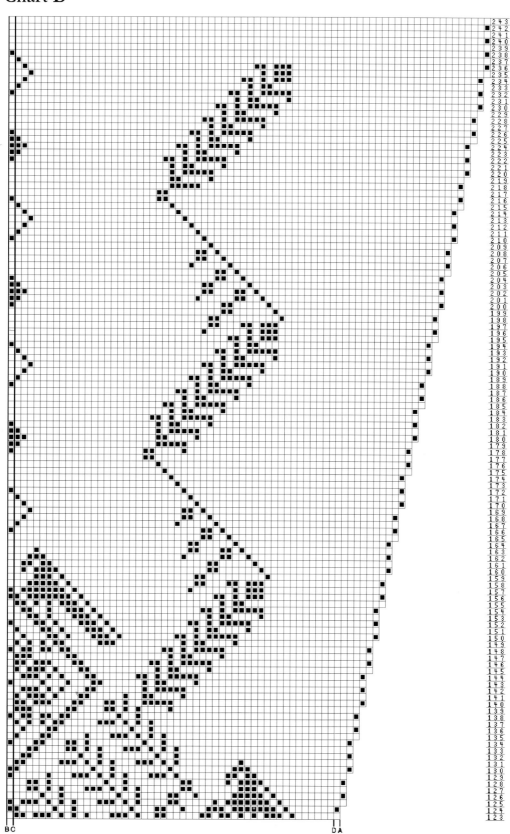

Circles

When I viewed the chart for this design on the computer screen, the circles in the design flashed in and out of my vision almost like a blinking neon light. The same phenomenon occurs when I look at the finished pullover. How could I not name the pullover "Circles" when they flashed before my eyes?

The design for the main portion of the garment was taken from Z. Ventaskrasts' book. I designed the bottom, neck and cuff border and used traditional Latvian braid and Meg Swansen's "Purl When You Can Technique."

Model Measurements and Gauges:
42" circumference, 28" long
32 stitches/36 rows = 4" (10 cm) in stranded knitting

Model Materials:
Color A—#36 Navy Jamieson & Smith Shetland Jumper Weight, Thirteen – 1 oz. skeins
Color B—#FC46 Ghilly Green Jamieson & Smith Shetland Jumper Weight, Nine – 1 oz. skeins
Color C—#121 Yellow Ochre Jamieson & Smith Shetland Jumper Weight, Three – 1 oz. skeins

Size Variations: The body has 336 stitches. Size may be varied by *Gauge* (page 14) or more or fewer 12 stitch pattern repeats. (*Design*, page 121) If you alter size by gauge, follow numbers given in pattern. If you alter size by pattern repeats, adjust the pattern numbers accordingly.

BODY

For a bottom border narrower than the body, use needle 1 or 2 sizes smaller than used for stranded knitting gauge. (*Needles*, page 19) With Color A, *Cast-On: Cable* (page 10), 336 stitches or your desired number.

Round 1: Place marker for beginning of round, join, being certain not to twist, and work knit 1, purl 1 ribbing around.

(The following braid instructions are from *Latvian Mittens* by Lizbeth Upitis.)

Round 2: Join Color B. Knit 1 Color B, knit 1 Color A around. The **Color B** stitches are above **knit** stitches and the **Color A** stitches are above **purl** stitches. (This row will surface in the center of the braid.)

Round 3: Bring both yarns **forward**. Purl 1 Color B, purl 1 Color A, keeping each color aligned with the same color as the round before. Keep colors alternating and always bring the yarn for next stitch to purl

over yarn used for the last stitch. This twists the yarn as you knit around.

To keep the yarn from twisting into knots, pull free several yards of both yarns and push the twist away from the knitting towards the yarn source. By the time your round is completed you will have a 2-color spun yarn dangling from your knitting. (This is possibly the most tedious means of producing a plied yarn yet discovered.)

Round 4: Purl 1 Color B, purl 1 Color A the entire round, but this time bring each color **under** the last stitch as you purl around. As you come to the end of the round, the last twist releases from the yarn, as if by magic! Break Color B.

The two rounds just worked are tedious, but I feel the marvelous result is well worth the effort, don't you?

Rounds 5–6: With Color A, knit 1, purl 1 around.

Round 7–27: Join Color C. Follow **Chart A** (following page) and repeat between Point A and B 28 times every round. Work **Chart A, Rows 1–5** one time, then **Rows 2–5** four times. Break Color C.

Rounds 28–29: Knit 1, purl 1 in ribbing around.

Rounds 30–32: Join Color B and repeat **Rounds 2–4.**

Round 33: With Color A, knit around. (It is not necessary to break Color B.)

Round 34: With Color A, knit until 6 stitches from beginning of round marker.

Round 35: Place marker, with Colors A and B follow **Chart B, Row 1** and work first 6 stitches, remove marker, work last 7 stitches of **Chart B, Row 1**, place marker. *Now follow **Chart C, Row 1**, and repeat between Point A and B 12 times, and between Point A and C 1 time.* Place marker, work **Chart B, Row 1** from Point A to B, place marker. Repeat between asterisks.

Note: Sweater may be personalized by adding name or message in side panel of body or sleeves. (*Alphabet & Number Chart*, page 6) Follow **Chart B** for panel before and after message. Model has my name in underarm panel.

Round 36 – to desired length for arm openings (approximately 10 inches shy of total length): Each round: *Slip marker, work **Chart B** from Point A to B,

Circles

Chart A	Chart B	Chart C
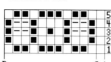	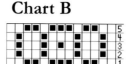	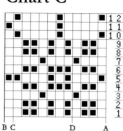

slip marker. Work **Chart C** Point A to B 12 times, Point A to C 1 time.* Repeat between asterisks.(**Chart B** rows repeat every 5 rounds. **Chart C** rows repeat every 12 rounds.) Model was knit with 11 repeats of **Chart C**'s 12 rows, plus Rows 1–5.

Arm Openings: *Slip marker, place next 13 stitches on hold. With Color A around thumb and Color B around index finger, *Cast-On: Long Tail* (page 11) a 10 stitch steek, place marker. (*Steeks*, page 21) Knit across in established pattern, **Chart C**, to marker.* Repeat between asterisks.

Following Rounds: Work steeks following *Steeks: Armhole Chart*, (page 33) and follow **Chart C** as established for a total of 16 repeats of **Chart C**'s 12 rows (or desired length to neck opening—approximately 4 inches shy of total length. Finish with Row 12, **Chart C**).

Front Neck Opening: Slip marker, work steek, slip marker, follow **Chart C, Row 1** and repeat between Point A and B 12 times, Point A and C 1 time (Back). Slip marker, work steek, slip marker, follow **Chart C** and repeat between Point A and B 5 times. (60 stitches) Place next 35 stitches on hold on a piece of yarn. Place marker, with Color A around thumb and Color B around index finger, *Cast-On: Long Tail*, a 10 stitch steek, place marker. The stitches on hold will form a *Kangaroo Pouch* (page 17). From **Chart C, Row 1**, knit stitch C/B, work chart between Point A and B 4 times, and Point A to C 1 time. (Front: 60 stitches each side of steek plus 10 steek stitches.)

Chart C Rounds 2–7: Front Neck Shaping. Slip marker, work armhole steek, slip marker, work from Point A to B 12 times, Point A to C 1 time, slip marker, work steek. Work in pattern to 3 stitches of center front steek marker, work 1 stitch with Color A, *Decrease: Left* (page 14) with Color A, slip marker, work *Steeks: Center Front Chart* (page 33) slip marker, *Decrease: Right* (page 14) with Color A, work 1 stitch with Color A, work in pattern to marker.

Chart C Round 8: Back Neck Opening. Slip marker, work armhole steek, slip marker, work **Chart C** from Point A to B 4 times, work 7 stitches (55 stitches). Place next 45 stitches on hold on a piece of yarn. Place marker, with Color A around thumb and Color B around index finger, *Cast On: Long Tail*, a 10 stitch steek, place marker. Work **Chart C** from Point D to B 1 time, Point A to B 3 times, Point A to C 1 time. (Back: 55 stitches each side of center steek, plus 10 steek stitches.) Finish round in pattern and work established decreases at center front steek.

Following Rounds: Front and Back Neck Shaping. Continue in pattern as established. Work back decreases and center steek the same as front. When there are 30 stitches between armhole steeks and center steeks, work even without decreases through **Chart C, Row 9**. (You arrive at 30 stitches between steeks on the front prior to the back so front decreases stop first.)

Chart C, Row 10: Work in pattern and work sleeve and center back steeks as established. At center front steek, bind off steek with alternate colors, and finish round in pattern.

Chart C, Row 11: Work as established to center back steek, bind off steek with alternate colors, work in pattern to end of second sleeve steek. Do **not** knit across front. Break yarns.

Steeks: Fold top of armhole steeks in half and *Kitchener Stitch: Graft* (page 17) the open steek stitches together. *Steeks: Slip Stitch Crochet* (page 21) all steeks. Cut center front and center back steeks.

Join Shoulders: Place front stitches onto another needle(s). Turn knitting inside out so right sides are facing. Hold the needles parallel, and use third **one size larger** than stranded knitting needle for binding off. *Start at side edge (the first stitches after the steek stitches). Follow **Chart C, Row 12** and work *Bind Off: Three Needle* (page 7) in pattern to center front steek. Break yarns* Turn your work and repeat between asterisks.

Circles

Tighten and weave in ends.

Neck Border: Use either a 16" or 2–24" needles (*Knitting Small Circumferences With Two Circular Needles*, page 18) one size smaller than used for body. Start at left shoulder with Color A and *Knit Up* (page 18) a stitch for every row along front steek (33 stitches), knit across 35 stitches on hold, *Knit Up* a stitch for every row along steek on opposite side (33 stitches). Total 101 front stitches.

Place marker. *Knit Up* a stitch for every row along back steek (27 stitches), knit across 45 stitches on hold, *Knit Up* a stitch for every row along steek on opposite side (27 stitches). Total 99 back stitches. Place marker. (The 2 extra stitches on the front become center stitches of double decreases after the braid has been knit.)

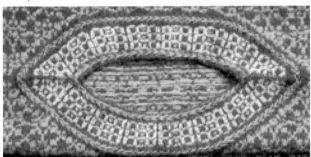

Front and Back Neck Border

Round 1: With Color A, knit 1, purl 1 around.

Rounds 2–5: Neck Border Braid. Join Color B and work **Body Rounds 2–5**, but end **Body Round 5** one stitch prior to marker at left shoulder. Break Color B.

Round 6: *Slip 1 stitch, remove marker, place slipped stitch back on left needle, *Decrease: Double* (page 14). Place safety pin into center stitch of double decrease. This stitch will be the center stitch of a double decrease in each of the following pattern rows. Work in established knit 1, purl 1 ribbing to 1 stitch prior to marker.* Repeat between asterisks, and end 1 stitch prior to marked stitch. 97 stitches each side of marked stitches.

Round 7: Join Color C. *Decrease: Double,* work **Chart A, Row 1** from Point C to B one time, from Point A to B 7 times.* Repeat between asterisks, and end 1 stitch prior to marked stitch. 95 stitches each side of marked stitches.

Rounds 8–19: *Decrease: Double* at each shoulder every round and continue in pattern **Chart A** as established through **Row 5** one time, then work **Rows 2–5** two

times. Every round the pattern on the chart starts one stitch to the left of the previous round. Break Color C.

Round 20: With Color A, knit around.

Round 21: With Color A, knit 1, purl 1 around in ribbing.

Rounds 22–25: Join Color B and work **Braid, Body Rounds 2–5**.

Bind Off: Sewn I (page 6) around. Break yarns and weave in ends.

SLEEVES

Model Measurement: 18" to Cuff, plus 2-1/2" Cuff

Model Gauge: 36 stitches/40 rows = 4" (10cm) in stranded knitting

Round 1: Knit Up Sleeves. (Armhole steeks may be cut before or after sleeve stitches are knitted up.) Use needle 1 size smaller than used for the body and with Colors A and B, knit 13 stitches on hold at underarms in established pattern, **Chart B**; i.e., knit 1, place marker, knit 11 in pattern, place marker, knit 1. *Knit Up* along steek 1 stitch for every row and follow **Chart C, Row 10**. Notice the sleeve pattern stitches **duplicate** the row pattern stitches they abut. The number of stitches in the sleeve varies with sleeve depth. Model has 194 stitches—13 underarm panel, last 7 stitches of Row 10, 14 repeats of Row 10 (168 stitches), plus first 6 stitches of Row 10.

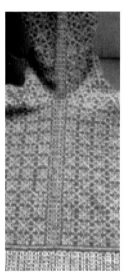

Side View and Underarm

Model Sleeves: (The sleeves are gradually decreased down the arm and the fullness at the bottom of the sleeve is suddenly decreased in one round just above the cuff.) Work **Rows 11–12, Chart C**, then work **Rows 1–12** fourteen times. Decrease at underarm panel every 5 rows 20 times and every 4 rows 17 times to 120 stitches. To decrease, work in pattern to 2 stitches before underarm panel marker, *Decrease: Right,* slip marker, work to next marker, slip marker, *Decrease: Left,* work in established pattern around. (*Decreases,* page 14, *Row Markers,* page 20)

When fourteen 12 row pattern repeats are complete,

Circles

work one round with Color A. Next round knit 2 together around—60 stitches.

Neck and Cuff

Sleeve Cuff Round 1: Cuff. Work in knit 1, purl 1 rib around.

Rounds 2–4: Work braid, **Body Rounds 2–4**.

Rounds 5–6: With Color A, knit 1, purl 1 around in ribbing.

Rounds 7–19: Join **Color C** and work **Chart A**, Point A to B 5 times each round. Work Rows 1–5 one time, Rows 2–5 two times. Break Color C.

Round 20: With Color A, knit around.

Round 21: With Color A, knit 1, purl 1 around in ribbing.

Rounds 22–24: Join Color B. Work braid, **Body Rounds 2–4**. Break Color B.

Round 25: With Color A, knit 1, purl 1 around in ribbing.

Alternate Sleeve Choices: The 60 stitch cuff is relatively snug, although I am able to push it up to my elbow. If you prefer a larger circumference cuff, decrease to 72 stitches and work 6 repeats of Chart A. If you do not want the bloused look above the cuff, (men may prefer not to have it) decrease at more frequent intervals down the sleeve so there is an even taper to the cuff. (*Spacing Decreases/Increases Evenly*, page 21)

Work *Bind-Off: Sewn I (*page 6). Weave in ends. Block. Wear with joy. It is a very interesting design if you are sitting or standing in front of someone for a long time. The phenomenon of the design keeps changing before their eyes. I have had knitters think they see a mistake because they do not see circles in one section, but if I move or they change the angle from which they are looking, there are the circles right where they were

missing before. With this movement of the pattern, it would be very exciting in bright colors.

CIRCLES SOCKS

For written details see *Toe to Top Sock*, (page 29) or *Top to Toe Sock*, (page 30). You choose which way you prefer to knit socks. Model was knit from *Toe to Top*. See below for deviations and cuff instructions. Sock may be knit with 60 or 72 stitches. Divide your ankle measurement into 60 or 72 to determine required gauge for your sock size.

Model Materials:
Color A—#36 Navy Jamieson & Smith Shetland Jumper Weight, Three – 1 oz. skeins
Color B—#FC46 Ghilly Green Jamieson & Smith Shetland Jumper Weight, One – 1 oz. skein
Color C—#121 Yellow Ochre Jamieson & Smith Jumper Weight, One – 1 oz. skein

Toe to Top: Follow written instructions and increase to 60 or 72 stitches. Work to approximately 2-1/2 inches short of total desired leg length. Work **Sock Cuff** below. When cuff is complete *Bind Off: Sewn I* (page 6).

Sock Cuff: Follow *Circles Sweater* instructions Rounds 2–6 (page 65). Work Latvian braid loosely, so it may be stretched. Join Color C. Follow **Circles Chart A**, Point A to B, 5 or 6 times, depending on number of stitches. Work Rows 1–5 one time, then Rows 2–5 four times. Break Color C. With Color A, knit 1 round, then knit 1, purl 1 in ribbing one round. Join Color B and Repeat *Circles Sweater* Rounds 2–5.

Top to Toe: *Cast On: Cable* (page 10) 60 or 72 stitches. Follow **Sock Cuff** above. When cuff is complete, follow written instructions.

CIRCLES GLOVES

Model Gauge:
32 stitches/44 rows = 4" (10 cm) stockinette stitch

Model Materials: See CIRCLES SOCKS

Follow *Basic Glove Pattern* (page 26) for 64 stitches. Cuff has 60 stitches.

Glove Cuff: Work **Sock Cuff** above. Work *Bind Off: Sewn I* (page 6).

Wear and wave for raves!

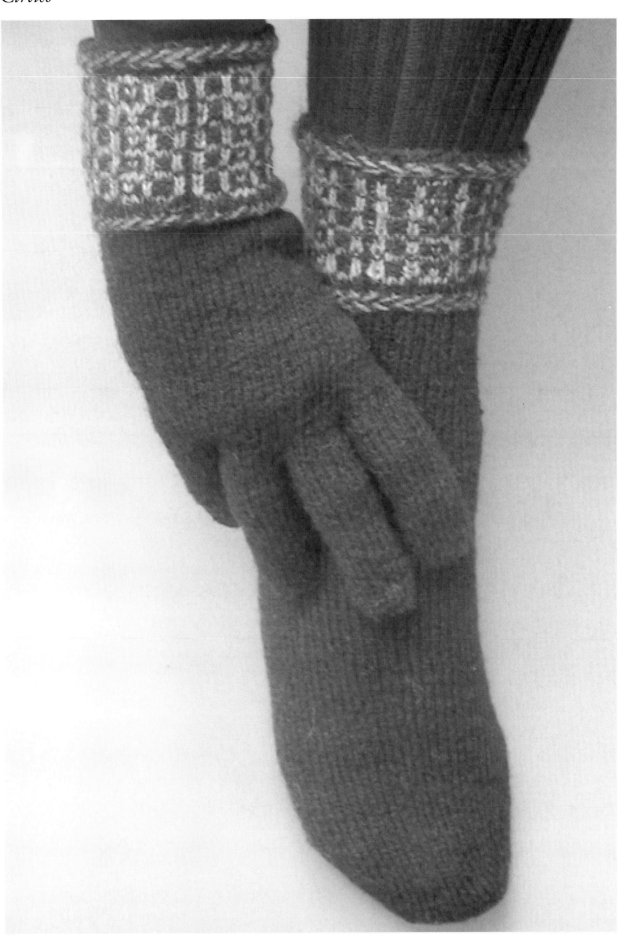

Cornfields

I live in the very hilly, back water area of the Mississippi River. This is an agricultural area with fields contour plowed and planted in strips of corn and alfalfa or grains to prevent erosion. This sweater is named "Cornfields" as the design reminds me of our fields and I used green and yellow yarn to carry out the theme. The design has great potential for many color combinations—brilliant colors to enhance its psychedelic look, or the subtle shading of the design could be spectacular knit with light and dark shades of the same color.

The design, from *A Joy Forever, Latvian Weaving* by Jane A. Evans, is from a blanket woven in Latvia and now at the Royal Ontario Museum, Toronto. I rotated the design 90 degrees and made slight changes in its proportions for a knitted garment. Variations of the design are familiar to weavers, some referring to it as the Swedish Snowflake.

Model Measurements and Gauge:
42" circumference, 25" long
32 stitches/40 rows = 4" (10 cm) in stranded knitting.

Model Materials:
Color A—#121 Yellow Ochre Jamieson & Smith Shetland Jumper Weight, Ten – 1 oz. skeins
Color B—#118 Moss Green Jamieson & Smith Shetland Jumper Weight, Ten – 1 oz. skeins

Size Variations: The body has 340 stitches. See *Gauge* (page 14) to determine the gauge and *Yarn Suggestions and Amounts* (page 24) for alternate sizes.

BODY

Hem: Use needle 2 to 3 sizes smaller than stranded knitting needle (*Needles*, page 19) and Color B, *Cast On: Invisible* (page 11) 340 stitches.

Hem Row 1: Knit.

Hem Round 2: Place marker. Join, being certain not to twist, and start to knit in the round.

Hem Rounds 3–12: Knit around.

Hem Round 13: (13 rows of knitting including the invisibly cast-on row) Purl.

Rounds 1–3: Knit.

Round 4: Begin stranded knitting. Use stranded knitting needle and join Color A. Slip marker, *knit Row 4 of **Chart A** (page 74) from Point A to B, Point

C to D,* place marker. Repeat between asterisks. Stitches A/D are side stitches and Stitches C/B are center back and center front stitches. You may wish to place a marker at Points B.

Rounds 5–13: Knit around as established in Round 4.

Round 14: Join Hem to Body. Use one size larger needle. In pattern knit body stitches together with invisibly cast-on stitches. (*Hems Knit In*, page 14)

Rounds 15–154: Use stranded knitting needle, follow **Chart A** as established and change to **Chart B** when required.

Round 155: Arm Openings. *Slip marker, place next stitch on hold. With Color A around thumb and Color B around index finger, *Cast On: Long Tail* a 10 stitch

Side View and Underarm

steek, place marker. (*Steeks*, page 21.) Knit from Point D to B, Point C to D.* Repeat between asterisks.

Rounds 156–210: Alternate Rows 1 and 2 of *Steek: Armhole Chart* (page 33) as you work **Charts B, C and D** as established.

Round 211: Center Front Neck Steek. Work armhole steeks as established, knit Row 211, **Chart C—Back**. Knit 81 stitches, Row 211, **Chart D—Front**, *Decrease: Right* (page 14), place 3 center front stitches on hold, place marker, with Color A around thumb and Color B around index finger *Cast On: Long Tail* a 10 stitch steek, place marker, *Decrease: Left* (page 14), complete Row 211, **Chart D**.

Rounds 212– 248: Work the armhole steeks as established and alternate Rows 1 and 2 of *Steeks: Center Front Chart* (page 33). Knit **Chart C** for the Back and **Chart D** for the Front. The front neck shaping consists of a decrease every round at each side of center front steek as established in Round 211.

Round 249: Knit as established to center front steek, bind off the center front steek with alternate colors, finish round.

Back Round 250: Knit **Chart C**, and bind off armhole steeks with alternate colors. Do **not** knit Front, **Chart D**. Break yarns.

Cornfields

Steeks: *Slip Stitch Crochet* (page 21) the 3 steeks, and cut center front steek. Place front stitches on same size or smaller needle(s).

Join Shoulders: *Have outsides facing each other and use needle one size larger. Begin at armhole edge and *Bind Off: Three Needle* (page 7) in pattern following Row 251 of **Chart C**. Break yarns.* Turn and repeat between asterisks for opposite shoulder.) The center back stitches remain on needle. Weave in ends.

Shoulder Join and Top of Sleeve (Can you spot the sleeve join?)

Finish Neck: Use a 16" or two 24" needles one size smaller than used for body. (*Knitting Small Circumferences With Two Circular Needles*, page 18) Looking at outside of back and using Color B, knit across back neck stitches, *knit 4, knit 2 together* 13 times, end knit 1 (66 stitches) , *Knit Up* (page 18) one stitch per row along front steek (38 stitches) , *Decrease: Double* (page 14) 3 center front stitches that were on hold, *Knit Up* along steek as on opposite side (38 stitches). 143 total stitches.

   Cast On: Cable (page 10) 3 stitches on left needle but bring yarn forward before placing the last stitch on needle. *I-Cord: Bind Off* (page 15) around. *Kitchener Stitch: Half-Graft* (page 18) 3 I-cord stitches to cast-on stitches. Weave in ends and tack down center front steek edges.

SLEEVES

Round 1, Chart E: Knit Up Sleeves. (Armhole steeks may be cut before or after sleeve stitches are knitted up.) Use two 24" needles 1 size smaller than used for body. (*Sleeve Gauge*, page 20 and *Knitting Small Circumferences With Two Circular Needles*, page 18) Follow **Chart E**, Round 1. Knit sleeve center underarm stitch to stitch on hold at body underarm. *Knit Up* one stitch for **every round** along armhole steek to Point B. Stitch B/C will be on the back of the sweater and you may

wish to mark this stitch. (**Note:** After the 5 underarm panel stitches have been knit, the knit-up stitches duplicate the selvage body stitches they abut.) *Knit Up* opposite side from Point C to Point D, place marker for start of round. *Knit Up* first 3 stitches of Round 2 to finish knitting up sleeve. You are at the center underarm, Round 2.

Knit Up sleeve

Round 2: Follow **Chart E**, knit 4, place marker, knit from Point D to B, Point C to D, slip marker. (**Note:** Rounds end at Point D.)

Round 3: Decreases start. Knit from Point A to D, slip marker, knit *Decrease: Left* , knit to Point B. Knit from Point C to 2 stitches before Point D, knit *Decrease: Right*, slip marker.

Rounds 4–175: Follow **Charts E** and **F** and knit around in pattern. (**Note:** Decreases alternate every 2 and 3 rounds as established in Round 3; i.e., *Decrease: Left* after first underarm panel marker and 2 stitches prior to second underarm panel marker *Decrease: Right*.)

<u>Optional Message In</u>
<u>Underarm Panel:</u> You may wish to write a name, date, or message, in the underarm panel (*Alphabet & Number Chart*, page 6). Use the underarm panel design before and after your message if it does not fill the entire length of the sleeve. (The model has my full name on one sleeve and "Cornfields" and year knit on the second sleeve.)

   After knitting Round 175, with Color B *Cast On: Cable* 3 stitches on left needle, but bring yarn

Underarm Message: Cornfields

Cornfields

forward before placing third stitch on needle. *I-Cord: Bind Off* around. *Kitchener Stitch: Half-Graft* the 3 I-cord stitches to cast on stitches.

    Tack down armhole steeks. Block.

    Wear and Enjoy!

CORNFIELD SOCKS

For written details see *Basic Pattern for Stranded Knit Socks (BPSKS)*, page 28. See below for **deviations**. Sock leg has 64 stitches. Divide your ankle measurement into 64 to determine required gauge for your sock size.

Model Gauge and Materials:

32 stitches/34 rows = 4" (10 cm) stranded knitting
Color A—#121 Yellow Ochre Jamieson and Smith Shetland Jumper Weight, Two – 1 oz.skeins
Color B—#118 Moss Green Jamieson & Smith Shetland Jumper Weight, Two – 1 oz. skeins

Hem: Because of design, have 31 stitches on Needle #1 and 33 stitches on Needle #2.

Pattern Round 1: After the purl round, work 2 rounds Color B before you start Pattern Round 1, **Cornfield Socks Chart,** page 79.

Round 7: Join Hem to Sock Body. See Round 9, *BPSKS.*

Rounds 8–48: See Rounds 10–48 *BPSKS.*

Round 108: Knit Needle #1 as established. Needle #2, *Decrease: Left*, knit to last 2 stitches, *Decrease: Right*.

Cornfields

Chart A

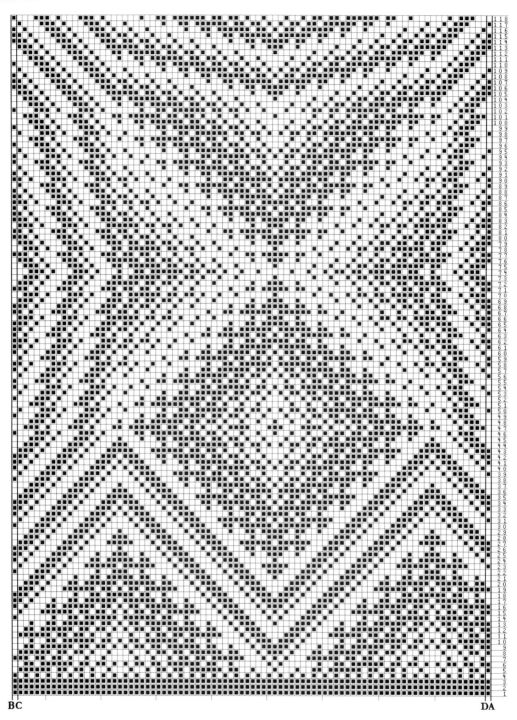

BC   DA

Chart B

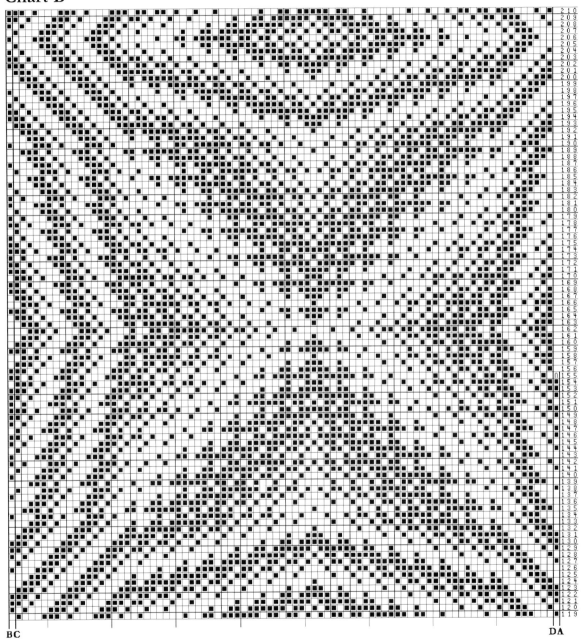

Chart D

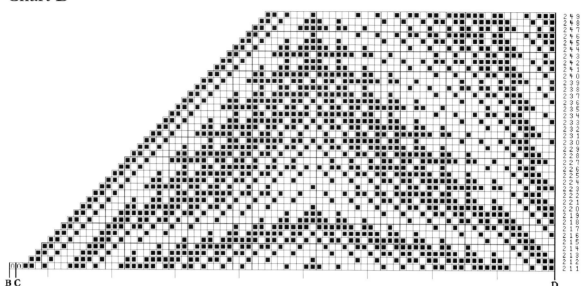

Chart C

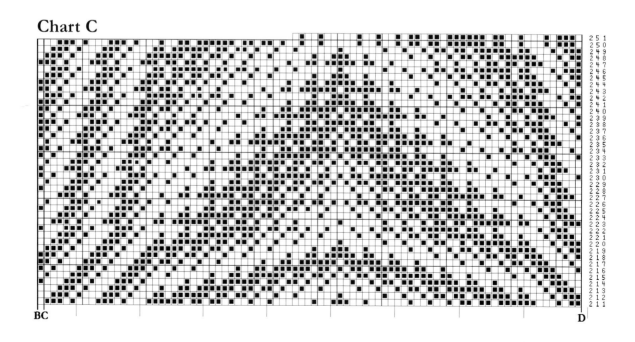

Chart E

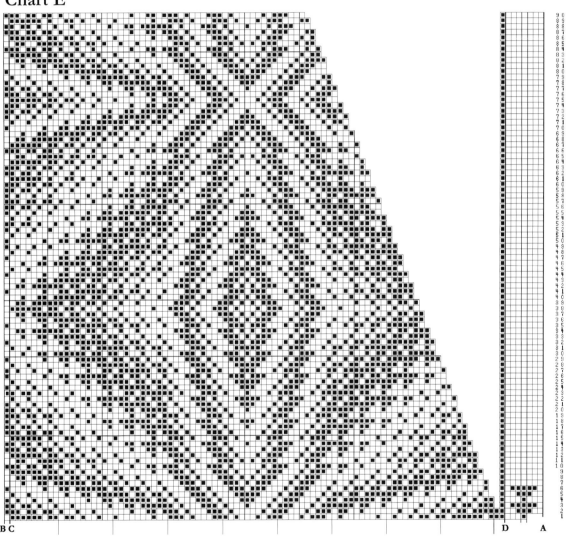

B C   D   A

Cornfields

Chart F

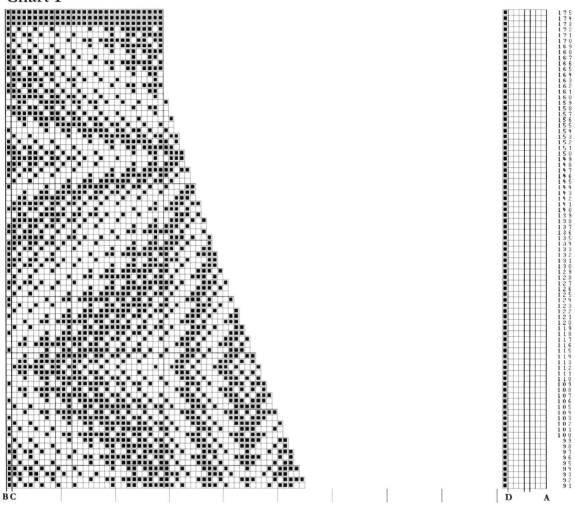

Socks Chart

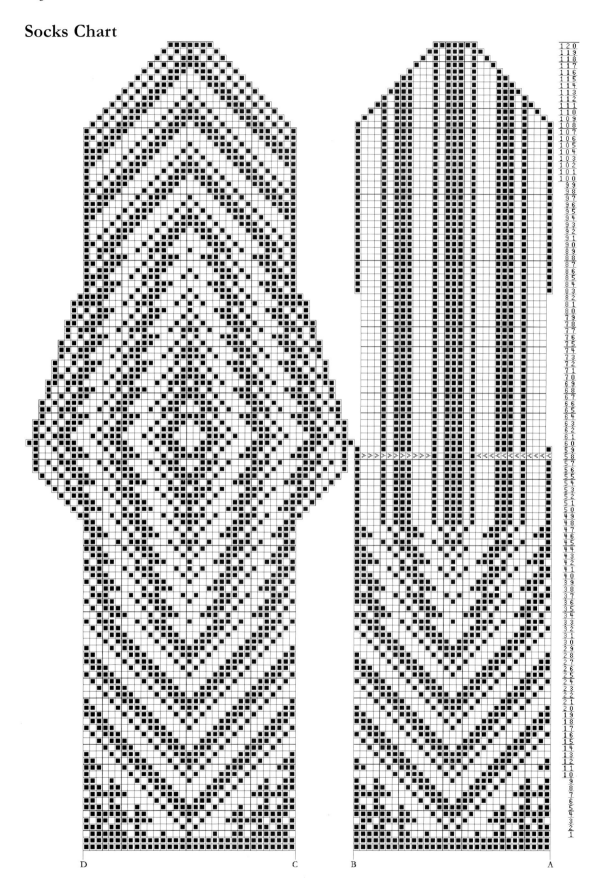

D   C   B   A

Don's Vest

I made this vest for my husband, but like many of my designs it is appropriate for either sex. The vest designs are from charts in A. Ventaskrasts' books. I used one design for the front and a second design for the back. I like a vertical delineation between two different patterns and the design on the back has a vertical stripe for this delineation. If you choose to use two different patterns and neither of them have a vertical line, you may introduce a third narrow pattern such as the six stitch vertical portion of the back pattern used in this vest.

To help the appearance of the single stitch vertical stripes in this vest, I reversed the color carried on top every round; i.e., *Round 1 carry Color A on top, Round 2 carry Color B on Top.* Repeat between asterisks. (*Two Color Yarn Carry*, page 4.)

Size Variations
(Measurements are rounded off to the nearest number.)

Gauge = sts/4" Stranded Knit	Body Circumferences		
	311 sts.	342 sts.	373 sts.
32	39"	43"	47"
31	40"	44"	48"
30	41"	46"	50"
29	43"	47"	51"
28	44"	49"	53"
27	46"	51"	55"
26	48"	53"	57"
25	50"	55"	60"
24	52"	57"	62"

Length: Your choice.

Shetland Jumper Weight may be used to attain these gauges, or you may use a yarn of your choice to attain gauge. (*Yarn Suggestions and Amounts*, page 24.)

Model Measurements and Gauge:
40" circumference, 24" long
31 sts = 4" (10 cm) in stranded knitting

Model Materials:
Color A—#FC56 Plum Heather Jamieson & Smith Shetland Jumper Weight, Six – 1 oz. skeins
Color B—#29 Green Lovat Jamieson & Smith Shetland Jumper Weight, Five – 1 oz. skeins

BODY

Ribbing: After you decide what size and gauge to knit your vest, you have a second decision to make. The number of stitches cast on for the ribbing is 10% less than the total number of stitches. But, if you knit the ribbing with the stranded knitting needle there is almost a straight line between the ribbing and body. For a more snug ribbing, use a needle 1 or 2 sizes smaller than the stranded knitting needle. (*Needles*, page 19) Ribbing on the model vest was knit with the stranded knitting needle.

With Color A, *Cast On: Long-Tail* (page 11) 280 [308, 336] stitches—for total stitches 311 [342, 373]. (See *Cast On: Purl*, page 13.)

Row 1: With Color A knit 2, purl 2 across.

Round 2: Place marker for start of round. Join, being careful not to twist, and knit ribbing in the round as established in Row 1.

Rounds 3–7: Work around in ribbing.

Round 8: With Color B, **knit all stitches.** (By knitting the ribbing purl stitches when you change color, the first color does not show through on the outside. The knit rows are not noticeable in the ribbing.)

Round 9: With Color B, work ribbing.

Round 10: With Color A, knit all stitches.

Rounds 11–12: With Color A, work ribbing.

Round 13: With Color B, knit all stitches.

Rounds 14–16: With Color B, work ribbing.

Round 17: With Color A, knit all stitches.

Round 18–19: With Color A, work ribbing.

Round 20: With Color B, knit all stitches.

Round 21: With Color B, work ribbing.

Round 23: With Color A, knit all stitches.

Rounds 24–29: With Color A, work ribbing.

Round 30: With Color A, **purl** all stitches.

Round 31: With Color A, knit, increasing 31 [34, 37] times evenly spaced. (Approximately every 9 stitches.) 311[342, 373] stitches.

Begin stranded knitting. Round 1: Slip marker, join Color B, knit Round 1, **Back Chart** (page 82) from Point A to C 10 [11, 12] times, end: knit from Point A to B, place marker. 156 [171, 186] Back stitches. Knit Round 1, **Front Chart**, from Point A to C 9 [10, 11] times, end: knit from Point A to B. 155 [171, 187]

Don's Vest

Front stitches. (Note the number of pattern rows varies between the back and the front.)

Front Chart

Back Chart

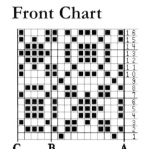
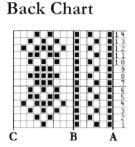

Following Rounds: Knit **Back** and **Front Charts** as established in Body Round 1 until desired length to bottom of armhole, less one inch.

Side View

Dividing for Armholes: Slip marker, *knit in established pattern to 10 stitches before marker, place next 20 stitches on hold on a piece of yarn. The stitches on hold form a *Kangaroo Pouch* (page 17). Place marker, with Color A around thumb and Color B around index finger, *Cast On: Long Tail*, a 10 stitch steek, place marker*. Repeat between asterisks. Back 136 [151, 166], Front 135 [151, 167] stitches. (*Steeks*, page 21.)

Armhole Shaping: (Alternate Rows 1 and 2 of *Steeks: Center Front Chart*, page 33.) Decrease 1 stitch before and after each steek **every other round** 16 times. (i.e. Decrease Rounds—*Knit steek, transfer marker, *Decrease: Right* (page 14), knit in established pattern to 2 stitches before marker, *Decrease: Left* (page 14), transfer marker.* Repeat between asterisks. After decreasing 16 times you start to knit the **Back Chart** at the 6th stitch after Point B and the **Front Chart** 1 stitch before Point B.

You have 104 [119, 134] back stitches. Divide your gauge into your number of back stitches and the answer is the width across your vest shoulders. You

add approximately 1 inch armhole ribbing on each edge. The shoulder width may be adjusted by having fewer or more stitches in the "kangaroo pouch" when you divide for the underarm, or you may decrease fewer or more times.

Simultaneously, divide for V-neck at the desired length for bottom of V-neck less 2" for ribbing. This is approximately 1" or more above the start of Armhole Shaping and after completing Row 16 [8, 16] of **Front Chart**.

Knit Back as established. Knit to center front stitch and place it on hold, place marker. With Color A around thumb and Color B around index finger *Cast On: Long Tail* a 10 stitch steek, place marker. Finish round in established pattern.

Begin center front decreases on an established armhole decrease round and decrease at center front **every other round** 25 times. (i.e.; knit in pattern and decrease at armholes as established, knit to 2 stitches prior to center front steek marker, *Decrease: Left*, slip marker, knit steek, slip marker, *Decrease: Right*, finish round and decrease at armhole edge as established.) After decreases, 26 [34, 42] shoulder stitches remain between armhole and center front steeks. Knit **even** to desired length of vest. It is preferable to end after completion of Row 8 or 16 of **Front Chart**.

V-Neck

V-neck Width Options: Divide your gauge into the 50 stitches decreased for the V-neck to obtain the width of your V. If you desire a narrower or wider V, decrease in fewer or more rounds and accordingly adjust the number of shoulder stitches given above. Keep in mind a 1" border is added to the V.

Steeks: With Color A, *Steeks: Slip Stitch Crochet* (page 21). Cut steeks.

Don's Vest

Shoulders: With Color A, *Kitchener Stitch: Graft* (page 17) shoulder seams together, leaving 52 [51, 50] center back stitches on the needle.

V-neck Ribbing: Start at left shoulder with needle 1 size smaller than stranded knitting needle. With Color A *Knit Up* (page 18) 3 stitches for every 4 rounds along straight portion of V. When V-neck decreases begin, *Knit Up* 1 stitch for every round to center front, knit center front stitch on hold and mark stitch with safety pin, knit up second side 1 stitch for every round to end of decreases, then *Knit Up* 3 stitches for every 4 rounds. Knit across back and decrease 5 stitches evenly spaced. Place marker for start of round.

Round 1: Purl and decrease as necessary to attain a total number of stitches divisible by 4, plus 3. (A number divisible by 4 is required for knit 2, purl 2 ribbing, and the 3 extra stitches allow for a balanced center front decrease.)

Round 2: Work knit 2, purl 2 ribbing to 1 stitch before marked center front stitch, *Decrease: Double* (page 14). Work up second side of V-neck with a mirror image of first side. (Example: If last stitches knit before the double decrease were knit 2, purl 1, you purl 1, knit 2 after the double decrease.) Work in established ribbing to end of round.

Rounds 3–5: Work around in ribbing with Color A, *Decrease: Double* at center front **every** round and continue to mirror image the ribbing each side of decrease.

Round 6: With Color B, **knit** and maintain center front decrease.

Round 7: With Color B, work ribbing and maintain decrease.

Round 8: With Color A **knit** and maintain decrease.

Round 9–10: With Color A, work ribbing and maintain decrease.

Round 11: Work ribbing and maintain center front decrease. After you reach the shoulder seam, purl 2 together across back at **every other** purl rib; i.e., *knit 2, purl 2, knit 2, purl 2 together,* repeat between asterisks.
  Bind Off: Sewn I (page 6). Tack down steek.

Armhole Ribbing: Place the 20 underarm stitches on hold onto a needle one size smaller than stranded knitting needle. With Color A, *Knit Up* 1 stitch every round along decreases, then *Knit Up* 3 stitches every 4 rounds to approximately 2 inches before shoulder join, *Knit Up* 1 stitch **every other** round to approximately 2 inches after shoulder join, and then knit up as on opposite side of armhole. (You pick up fewer stitches around the shoulder to contour the shape.) Knit 10 stitches that had been on hold (to center underarm), and place marker for beginning of round.

Round 1: Purl and decrease as necessary to attain a total number of stitches divisible by 4.

Rounds 2–5: Work around in knit 2, purl 2 ribbing.

Round 6: With Color B, **knit.**

Round 7: With Color B, work ribbing.

Round 8: With Color A **knit.**

Round 9–10: With Color A, work ribbing.

Round 11: Decrease by purl 2 together at **every other** purl rib.
  Work *Bind Off: Sewn I* around. Tack down steek.
Weave in ends.
  Work other armhole ribbing.
  Block.
  Wear and enjoy.
  This could be a time to turn your back on someone.

Joyous Jacket

I wished to call this "The Geiger Jacket," but it seems someone with that name already used it! So I decided I would give it a deviation of my name. The twisted I-cord trim on this jacket gives the appearance of a separate underarm panel, but the fronts and back are knit (garter stitch) in one piece to underarms. Then underarm stitches are placed on hold and fronts and back are knit separately. The stranded knit sleeves begin at the top and are saddled to body underarm stitches until sleeve underarm panel begins. Then sleeves are knit in the round to cuff. Sleeves are bound off in I-cord, and a decorative I-cord is applied at top of cuff. A collar is added, then twisted I-cord is applied around jacket. The design for the sleeves is from Z. Ventaskrasts' books.

Measurements and Gauges:

36" [40", 44", 48", 52"] circumference (does not include twisted I-Cord Trim), 21" [23", 25", 27", 29"] long (or your choice. This style also looks very nice at a length just below the waist.), 23" bloused sleeve length – all sizes (again you have a choice)

20 stitches/40 rows = 4" (10 cm) in garter stitch

24 stitches/26 rows = 4" (10 cm) in stranded knitting

Materials:

Color A—#99 Black Quebecoise, 8 [9, 10, 11, 12] – 3.5 oz. skeins

Color B—#53 Red Quebecoise, 4 [5, 6, 7, 8] – 3.5 oz. skeins

6 [7, 7, 7, 8] Buttons

BODY

Use Color A and garter stitch needle, *Cast On: Invisible* (page 11) 175 [195, 215, 235, 255] stitches.

Row 1: Knit to last three stitches, yarn forward, slip 3 as if to purl. Turn. As you start to knit back, working yarn for first stitch comes behind your work from fourth stitch on left needle. (After you complete several rows, the 3 edge stitches have the appearance of stockinette stitch I-cord.)

Lower Front Curve

Rows 2–11: Increase. Knit 3 I-cord stitches, *Increase* 1 (page 16), knit to last 3 stitches, slip 3 as if to purl. Turn. 185 [205, 225, 245, 265] stitches.

Rows 12–27: Knit even with established I-cord edges.

Sizes 36, 40, 44 make buttonhole following Rows 28–31 directions. **Sizes 48 and 52** work to Row 32, **then** make buttonhole following Rows 28–31 directions.

Row 28: Knit to last 3 stitches. **Turn**. Do **not** slip or knit I-cord stitches. (You are at right edge of jacket.)

Row 29: Knit across and slip last 3 stitches as established.

Row 30: Knit across to last 3 stitches. With yarn forward, slip 3 stitches as if to purl, turn.

Row 31: Knit 3 stitches, place them back onto left needle and work them again with knit 2, slip 1. There is a loose strand between slipped stitch and next stitch on left needle. Place this strand onto left needle, place slipped stitch onto left needle with left side forward, and knit 2 **together** through back loops (*Decrease: Left*, page 14). Work across as established.

Rows 32–110 [130, 150, 160, 180]: 55 [65, 75, 80, 90] ridges, or desired length to underarm. (Armhole depth is 10 inches for first 3 sizes and 11 inches for last 2 sizes.) Work as established, placing buttonholes at right edge every 14 [13, 15, 16, 15] ridges (count from first ridge at top of buttonhole). Buttonholes are approximately 3 inches apart.

Row 111 [131, 151, 161, 181]: Divide for underarm panel. Work 40 [43, 48, 50, 53] stitches. Break yarn. *Place next 15 [20, 20, 25, 30] stitches on hold on a piece of yarn.* Join new yarn. Knit across 75 [80, 90, 95, 100] stitches. Repeat between asterisks. Place last 40 [42, 47, 50, 52] stitches on hold on separate piece of yarn. (Yes, some sizes do have one more stitch on right front than on left.)

Note: Here you may customize jacket to fit your shoulder size. Measure across your back from shoulder edge to shoulder edge. Multiply answer by 5 (gauge) for number of back stitches required. For button overlap, add 5 to number of back stitches and divide by 2 for number of stitches for each front. If uneven number, use extra stitch on right front. Add together total number of front and back stitches. Subtract answer

Joyous Jacket

from 185 [205, 225, 245, 265] stitches, then divide answer by 2 to determine number of stitches in each underarm panel.

Back: Knit every row (no I-cord edge) to total length of 210 [230, 250, 270, 290] rows. 105 [115, 125, 135, 145] ridges. End with wrong side row (ridge row on outside of jacket.) Break yarn. Place Back stitches on hold.

Fronts: Start at armhole edge (no I-cord) and knit to front edge. Work I-cord and buttonholes at front edge as established. Knit 70 [70, 70, 80, 80] rows from start of underarm panel. 35 [35, 35, 40, 40] ridges.

Neck Shaping: Start at front edge and *I-Cord: Bind Off* (page 15) 8 [8, 10, 10, 12] stitches. Finish row as established. Work rows from arm edge to front as established. Rows that start at front edge, *I-Cord: Bind Off* 1 stitch as follows: 36" – 12 times, 40" – 12 times left side, 13 times right side, 44" – 12 times, 48" – 13 times, and 52" – 12 times left side, 13 times right side. 20 [22, 26, 27, 28] shoulder stitches.

Knit even to total of 30 rows from start of neck shaping. 15 ridges.) Total jacket length 105 [115, 125, 135, 145] ridges. End with wrong side row (ridge row on outside of jacket).

Join Shoulders: Place fronts and back on separate needles. With right sides facing each other, start at **left** arm edge and *Bind Off: Three Needle* (page 7) across shoulders up to 3 I-cord stitches at front edge.* Break yarn. Start at right arm edge and repeat between asterisks. Turn jacket to outside. Place 3 I-cord stitches from front onto back needle. *I-Cord: Bind Off* (page 15) across back stitches. *Kitchener Stitch: Graft* (page 17) the 3 I-cord stitches to 3 front I-cord stitches.

I-Cord Bind Off Bottom Edge: Place invisibly cast on stitches onto needle. With Color A, *I-Cord: Bind Off* across bottom. *Kitchener Stitch: Graft* 3 I-cord stitches to 3 front I-cord stitches.

Weave in ends.

SLEEVES

With **stranded knitting needle** and Color A, *Cast On: Long-Tail* (page 11) 3 stitches, then *Knit Up* (page 18) along body at arm edge 109 [109, 109, 121, 121] stitches (1 stitch for every ridge plus 4 [4, 4, 5, 5] evenly spaced each side plus 1 at shoulder join), *Cast On: Cable* (page 10) 3 stitches. Total 115 [115, 115, 127,

127] stitches. (You start to knit up from back on right sleeve and from front on left sleeve.) **Turn**.

I suggest that you *Knit Onto Left Needle* (*KOLN*, page 4) as I did rather than purling top portion of sleeve that is knit flat. However, I realize many knitters are not familiar with the technique so instructions are to purl back. I assume if you knit onto your

Sleeve and Body Join

left needle, you will translate purl instructions to knitting back. The 3 additional stitches form an I-cord edge to conceal trapped second color where sleeve joins underarm panel.

With Color A and yarn in front, slip 3, purl 109 [109, 109, 121, 121], yarn in front slip 3. Turn. Place underarm stitches on hold onto second circular needle. (May be a smaller size.)

Start stranded knitting. Row 1: Use needle holding knit up sleeve stitches, knit 2 (yarn for first stitch will come from 4th stitch on needle), slip 1, place stitch from underarm panel onto left needle, place slipped stitch onto left needle and *Decrease: Left* (joining underarm panel stitch to sleeve). Join Color B, and follow **Chart A** (page 88), **Row 1. Sizes 36", 40", and 44":** Knit from Point C to B, 1 time, Point A to B 8 times, Point A to D 1 time. **Sizes 48" and 52": Knit** from Point A to B 10 times, Point A to E 1 time. **All sizes:** Place stitch from underarm panel onto left needle, place Color B over Color A (trapping it) and *Decrease: Right*, Color A (joining underarm panel stitch to sleeve), knit 2. Turn.

Row 2: With yarn in front slip 3, follow **Chart A, Row 2. Sizes 36", 40", and 44": Purl** from Point D to A 1 time, Point B to A 8 times, Point B to C 1 time, slip 3 with yarn in front. **Sizes 48" and 52": Purl** from Point E to A 1 time, Point B to A 10 times, slip 3 with yarn in front.

Uneven Rows 3–5 [9, 9, 15, 19]: Knit rows – join

underarm stitches. Work as established in Row 1, **but** place Color B (trapping it) over Color A when you knit first stitch. Continue to work **Chart A**, Rows 1–12, and repeat when necessary.

Even Rows 4–[10, 10, 16, 20]: Purl Rows. Follow Chart A with established repeats **as in Row 2.** 9 [10, 10, 9, 10] stitches remain in underarm panel. On left sleeve do **not** work last purl row.

Start to knit in the round: Place remaining underarm panel stitches onto left needle. Place 3 I-cord stitches last knit onto left needle. With Color A, knit 1, place marker, *Decrease: Left.* (The 3 I-cord stitches are reduced to 2 on each side and become pattern stitches in underarm panel.) Follow **Chart B, Row 1** and work between Points C and D. With Color A, *Decrease: Right* 1 [2, 2, 1, 2] times. Sizes that decrease 2 times work I-cord stitch with underarm panel stitch, place marker, knit 2 I-cord stitches together. Sizes that decrease one time, work 2 I-cord stitches together, place marker, knit 1. (There are 13 stitches in underarm panel, but markers are placed 1 stitch in on each side to accommodate later decreases.) Knit around sleeve in established pattern, **Chart A**, to 1 stitch prior to underarm marker.

Following rounds: Work **Chart B** Point A to B; i.e., knit 1, slip marker, knit 11, slip marker, knit 1. Repeat Rows 1 to 6 as required. Knit sleeve stitches in established pattern, **Chart A**, and repeat Rows 1 to 12 as required. Use a second circular when required. (*Knitting Small Circumferences With Two Circular Needles*, page 18)

Decrease rounds: Decrease every 4th round 19 times 84 [84, 84, 96, 96] stitches. Decrease every 5th round 12 times. 60 [60, 60, 72, 72] stitches. To decrease, knit to 2 stitches prior to first underarm marker, *Decrease: Right*, slip marker, follow **Chart B** and knit 11, slip maker, *Decrease: Left*. Finish round in established pattern, **Chart A**. If longer or shorter sleeves are desired, adjust decreases accordingly. Remember to allow for a 2 inch cuff. (*Spacing Decreases/Increases Evenly*, page 21) The model sleeves end 4-1/2 inches **below** the wrist. Break Color B.

Note: You may personalize jacket in underarm panel. Model has my first name on one sleeve, and last name and date on second sleeve. Place writing on panels so as you look at names you may read from left to right. Model is reversed—learn from my mistake! (*Alphabet*

Sleeve Cuff and Underarm

& Number Chart, page 6.)

Cuff: Size Options. With Color A, decrease to 30, 35, 40, 45, or 50 stitches (6, 7, 8, 9 or 10 inch circumferences). Size 40" model has 30 stitches. With garter stitch needles, knit 1 round, purl 1 round (garter stitch knit in the round) for 20 rounds (10 ridges). Break Color A.

Cuff Bind Off: With Color B, *Cast On: Invisible* 3 stitches. Work *I-Cord: Applied Contrasting Color* (page 15) to bind off around. *Kitchener Stitch Graft* (page 17) 3 I-cord stitches to the 3 invisibly cast on I-cord stitches. Work *I-Cord: Applied Contrasting Color* around top of cuff. Weave in ends.

Work second sleeve.

Collar: Use Color A and stranded knitting needle. Begin at start of curve on front neck edge and *Knit Up* along front and back to end of curve on opposite front 69 [69,81,81,93] stitches evenly spaced. (Count the number of I-cord rows where you knit up. See *Spacing Decreases/Increases Evenly*, page 21.) Turn.

(I do not want to hear complaints that you have to do some math. The technique to determine spacing is among the most useful I have learned at Knitting Camp. I want you to do the math to understand how the technique works. If this technique is not in your repertoire, you will thank me.)

Collar

Joyous Jacket

With Color A, **purl 1 row.**

Join Color B.

Uneven Rows 1–5: Follow **Chart C, knit** from Point A to B 5 [5, 6, 6, 7] times, from Point A to C 1 time.

Even Rows 2–6: Follow **Chart C, purl** (or KOLN) from Point C to A 1 time, Point B to A 5 [5, 6, 6, 7] times.

Uneven Rows 7–9: With Color A, *Decrease: Left*, knit across in established pattern to last 2 stitches, with Color A *Decrease: Right*.

Even Row 8: With Color A, *Decrease: Left*, purl across in established pattern to last 2 stitches, with Color A *Decrease: Right*. At completion of Row 9, break Color B.

Row 10: With Color A, purl. Place stitches on hold.

Finishing: Sleeve Edge and Underarm Panel Twisted I-Cord Trim: Start at lower edge of body sleeve join and slide a circular needle (small size) through top loop of garter stitches in straight line to bottom of jacket. (For right side of jacket start at back, and for left side start at front.)

With Color B, start at bottom edge and apply *I-Cord: Twisted* (page 15) using *Contrasting Color* technique up to sleeve edge, around sleeve, and down to bottom on opposite side. Mirror image twists on each side; i.e., on right side of jacket carry the free I-cord in back, and on left side of jacket carry free I-cord in front.

Twisted I-Cord Trim Around Outer Edges: Start at lower center back with Color B and apply *I-Cord: Twisted* using *Contrasting Color* technique around. To match twist on sleeves, start with free I-cord behind. At collar edge, apply one I-cord along lower collar edge. Apply second I-cord along front edges of collar and to stitches on hold at top of collar. At opposite end of collar, mirror image twist and start to carry free I-cord in front. At end of application, *Kitchener Stitch: Graft* the 6 I-cord stitches to 6 invisibly cast on I-cord stitches.

Weave in ends. Sew on buttons. Give the jacket your name and wear with pleasure.

Chart C

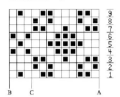

Chart B

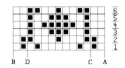

Chart A

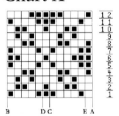

Morocco

Morocco may seem a very strange name for a garment with a Latvian weaving pattern, but the border design reminded me of architecture and designs I saw in Morocco. I knit this jacket after all the knitting for the book was supposedly complete, but Meg and Lizbeth insisted the pattern go into the book. (Bossy publisher and editor!)

The chart for this design, meant to be a woven bed coverlet, is another one from Z. Ventaskrasts' books. This cardigan jacket is knit in the round with center front steek, mitered hem and front facing. Sleeves are set in to shoulder width and are knit from the top down to the hemmed cuff. An I-cord is applied around the entire jacket and used to make buttonholes.

Sizes: Size variations for this unisex design are practical only through change of gauge. To maintain pattern integrity it would be necessary to add or subtract 50 stitches to adjust sizes with stitch numbers. Divide 397 (total number of body stitches) by the circumference of your choice and your answer will be the gauge required to achieve that circumference. Select yarn and needle sizes to attain your gauge. (*Yarn Suggestions and Amounts*, page 24) To determine your finished lengths, divide your body row gauge into 285 (total number of rows)and sleeve row gauge into 222. Note the variation in body/sleeve gauges below.

Model Measurements and Gauges:
44" circumference, 30" long, 23"sleeve length
36 stitches/34 rows = 4" (10 cm) in stranded knitting
38 stitches/40 rows = 4" (10 cm) sleeves in stranded knitting

Model Materials:
Color A—#151 Charcoal Spun Lace Weight Icelandic Wool, Seven – 1.75 oz. balls
Color B—#885 Medium Brown Spun Lace Weight Icelandic Wool, Seven – 1.75 oz. balls
6 Buttons

Steek: Rounds begin at center of front steek. For hem, work steek in Color A. (*Steeks*, page 21).

Hem Note: First, see **Hem Note** in *The Star* pattern, (page 115). Then, see *Hems: Knit In* (page 14). This jacket was knit with the same yarn as *The Star* (except change in pattern color), but I chose to knit the hem to the body in this jacket. Knitter's choice!

BODY

Hem: Use needle 2–3 sizes smaller than body stranded knitting needle and Color A, *Cast On: Invisible* (page 11) 387 stitches. This number includes 10 steek stitches.

Hem Row 1: Knit and increase 1 at each side of steek. (i.e. Knit 5 steek stitches, place marker, *Increase Right* (page 16), knit to last 5 stitches, *Increase: Left* (page 16), place marker, knit 5 steek stitches.) The increases at each side of the steek form a mitered corner inside the hem. (*Mitered Corners Knit in the Round*, page 19.)

Hem Round 2: Join, being certain not to twist, and start to knit in the round. Knit 5 steek stitches, slip marker, *Increase: Right*, knit to the next marker, *Increase: Left*, slip marker, and knit 5 steek stitches.

Hem Rounds 3–10: Knit, increase 1 stitch each side of steek as established. The miter will bunch up and look funny before cutting, but unbunches when steek is cut. Believe me!

Hem Turning Round 11: Knit 5 steek stitches, slip marker, *Increase: Right*, purl around to next marker (397 stitches), *Increase: Left*, slip marker, knit 5 steek stitches. 409 stitches

Round 1: Begin stranded knitting. Row 1 on Chart A and Chart B (pages 95 and 94)**.** Use **stranded knitting needle** and join Color B. (For this and following rounds, alternate Rows 1 and 2 of *Steeks: Center Front Chart*, page 33.) Work 5 steek stitches, slip marker, with Color A *Increase: Right* 1, purl 1, place marker for start of pattern. Follow **Chart A**, and knit from Point C to B 1 time (39 stitches), place marker. Follow **Chart B**, and knit from Point A to B 5 times, Point A to C 1 time (121 stitches), place marker. Follow **Chart A** and work from Point A to B 1 time (77 stitches), place marker. Follow **Chart B** and work from Point A to B 5 times, Point A to C 1 time (121 stitches), place marker. Follow **Chart A** and work from Point A to D (39 stitches), place marker. With Color A purl 1, *Increase: Left* 1, slip marker, work 5 steek stitches.

Rounds 2–8: Work 5 steek stitches, slip marker, with Color A *Increase: Right* 1, knit to 1 stitch of start of pattern marker, purl 1, slip marker. (The facing stitches between steek and start of pattern are worked in Color A to top of jacket. The stitch at each side of front edge next to pattern are purl stitches to top.) Work pattern repeats around as in Round 1. Markers were placed where changes are made from **Chart A to B** or **Chart B to A**. Slip marker at end of color pattern, purl 1, knit to steek marker, *Increase: Left* 1, slip marker, work 5 steek stitches.

There will be some long carries of Color B across back of facing. Facing is turned to inside at purl stitch and long carries are concealed and need not be trapped, but make sure stranded carry of Color B is long enough. Stretch knitting out on right needle before knitting first Color B pattern stitch. Increases end with Round 8. 425 stitches – 10 steek stitches, 8 facing stitches each front (16), 1 purl stitch next to pattern each front (2), and 397 pattern stitches.

Rounds 9–11: Work around as established, but without increasing.

Round 12: Join hem. Fold hem to inside on purl round and knit **in pattern** the body stitches to the invisible cast-on stitches where possible. Use **needle 1 size larger** than stranded knitting needle for this joining round. (*Knitting in Mitered Hems,* page 19)

Bottom of Center Back

Rounds 13–77: Use **stranded knitting needle** and work in pattern as established.

Round 78: Work steek, slip marker, work facing, slip marker. Follow **Chart C, Row 1** and knit from Point C to B 1 time, slip marker. Knit 1 Color A, follow **Chart D, Row 1** and knit from Point A to B 20 times, with Color A increase 1, slip marker. Follow **Chart C, Row 1** and work from Point A to B, slip marker. With Color A increase 1, follow **Chart D**, Row 1 and work from Point **B to A** 20 times, with Color A knit 1, slip marker. Follow **Chart C, Row 1** Point A to D 1 time.

Next Rounds: Work as established in Round 78 until

you have completed **Chart C, Rows 1–24 four** times. Repeat **Chart D, Rows 1–6** as required. (There is 1 Color A stitch at each edge of panel with the 20 pattern repeats from **Chart D**.) Total 427 stitches: 10 steek, 8 facing each side (16), 1 purl each front (2), 39 in each front border (78), 1 Color A at each edge of **Chart D** pattern repeats (4), 120 stitches for **Chart D** repeats each side (240) and 77 stitches in center back panel.

Note: Model armholes are inset to shoulder width. However, this requires some manipulation to maintain pattern design sequence with underarm pattern when you start to knit sleeves. It also involves more ends to weave in. If you desire a simpler method, change armholes to drop shoulder.

Next Round: Divide for underarms. Work 5 steek stitches, slip marker, with Color A knit 8, purl 1, slip marker. Follow **Chart C, Row 1** (where you should be) and knit from Point C to B (39 stitches), slip marker, *with Color A knit 1, follow **Chart D** as established and knit 44 (45 stitches after marker). Place next 32 stitches on hold on a piece of yarn. (The underarm stitches on hold will form a *Kangaroo Pouch*, page 17.) Place marker. With Color A around thumb and Color B around index finger, *Cast On: Long-Tail* , (page 11) a 10 stitch steek, place marker. Follow **Chart D** as established and knit 44 stitches in pattern, knit 1 Color A, slip marker.* Follow **Chart C, Row 1** and knit 77 stitches, slip marker. Repeat between asterisks. Follow **Chart C, Row 1**, and knit from Point A to D, slip marker, with Color A purl 1, knit 8, slip marker, work 5 steek stitches.

Next Rounds: Decrease at arm edges. Work as established, but decrease **every** round at armhole edges 10 times; i.e., *work in established pattern to armhole steek, *Decrease: Left* (page 14), slip marker, follow *Steeks: Armhole Chart*, (page 33) alternating Rows 1 and 2 in following rounds, slip marker, *Decrease: Right* (page 14).* Repeat between asterisks, and finish round as established. 25 stitches each side of sleeve in **Chart D** sections.

Following Rounds: Work even in pattern through **Row 23** of the **seventh** repeat of **Chart C** and work **Chart D** as established.

Next Round: Prepare for front neck opening. Bind off 5 center front steek stitches, bind off 8 facing stitches, plus 1 purl stitch. Work around as established to front facing. Bind off 1 purl stitch and 8 facing stitches, bind off 5 steek stitches.

Next Round: Front Neck Opening. Place 28 stitches on hold on piece of yarn. Place marker, and with Color A around thumb and Color B around index finger, *Cast On: Long Tail* 5 steek stitches, place marker. Follow **Chart C, Row 1** and work from Point E to Point B, slip marker. *Follow **Chart D** and work 25 stitches as established, slip marker.* Work armhole steek, slip marker. Repeat between asterisks. Follow **Chart C, Row 1** from Point A to B, slip marker. Work between asterisks again, then work armhole steek, slip marker, and repeat between asterisks **again**. Follow **Chart C, Row 1** from Point B to E, place next 28 stitches on hold on piece of yarn. Place marker, with Color A around thumb and Color B around index finger, *Cast On: Long Tail* 5 steek stitches.

Next Round: Back to Charts A and B. Work 5 steek stitches, slip marker. Follow **Chart A, Row 1** and work from Point E to Point B. *Follow **Chart B, Row 1** and work from Point A to B, Point A to C*, slip marker, work armhole steek, slip marker. Repeat between asterisks. Follow **Chart A, Row 1** and work from Point A to B. Repeat between asterisks again. Slip marker, work armhole steek, slip marker. Work between asterisks again. Follow **Chart A, Row 1** and work from Point B to E, slip marker, work 5 steek stitches.

Following Rounds Through Row 38, Chart A and B: Work as established above. When working **Row 38**, bind off center front steek stitches. Do **not** bind off armhole steeks.

Break yarns. Place front body stitches on separate needle(s) which may be smaller to prepare for three needle bind off at shoulders. Place 5 front sleeve steek stitches at each side of front on hold.

Back: Join Colors A and B and work 5 armhole steek stitches, slip marker. Work Back across Row 39 from established charts, slip marker, work 5 steek stitches. Place 5 steek stitches at each edge on hold.

Join Shoulders: With outsides together, *Bind Off: Three Needle* (page 7) across shoulders with needle one size larger than stranded knitting needle. Start at arm edge and leave tail of Color A long enough to graft armhole steeks. For the bind off, follow Row 39 of **Charts B and A** to center steek. Break yarns and repeat on other

side. *Kitchener Stitch: Graft* (page 17) front and back armhole steeks together.

Center Front and Outer Edge Finishing: *Steeks: Slip Stitch Crochet* (page 21) all steeks. Cut center front steeks. Fold to inside and tack down neck edge steeks, facings and hem stitches where required. With Color A, work 3 stitch *I-Cord: Applied* (page 14)) to purl turning stitches around edges of jacket and to stitches on hold at neck fronts and center back stitches. Make *I-Cord: Buttonholes*, (page 15) opposite Row 1, **Chart C** at appropriate front edge. *Kitchener Stitch: Graft* (page 17) I-cord ends together. Sew on buttons.

SLEEVES

Here some manipulation takes place so underarm sleeve pattern is uninterrupted. Sleeve steeks may be cut before of after picking up sleeve stitches.

Sleeve and Body Join

Knit Up Right Sleeve Stitches: Use **stranded knitting needles** to obtain sleeve gauge, page 91. (See *Sleeve Gauge*, page 20.) Start at back at sleeve edge adjacent to **Chart B, Row 1**. Follow **Chart C, Row 2** from Point A to B and *Knit Up* (page 18) along steek in pattern 1 stitch for every row, place marker. The knit up stitches should line up with those of **Chart C, Row 1**. *With Color A increase 1. Follow **Chart D, Row 1** and *Knit Up* 1 stitch for every row to start of curve, *Knit Up* 8 stitches along curve. 68 stitches*. You will be on the front at underarm stitches on hold and pattern will line up with underarm pattern stitches. The knit up stitches will blend with body pattern, but **not** duplicate body stitches they abut as in some patterns. Break yarns. Slide stitches to right end of needle. Join Colors A and B, place marker. Repeat between asterisks on back side of armhole steek. Follow

Morocco

Chart D, Row 1 and work across 32 underarm stitches on hold in established pattern. Total 247 stitches. Break yarns.

Knit Up Left Sleeve Stitches: Start at front at sleeve edge adjacent to **Chart B, Row 1**. Follow **Chart C, Row 2** from Point A to B and *Knit Up* along steek in pattern 1 stitch for every row. The knit up stitches should line up with those of **Chart C, Row 1**, place marker. *With Color A increase 1. Follow **Chart D, Row 1** and *Knit Up* 1 stitch for every row to start of curve, *Knit Up* 8 stitches along curve. 68 stitches*. You will be on the back at underarm stitches on hold and pattern will line up with underarm pattern. Follow **Chart D, Row 1** and work across 32 underarm stitches on hold in established pattern. Break yarns. Slide stitches to right end of needle. Join Colors A and B, place marker, and repeat between asterisks on front side of armhole steek. Total 247 stitches. Break yarns.

Both Sleeves: (Note decrease rounds below.) Slip stitches so rounds begin at marker at start of **Chart C**. Join yarns, work in pattern across **Chart C**, slip marker, work **Chart D** in established pattern to start of round. Repeat **Chart D, Row 1–6** as required. Repeat **Chart C, Rows 1–24** six times, work **Row 1** one time. Change to **Chart A** and work Point A to B until last decrease, then work Point A to F through Round 77. (You will have decreased all **Chart D** stitches.) Change to second circular needle when required. (*Knitting Small Circumferences With Two Circulars*, page 18.)

Decrease Rounds:

Decrease every second round 73 times (146 stitches), then every third round 12 times. Next round decrease 1. 76 stitches remain. Decreases are made along the edge of **Chart C** then **Chart A**. On decrease rounds, transfer start of round marker, work **Chart C** or **A**, transfer marker, with Color A, *Decrease: Left*, work in established pattern **Chart D** to 2 stitches before start of round marker, with Color A, *Decrease: Right*.

Lower Sleeve Underarm

On completion of **Chart A**, Row 77, break Color B. With Color A, knit 1 round, purl 1 round, then knit 10 rounds for hem. With blunt needle run a length of Color A through stitches. Fold hem to inside at purl ridge and tack down, catching each open loop stitch. Weave in ends. I warned you!

Block.

Sew on buttons.

Wear or give with pride.

Chart D

B   A

Chart B

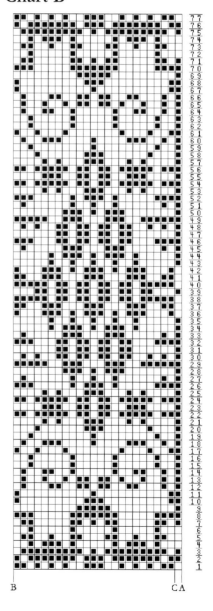

Chart C

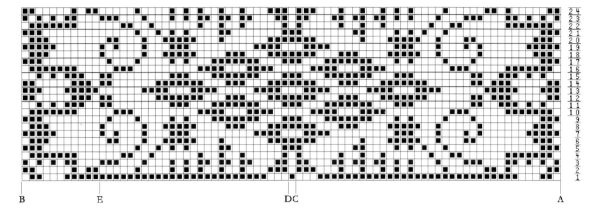

Chart A

Park High Pullover

I found the stitch pattern for this pullover in *A Joy Forever, Latvian Weaving*, by Jane A. Evans. The pattern is from a twill tablecloth that is part of the collection at the Royal Ontario Museum, Toronto, Canada. This pullover received its name because blue and gold, the colors I used for the pullover, were Park High colors, my school in Racine, Wisconsin.

To give the garment the desired width and length and to fit the pattern to knitting, I turned the pattern on its side and added repeats in the center section both horizontally and vertically. The sleeves are a mirror image of the top portion of the sweater, again with added repeats of the center pattern for wanted length.

Sizes: Because this sweater does have a section with a 10 stitch or 10 row pattern repeat, the size may be adjusted by additional or fewer pattern repeats. If you adjust pattern repeats for circumference, keep in mind you need to add or subtract stitches in increments of 10 to **both** front and back. Thus, the sweater will increase or decrease in size by 20 stitches for each pattern repeat added or subtracted. This does not apply if you add rows, so the length may be changed by increments of 10 rows. (*Design*, page 121.)

As with all designs in this book, yarn and gauge are your choice, so sizes may be changed by a change of gauge. The body has 340 stitches. (*Gauge: Determining*, page 14 and *Yarn Suggestions and Amounts*, page 24.)

Model Measurements and Gauge:
42"circumference, 27" long
32 stitches/32 rows = 4" (10 cm) in stranded knitting

Model Materials:
Color A—#121 Yellow Ochre Jamieson and Smith Shetland Jumper Weight. Ten – 1 oz. skeins
Color B—#135 Prussian Blue Jamieson and Smith Shetland Jumper Weight, Ten – 1 oz. skeins

BODY

Hem: Use needle 2 to 3 sizes smaller than stranded knitting needle (*Needles*, page 19) and Color B, *Cast On: Invisible* (page 11) 340 stitches or your desired number. (*Hems: Knit In*, page 14)

Hem Row 1: Knit.

Hem Round 2: Place marker. Join, being certain not to twist, and start to knit in the round.

Hem Round 3–14: Knit around.

Hem Round 15: Purl.

Round 1: Knit around.

Round 1: Begin stranded knitting. Use **stranded knitting needle** and join Color A. Slip marker, *knit Row 1 of **Chart A** from Point A to B, Point C to D*, place marker. Repeat between asterisks. Stitches A/D are side stitches and Stitches C/B are center back and center front stitches. You may wish to place a marker at Points B.

<u>**Size Variations by Stitch Adjustment:**</u> Knit more or fewer 10 stitch pattern repeat outlined in chart.

Rounds 2–13: Follow **Chart A** as established in Round 1.

Round 14: Knit in Hem. With needle one size larger, knit in pattern the invisibly cast on stitches together with body stitches.

Rounds 15–63: Use **stranded knitting needle** and continue with **Chart A**.

Rounds 64–148: Work Rows 54–63 of **Chart A**, as established, 8 times more (Round 143) or until desired length to underarm (approximately 11 inches short of total length). If more or less length is desired, knit the 10 row repeat more or less times. Then, knit Rows 54–58.

Side View

Round 149: Chart B, Arm Openings. *Slip marker, place next stitch on hold. With Color A around thumb and Color B around index finger, *Cast-On: Long Tail* (page 11) a 10 stitch steek, place marker. Knit from Point D to B, Point C to D.* Repeat between asterisks. (*Steeks*, page 21)

Park High Pullover

Rounds 150–222: Work **Chart B** as established, and repeat Rows 1 and 2 of *Steeks: Armhole Chart* (page 33) between steek markers.

Round 223: Front Neck Steek. Work steek, then work **Chart C** (back) from Point D to B, Point C to D. Work steek, then work **Chart B** (front) from Point D to stitches to be placed on hold. Place 27 stitches on hold on a piece of yarn, place marker. With Color A around thumb and Color B around index finger, *Cast-On: Long Tail* a 10 stitch steek, place marker. Work pattern in reverse to Point D.

<u>Note for Size Variations:</u> Thirteen stitches are decreased on each side of the front neck opening for a total neck width of 53 stitches. Divide your gauge into 53 to determine the width of your neck opening. Adjust the number of center front stitches on hold for a wider or narrower neck opening, but keep in mind that 26 additional stitches are decreased.

Rounds 224–236: Front Neck Shaping. Work steek, knit **Chart C** in both directions, work steek. On **Chart B**, knit until two stitches before front neck steek marker, work *Decrease: Right* (page 14), slip marker. Alternate Rows 1 and 2 of *Steeks: Center Front Chart* (page 33) in this and following rounds. Slip marker, *Decrease: Left* (page 14), and finish round.

Rounds 237–239: Work around as established, but do not decrease at front neck. On **Round 239,** with alternating colors, bind off 10 center front steek stitches.

Round 240: Bind off 10 steek stitches, knit **Chart C** in both directions, bind off 10 steek stitches. Break yarns. (Do not knit across **Chart B**–front.) *Steeks: Slip Stitch Crochet* (page 21) the 3 steeks.

Shoulder and Top of Sleeve

Join Shoulders: Place front stitches onto another needle(s). Turn knitting inside out so right sides are facing. Hold the two needles parallel, and use third needle **one size larger** than stranded knitting needle to work the bind-off.

*Start at side edge, repeat **Row 240, Chart C**, and work *Bind Off: Three Needle* (page 7) in pattern to center front steek. Break yarns.* Turn your work and repeat between asterisks. Center back stitches remain on needle. Tighten and weave in ends.

Neck finishing: Cut center front neck steek. Use either a 16" or 2 - 24" needles (*Knitting Small Circumferences With Two Circular Needles,* page 18) the same size as used for hem to pick up stitches around neck. With outside of back facing and Color B, knit across 53 back neck stitches, *Knit Up* (page 18) 16 stitches along front steek, knit across 27 center front stitches on hold, knit up 16 stitches along steek. (112 stitches.)

With Color B *Cast-On: Cable* (page 10) 3 I-cord stitches and bring yarn forward before placing third stitch onto left needle. *I-Cord Bind Off* (page 15) around neck. *Kitchener Stitch: Half-graft* (page 18) the 3 I-cord stitches to cast-on stitches. Weave in ends and tack down center front steek edges.

SLEEVES

Round 1: Chart D. Knit Up Sleeves. (Armhole steeks may be cut before or after sleeve stitches are knitted up.) Use either 1–16" or 2–24" needles one size smaller than used for body. (*Sleeve Gauge,* page 20) Follow **Chart D**, Round 1 and knit first stitch into stitch on hold at underarm, knit second stitch of pattern into a twisted picked up loop, then *Knit Up* one stitch for **every round** along armhole steek to Point B. Stitch B/C will abut top stitch on pullover back. You may wish to mark this stitch. (Note: After the 5 underarm panel stitches have been knit, the knit-up stitches duplicate the selvage body stitches they abut.) *Knit Up* opposite side of armhole and follow **Chart D** from Point C to Point D, place marker. Knit first 3 stitches of Round 2 to finish knitting up sleeve. You are at the center underarm, Round 2.

Round 2: Follow **Chart D**, knit 4, place marker, knit from Point D to B, Point C to D, slip marker. (Note: Rounds end at Point D.)

Round 3–13: Knit from Point A to D, slip marker,

Park High Pullover

knit from Point D to B, from Point C to D, slip marker.

The underarm panel is a good place to write a name, message, date, etc. if you wish to do so. (*Alphabet & Number Chart*, page 6) I suggest messages end before Round 164. Fill in before and after your message with the underarm panel design from **Charts D and E**.

Round 14: Decreases Start. Knit from Point A to D, slip marker, work *Decrease: Left*, knit to point B. Knit from Point C to 2 stitches before Point D, work *Decrease: Right*, slip marker.

Rounds 15–183: Follow **Charts D and E** and decrease in rounds indicated on charts. Decrease rounds change in intervals to accommodate the design on top of sleeve.

<u>Note for Size Variations:</u> To shorten or lengthen sleeves, eliminate or add one of the 10 row pattern repeats in center of sleeve. Adjust decreases accordingly.

After knitting Round 183, with Color B *Cast On: Cable* 3 stitches onto left needle, but bring yarn forward before placing third stitch on needle. *I-Cord: Bind Off* (page 15) around. *Kitchener Stitch: Half-graft* (page 18) the 3 I-cord stitches to cast on stitches.

Tack down sleeve steeks.

Block (page 7).

Wear, and wait for comments. You may notice when people first see it they do not comment on it, but after being around for awhile the pattern nuances start to be noticed and the favorable comments start to flow. As an example, the first time I wore this sweater on the golf course it was the seventh hole before my golf partner commented that she had been noticing my sweater and thought it was wonderful.

PARK HIGH SOCKS

For written details see *Toe to Top Socks*, page 29 or *Top to Toe Socks*, page 30. You choose which way you prefer to knit socks. Model was knit from Toe to Top. See below for variations and cuff instructions. Sock may be knit with 60 or 70 stitches. Divide your ankle measurement into 60 or 70 to determine required gauge for your sock size.

Model Materials:
Color A—#121 Yellow Ochre Jamieson & Smith Shetland Jumper Weight, One – 1 oz. skeins
Color B—#135 Prussian Blue Jamieson & Smith Shetland Jumper Weight, Three – 1 oz. skeins

(One additional skein of each color may be required for larger sizes.)

Toe to Top: Cast on with Color B. Follow written instructions for *Toe to Top Socks*, and increase to 60 or 70 stitches. Work to approximately 1–2 inches above short row heel turn. Work **Sock Chart**. With 60 or 70 stitches, work from Point A to B two times, then if 70 stitches work from Point A to C. When chart is complete, bind off with *Bind Off: Sewn* (page 6).

Top to Toe: Cast on 60 or 70 stitches. Work **Sock Chart** from top to bottom. With 60 or 70 stitches, work from Point A to B two times, then if 70 stitches work from Point A to C. When chart is complete, follow written instructions for *Top to Toe Socks* working with Color B.

Sock Chart

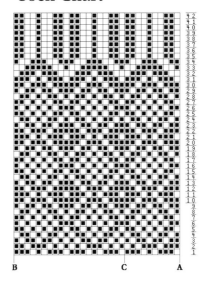

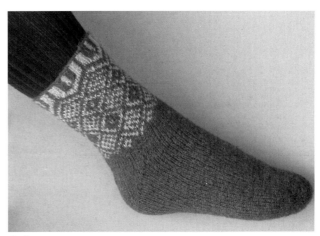

Sock

Chart A

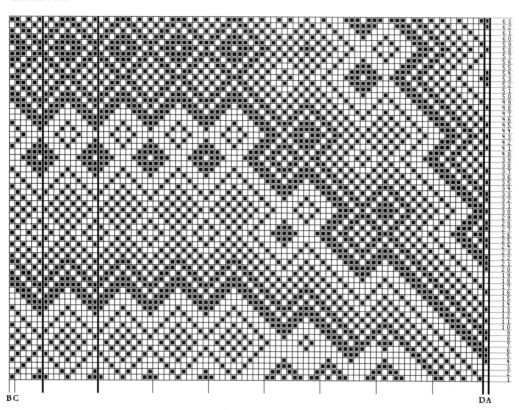

Chart C

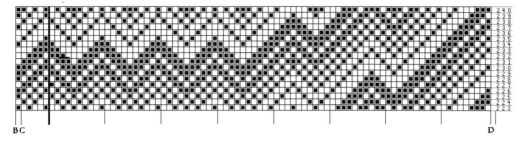

Chart B

Chart D

Chart E

B C

D   A

Snowflake Cardigan

This cardigan was the first garment I designed with a Latvian motif, and was knit long before I had any idea I would write a book on the subject. The snowflake or star used in the border of this cardigan is common in Latvian weaving and knitting patterns and also in Scandinavian patterns. The overall pattern is from a mitten in *Latviesu Rakstainie Cimdi* by Mirdza Slava which Lizbeth Upitis has in her book collection.

Usually I knit socks to match a sweater after the sweater has been knit. In this case the procedure was reversed. Using navy and red Guernsey wool, I knit knee socks with a snowflake design to wear with knickers for cross country skiing. The knee socks were my first experience using Guernsey wool for stranded knitting. I was thrilled with the results, liked the colors, and decided to make a matching cardigan.

This pattern may interest adventurous knitters as the construction of this cardigan frequently deviates from common methods of knitting cardigans. I merrily knit along on this garment doing things my (strange?) way never thinking that one day I would write down the pattern for a book.

This cardigan is knit in the round and cut (common). The solid color border is knit right along with the sweater (uncommon). I was not sure this would work. My friends said it would not work. But, I figured all I had to lose was time and yarn. If I was not satisfied with the finished border, I would simply turn it into a steek, cut the original steek and part of the border away, and add a new border in the conventional manner.

The body is stranded knitting, so double thickness. I wanted the solid color border to be double thick also so it is hemmed and faced. To avoid bulk when hem and facing are folded at the corners, I "unvented" a mitered corner hem while knitting in the round. (*Mitered Corners Knit in the Round*, page 19)

The sleeves are knit from the cuff up, and half grafted to the body from the underarm to the border (top of sleeve) design. Decreases are made along edge of design on sleeve top so as not to interrupt the underarm design. Border pattern continues as an I-cord edged saddle shoulder to join front and back of cardigan as it is knit. (There are decreases near the top of the body at the arm opening edges to give a gentle curve to the start of the saddle.)

Model Measurements and Gauges:

42" circumference, 25" long, 30" sleeve length from center back.

24 stitches/34 rows = 4" (10 cm) stockinette stitch.
24 stitches/26 rows = 4" (10 cm) stranded knitting

Model Materials:

Color A—Navy Guernsey Wool, Seven – 3.5 oz. skeins
Color B—Red Guernsey Wool, Six – 3.5 oz. skeins
5 or 9 Buttons

Because the rather large border pattern repeat goes up the top of the sleeve and across the shoulder, it is difficult to adjust size by pattern repeats without interfering with the integrity of the design. One more or less pattern repeat would be feasible around the body, but would not be feasible for sleeve lengths. Circumferences may vary from 54 to 34 inches by changes of gauge – anywhere from 20 to 32 stitches per 4 inches (10 cm).

GAUGE	Circumference	Length	Sleeve Length from center back
20 sts/22 rows = 4" (10 cm)	54	33	35
24 sts/26 rows = 4" (10 cm)	45	27	30
28 sts/30 rows = 4" (10 cm)	39	24	26
32 sts/34 rows = 4" (10 cm)	34	21	23

BODY

Steek: Rounds begin at center of *Center Front Steek*. For hem and border use Color A. For stranded knitting alternate Rows 1 and 2 of *Steeks: Center Front Chart* (page 33). Stitch numbers in pattern do not include steek stitches unless otherwise noted.

Hem: Use needle 1 or 2 sizes smaller than stockinette needle and Color A, *Cast On: Invisible* (page 11) 257 stitches. This includes 10 steek stitches. (*Needles*, page 19, *Yarn Suggestions and Amounts*, page 24)

Row 1: Knit, and increase 1 stitch each side of steek; i.e., knit 5 steek stitches, place marker, *Increase: Right* (page 16), knit to last 5 stitches, *Increase Left* (page 16), place marker, knit 5 steek stitches. The increases at each side of the steek form a mitered corner inside the hem.

Round 2: Join, being certain not to twist, and start to knit in the round. Knit 5 steek stitches, slip marker, *Increase: Right*, knit to the next marker, *Increase: Left*, slip marker, and knit 5 steek stitches.

Rounds 3–11: Knit, increase 1 each side of steek, as established.

Round 12: (You have 12 rows of knitting, including invisibly cast-on row. The center front looks bulky and funny. Just wait. It gets funnier looking.) **Purl all hem stitches** (not steek), increasing 1 each side of steek as established. 281 stitches

Round 13: Body. Change to **stockinette** needle. Knit, increasing as established.

Round 14: Knit steek stitches, slip marker, increase 1, purl 1, knit to last stitch before steek marker, purl 1, increase 1, slip marker, knit steek stitches. (The 2 purl stitches are turning stitches for the facing of the cardigan. These stitches are purled every round—see **Chart A**, page 111.)

Rounds 15–21: Knit around. Increase and purl as established. Increases are complete with Round 21. 299 stitches which includes 10 steek stitches.

Rounds 22–23: Knit around without increases, but maintain purl stitches at the front.

Round 24: (There are 11 knit rounds after the purled round.) Fold hem on purl round and knit the body stitches to the invisibly cast-on stitches where possible. **Use needle one size larger** than stockinette needle for this joining round. (*Knitting in Mitered Hems*, page 19)

Round 25: Begin stranded knitting. Use **stranded knitting needle** and join Color B. Knit 5 steek stitches, slip marker. Follow **Chart A** and work Point A to B 1 time, Point B to C 5 times, Point D to A (reading left to right), slip marker, knit 5 steek stitches.

Round 26: Make Buttonholes. Work around as established in Round 25, but work buttonholes of your choice on facing and solid border where indicated. I recommend the Roberta Center Buttonholes. (*Buttonholes*, page 8) If the cardigan is for a woman, work the buttonholes at start of round, for a man work the buttonholes at end of round. (Buttonholes on photographed model are not positioned as in instructions. The model buttonholes are placed 3–1/2 inches apart and are not aligned with the design. To improve appearance, buttonholes are aligned with the design in instructions. Additional buttonholes could be placed midpoint of each design.)

Rounds 27–61: Follow **Chart A** and work as established.

Rounds 62–63: Use **stockinette needle** and Color A. It is not necessary to break Color B.

Round 64: Knit around working buttonholes as established.

Round 65: Work around as established, but decrease 1 anywhere in back. 58 stitches between Point A and B, 172 stitches between Point B and B, and 58 stitches between Point B and A, plus 10 steek stitches equal 298 total stitches.

Round 66: Follow **Charts A and B**. With **stranded knitting needle** work steek, slip marker, follow **Chart A, Row 25** Point A to B. Follow **Chart B, Row 1** Point A to B 12 times, Point A to C 1 time. Follow **Chart A, Row 25** Point B to A, slip marker, knit steek.

Round 67: Knit steek, slip marker, work **Chart A, Row 26** from Point A to B but do **not** work buttonholes. Follow **Chart B, Row 2** and repeat as established in Round 66. Follow **Chart A** and work from Point B to A, slip marker, knit steek.

Rounds 68–99: Work in pattern as established through **Row 58, Chart A**, and repeat **Rows 1–10, Chart B** as required.

Rounds 100–120: Work **Rows 25–45, Chart A** as established (work buttonholes in Row 26), and work **Chart B** as established.

Round 121: Arm Openings. Work steek, slip marker, knit **Row 46, Chart A** Point A to B. Follow **Chart B**, (you should be on Row 6) and knit 21 stitches in pattern. *Knit 1 Color A, place marker, place next 2 stitches on hold. With Color A around thumb and Color B around index finger, *Cast On: Long Tail* (page 11) a 10 stitch steek, place marker, knit 1 Color A.* Knit 122 stitches in pattern (25 stitches prior to Point B, Chart A). Repeat between asterisks. Knit 21 stitches in pattern. Knit **Chart A** Point B to A, slip marker, work steek.

Round 122: Work steek, slip marker, continue on **Chart A** and work Point A to B. *Follow **Chart B** and work in established pattern to 1 stitch prior to armhole steek, knit 1 Color A, slip marker, follow *Steeks: Armhole Chart* (page 33) and work steek, slip marker, knit 1 Color A.* Repeat between asterisks. Work **Chart**

Snowflake Cardigan

B as established and then follow **Chart A** and knit Point B to A, slip marker, work steek.

Rounds 123–164: Work as established in Round 122. Knit **Chart A** through **Row 58**, then repeat **Rows 25 through 55** (work buttonholes in Row 26). Repeat **Chart B** rows as required.

Rounds 165–169: Decrease at arm edges. *Work as established to 3 stitches before armhole steek, knit 1 Color A, *Decrease: Right*, slip marker, work steek, slip marker, *Decrease: Left*, knit 1 Color A.* Repeat between asterisks. Finish round as established. Work **Chart A** through **Row 60, but** place buttonholes in **Row 60**.

Round 170: Work around in pattern **Chart A, Row 61** and **Chart B** without decreases. Break Color B.

Round 171: With Color A, work around. Break yarn.

Round 172: Place steek and next 37 stitches on hold (to center of border design). *With Color A, knit 2 together to armhole steek, bind off steek.* Repeat between asterisks. Knit 2 together the next 38 stitches—37 stitches plus 5 steek stitches remain. Place all stitches on hold.

Steeks: *Slip Stitch Crochet* (page 21) **armhole** steeks.

SLEEVES

Use needle 1 or 2 sizes smaller than stockinette needle and Color A, invisibly cast on 45 stitches. Use Color A through Round 24.

Row 1: Prepare to knit in the round by knitting 22 stitches with needle used to cast on and 23 stitches with a second circular needle of the same size. (*Knitting Small Circumferences With Two Circular Needles*, page 18)

Round 2: Join, being certain not to twist, and knit in the round.

Rounds 3–11: Knit.

Round 12: Purl.

Rounds 13–23: Change to stockinette needles and knit around.

Round 24: Join Hem. Use **one size larger needles** than stockinette needles. Knit the cast-on stitches together with the working stitches to form a hem. (*Hems: Knit*, page 14)

Rounds 25–27: Begin Stranded Knitting. Use **stranded knitting needles** and join Color B. Follow **Chart C** and knit 43 top of sleeve stitches and 2 underarm stitches (triangle point on chart).

Lower Sleeve Underarm

Round 28: Work **Chart C, Row 28** across 43 top of sleeve stitches, *Increase: Right* 1, knit 2 underarm stitches, *Increase: Left* 1.(To maintain a more even number of stitches on each needle as you increase, *Increase: Right* 1, knit 1 with second needle. With first needle knit 1, *Increase: Left* 1. Your stitches will be divided at the top and underarm of the sleeve.)

Rounds 29–87: Follow **Chart C** and increase every 3 rounds as established in Round 28.

Rounds 88–133: Continue in pattern as established, but increases now occur every 2 rounds.

Round 134: Knit 43 top of sleeve pattern stitches. With **Color A** *Increase: Right* 1 **and** knit underarm stitches, *Increase: Left* 1.

Attach Sleeves: You may cut armhole steek before or after half-grafting sleeves to the body. (My preferred method is cutting after half-grafting sleeves to body.)

Place 43 top of sleeve pattern stitches on hold. Use Color A and leave about a 12 inch tail. Seven rows from top of body (last row before decreases start), *Kitchener Stitch: Half Graft* (page 18) 44 sleeve stitches to 44 adjoining body stitches along armhole steek (44 rows), *Kitchener: Graft* (page 17) the 2 center underarm stitches to the 2 stitches on hold at body underarm, half graft 44 sleeve stitches to 44 adjoining body stitches. With circular needle *Knit Up* (page 18) 7 stitches along decreases at edge of steek. Break yarn. Place front or back body stitches on hold (dependent on sleeve) onto needle with the 7 stitches just knit up. With second circular needle and tail left on opposite side, knit up 7 stitches in same manner and place front or back stitches on needle with the second 7 stitches.

Snowflake Cardigan

The two needles holding the knit up and front and back stitches may be smaller size needles.

Transfer 43 top of sleeve stitches on hold onto stranded knitting needle. The top of the sleeve now becomes a saddle and joins front and back of cardigan together.

I-Cord Edged Saddle Shoulder

Row 135: Begin I-Cord Edged Saddle Shoulder. Unknit the first 3 stitches on left needle holding top of sleeve stitches. (To unknit, place tip of right needle into stitch in row below and remove working yarn from stitch.) Place the 3 stitches back onto left needle in proper working position. Bring Color B over Color A (trapping Color B) and knit 1 stitch with Color A (working yarn for first stitch will be coming from third stitch on left needle, *Increase* 1, knit 1. With Color A in front of left needle, place knit up stitch from first decrease row onto left needle (first stitch on needle holding the front or back), *Decrease: Right*. Work **Chart C, Row 135** (you are now at the fifth stitch) to last 3 stitches. With Color A in back, slip 1 as if to knit, place stitch from back body onto right needle. Place Color B over Color A, insert tip of left needle into front of the 2 slipped stitches on right needle, and knit the 2 stitches together through back loops with Color A *(Decrease: Left)*, knit 1, increase 1, knit 1. Turn.

Row 136 and all even numbered rows through 184: Work **Chart C** from left to right (actually the same in either direction) by either knitting onto your left needle or purling; i.e. slip 3 stitches, work across in pattern, slip 3 stitches.

Row 137 and odd numbered rows through Row 185: Place Color B over Color A, knit 3 with Color A. With Color A in front of left needle, place stitch from body onto left needle, *Decrease: Right*. Knit across in pattern to last 4 stitches. Slip 1 as if to knit, place stitch from body onto right needle, place Color B over Color A, insert tip of left needle into front of 2 stitches on right needle, and knit the 2 together through the back loops with Color A *(Decrease: Left)*, knit 3. Turn.

Row 186: Start front neck shaping. Work 24 stitches in pattern. Place 21 remaining stitches on hold.

Rows 187–205: Odd rows. Bring Color B over Color A for first stitch, work across in pattern to last 4 stitches, attach to back as established.

Rows 188–204: Even rows. Slip 3, knit back or purl in pattern across.

Place center back saddle stitches on hold.

Work second sleeve.

With Color A, *Kitchener Stitch: Graft* the center back stitches together.

Knit Up Neck Border: With stockinette needle(s) and Color A, knit 5 center front steek stitches, place marker, work 37 front neck stitches on hold (purl the established turning stitch). *Decrease: Right* first 2 I-cord stitches, place a pin on stitch just knit to mark it as center of future double decreases. Knit remaining 19 stitches on hold at side of neck. Between first and second stitch at selvage, *Knit Up* (page 18) 35 stitches evenly spaced across back of neck. Knit 19 stitches on hold at side of neck, *Decrease: Left* the 2 I-cord stitches and place a pin on stitch. Work 37 stitches to steek (purl the established turning stitch), place marker, and knit 5 steek stitches. 159 stitches.

Rounds 5–11: Knit steek, slip marker, *Decrease: Left*, *knit to 1 stitch before stitch marked with pin, *Decrease: Double*. Repeat between asterisks. Work to 2 stitches before steek marker, right decrease, slip marker, knit steek. *(Decreases, page 14)*

Round 12: Knit steek, slip marker, *Decrease: Left*, **purl** to 1 stitch before marked stitch, *Decrease: Double*. Repeat between asterisks. Purl to 2 stitches before steek marker, *Decrease: Right*, slip marker, knit steek.

Rounds 13–23: Reverse shaping for neck facing. (Now **increase** 1 each side of marked stitch at front neck corners.) Knit steek, slip marker, *Decrease: Left*, *knit to marked stitch, *Increase: Right* 1, knit marked stitch, *Increase: Left* 1*. Repeat between asterisks. Work to 2 stitches before steek marker, *Decrease: Right*, slip marker, knit steek. (*Increases*, page 16)

Finishing: Slip stitch crochet center front steek. Cut. If Roberta Center buttonholes were worked, finish buttonholes. Fold to inside and tack down all facings. If Roberta Center buttonholes were not used, tack border and facing together around each buttonhole. With Color A, apply 2 stitch I-cord around entire outer edge. Sew on buttons. Block.

Wear or give with pleasure.

SNOWFLAKE SOCKS—KNEE HIGH OR SHORT

These socks have a Snowflake pattern that continues from the ribbing down to tip of toe so they are an excellent choice to wear with sandals. The center back panel also continues to tip of toe so gives an attractive appearance when worn with sandals or clogs, or when sitting with your shoes off and feet up.

These socks are knit from top to toe using my method for gusset and heel. Toe stitches are grafted together. (*General Sock Information*, page 28)

Gauge:

24/22, 26/28, 28/30, 30/32 or 32/34 stitches/rows = 4" (10cm) in stranded knitting. (Sizes vary by gauge, not number of stitches.)

Knee High Calf Circumference: 13", 12", 11", 10.5", 10"

Ankle Circumference: 9", 8.5", 8", 7.5", 7"

Materials (All Lengths):
Color A—Navy Guernsey Wool, One – 3.5 oz. skein
Color B—Red Guernsey Wool, One – 3.5 oz. skein
Note: If you use gauge for 2 larger sized knee highs, you may wish to order an extra skein of each color. Also, see **Cuff Note** below.

KNEE HIGH

(**Short Sock**, see end of pattern.) With needle 1 to 2 sizes smaller than stranded knitting needle and Color A, *Cast On: Long Tail* (page 11) 80 stitches. With needle used to cast on, work 40 stitches in knit 2, purl 2 ribbing. With second needle of same size knit 40 remaining stitches in knit 2, purl 2 ribbing. (*Cast-On: Purl*, page 13, *Knitting Small Circumferences With Two Circular Needles*, page 18.)

Join, being certain not to twist, and work around in established ribbing to desired ribbing length (approximately 2"). The model has an eight inch cuff so sock comes up over knees when worn with knickers. (**Cuff**

Note: An additional skein of Color A is required for long cuff.)

Pattern Round 1: Begin Stranded Knitting. Join Color B and use stranded knitting needles. Follow **Sock Chart A, Row 1** (page 113). With **Needle #1**, from Point A knit 4, place marker, knit to Point B. With **Needle #2** knit from Point C to last 3 stitches, place marker, knit to Point D. (Markers designate center back panel, but are placed one stitch in from edge of panel to accommodate later decreases.) Stitch A/D is center back, and Stitch B/C is center front.

Rounds 2–24: Knit around as established in Pattern Round 1.

Round 25: Begin Decreases. With Needle #1, from Point A knit 4, slip marker, *Decrease: Left*, knit to Point B. With Needle #2, knit from Point C to 2 stitches before marker, *Decrease: Right*, slip marker, knit to Point D. (*Decreases*, page 14.)

Rounds 26–58: Work pattern and decrease every third round as established in Round 25. 56 stitches.

Rounds 59–84: Knit around in pattern.

Round 85, Sock Chart B: Begin gusset and rearrange stitches on needles. With Needle #1, from Point A (Start of Round) knit 4 to marker, (**Short Socks**, knit 5 to marker) remove marker, knit to Point B. (You are at Point E indicated at top of **Sock Chart A**.) **Using Needle #2** and Color B, make an *Increase: Loop—Right Slanted* (page 16), place marker. Tighten increase up to last stitch knit with Needle #1. Knit from Point C to D, place marker. With Color B make an *Increase: Loop—Left Slanted* (page 16). **With Needle #1**, knit from Point E to marker, remove marker, knit 3 to Point A, (**Short Socks**, knit 4) place marker for start of round. 27 stitches Needle #1, 31 stitches Needle #2. **Rounds continue to start** at center of back panel. (Point A, center of Needle #1)

Rounds 86–92: Work as established in Round 85 with a Color B increase at each end of Needle #2.

Round 93: Short Row Heel Turns. Needle #1, work short rows **in established pattern**. Make first turns one stitch in from each edge. End turns when you reach center back panel as seen on chart. (*Rounds 58–59 Short Row Heel Turn*, page 29) Work to Point B and work short row yarn overs together with proper adjoining stitches. Work Needle #2 as established. As

Snowflake Socks

you work Needle #1 from Point E to A, work short row yarn overs together with proper adjoining stitches.

Round 94: Knit around as established.

Round 95: Rearrange stitches. Work as established, **but** place Color A stitch at each end of Needle #1 onto each end of Needle #2. 25 stitches Needle #1, 47 stitches Needle #2.

Round 96: Begin Gusset Decreases. Knit **Needle #1** as established. **Needle #2**, *Decrease: Left*, knit to last 2 stitches, *Decrease: Right*.

Rounds 97–117: Knit Needle #1 as established. Needle #2, decrease every third round as established in Round 96.

Round 118: Rearrange stitches. Work as established, **but** place Color A stitch at each end of Needle #2 onto each end Needle #1. If you have not previously done so, remove markers on Needle #2. 27 stitches Needle #1, 29 stitches Needle #2.

Rounds 119–129: Knit around in pattern.

Round 130: Start Toe Decreases. Knit **Needle #1** as established. **Needle #2**, *Decrease: Left*, knit across to last 2 stitches, *Decrease: Right*.

Round 131: (Remember start of round is at Point A.) **Needle #1**, knit to last 2 stitches, *Decrease: Right*. **Needle #2**, *Decrease: Left*, knit to last 2 stitches, *Decrease: Right*. **Needle #1**, *Decrease: Left*, knit to end of round.

Rounds 132–140: Decrease every round as established in Round 131. 7 stitches remain on each needle. Break Color B.

   With Color A *Kitchener Stitch: Graft* (page 17) top of foot stitches to sole stitches. Weave in ends.

SHORT SOCK

   With needle 1 to 2 sizes smaller than stranded knitting needle and Color A, *Cast On: Long Tail* (page 11) 56 stitches. (*Cast On: Purl,* page 13)

Row 1: With needle used to cast on, work 28 stitches in knit 2, purl 2 ribbing. With second needle of same size knit 28 remaining stitches in knit 2, purl 2 ribbing. (*Knitting Small Circumferences With Two Circular Needles,* page 18.)

Round 2: Join, being certain not to twist and work around in established ribbing.

Rounds 3–5: Knit around in ribbing.

Rounds 6–8: Join Color B, knit 2 Color A, purl 2 Color B around. (I wanted Color A "blip" to show in Color B purl stitches. If you choose not to have "blip", knit 2 Color A, knit 2 Color B in Round 6.)

Rounds 9–13: With Color A, knit 2, purl 2 around. (If "blip" not desired, knit all stitches in Round 9.)

Round 14: Begin Stranded Knit Pattern. Follow **Chart A, Row 57, Needle #1**. Start at Point A and knit 5 stitches, place marker, skip next stitch on chart, knit to Point B. With **Needle #2** start at Point C and knit to last 4 stitches, skip next stitch on chart, place marker, knit to Point D. 28 stitches Needles #1 and #2.

Follow **Knee High Instructions** from **Round 58** (no decrease needed) to end of pattern.

Short Socks
(see cover for knee high photo)

Chart B

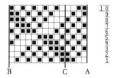

Chart A

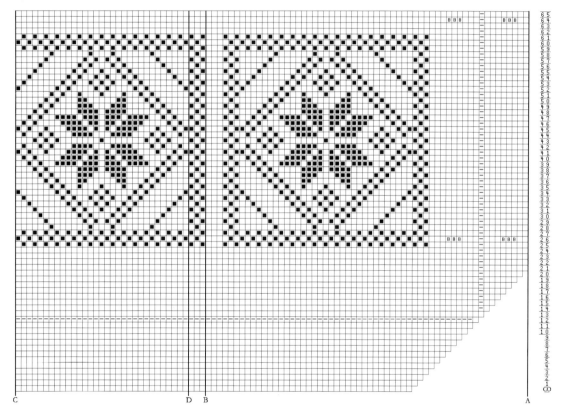

Chart C

Chart B

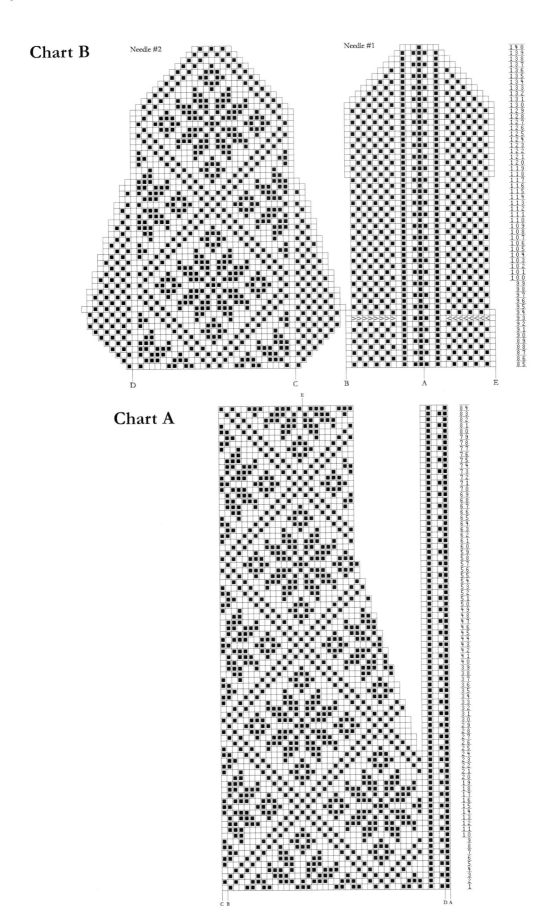

Chart A

The Star

This design is from a twill tablecloth found in Jane A. Evans book, *A Joy Forever, Latvian Weaving.* The tablecloth was woven in Latvia and is at the Royal Ontario Museum in Toronto. I call this jacket "The Star" as it reminds me of the 4-pointed star used on maps to indicate directions. The large motif is repeated on the front and back of the jacket. The semi set-in sleeves are knit in one color from the armhole down. This jacket has the appearance of a vest and could be knit as such by eliminating the sleeves. The hem and front facing are knit at the same time as the jacket body.

Sizes: Divide 369 (the total number of body stitches) by the circumference of your choice and your answer will be the gauge required to achieve that circumference. Select yarn and needle sizes to attain your gauge. (*Yarn Suggestions and Amounts*, page 24.) Divide your row gauge into 249 and you will know the length of your jacket. It will take the same amount of time to knit this jacket whether you are using a Size 0 or a Size 6 needle to attain your gauge as the same number of stitches have to be knit no matter what the needle size.

Model Measurements and Gauges:
42" circumference, 29" long, 21" sleeve length
35/34 rows = 4" (10 cm) in stranded knitting
24 stitches/34 rows = 4" (10 cm) in double strand stockinette stitch

Model Materials:
Color A—#1027 Medium Gray Spun Lace Weight Icelandic Wool, Five – 1.75 oz. balls
Color B—#151 Charcoal Spun Lace Weight Icelandic Wool, Eight – 1.75 oz. balls
7 Buttons

Steek: Rounds begin at center of **Center Front Steek.** For hem use Color B. For stranded knitting alternate Rows 1 and 2 of *Steeks: Center Front Chart* (page 33). Stitch numbers in pattern do not include steek stitches unless otherwise noted.

Hem Note: Some garments in the book have the invisibly cast on hem stitches knit together with the body stitches to eliminate the need to later tack down the hem. I chose not to knit the hem to the body of this jacket, because the fuzzy Icelandic charcoal yarn used makes it difficult to knit the invisibly cast-on stitches together with the body stitches. But, if you choose to knit the hem together with the body stitches,

use *Cast On: Invisible* and knit the hem to the body in Round 11 of Chart A.

BODY

Hem: Use needle 2–3 sizes smaller than stranded knitting needle and Color B, *Cast On: Purl* (page 13) 359 stitches. This figure includes 10 steek stitches.

Hem Row 1: Knit and increase 1 stitch each side of the steek. (i.e. Knit 5 steek stitches, place marker, *Increase: Right*, knit to the last 5 stitches, *Increase: Left*, place marker, knit 5 steek stitches.) The increases at each side of the steek form a mitered corner inside the jacket. (*Increases*, pages 16–17)

Hem Round 2: Join, being certain not to twist, and start to knit in the round. Knit 5 steek stitches, slip marker, *Increase: Right*, knit to the next marker, *Increase: Left*, slip marker, and knit 5 steek stitches.

Hem Rounds 3–10: Knit, increase 1 stitch each side of steek as established. 369 body stitches. The miter is bunched up and funny looking before being cut. Believe me! This unbunches when the steek is cut.

Hem Round 11: Purl all stitches (except steek) and increase each side of steek as established.

Chart A, Round 1: Begin stranded knitting. Use stranded knitting needle and join Color A. Knit the 5 steek stitches, slip marker, with Color B increase 1, purl 1, place marker. *Knit Round 1 of **Chart A** (page 118) from Point A to B (side), Point C to D* (center back). Repeat between asterisks but end knit to Point A (center front), place marker, with Color B purl 1, increase 1, slip marker and knit 5 steek stitches. If you wish, place markers at the sides and center back.

Rounds 2–10: Work as established in Round 1; i.e. with Color B increase 1 on each side of steek, knit the facing but purl the stitch that abuts the stranded knitting on each side of the front. The purled stitches are the turning stitches for the front edge and will be purled the entire length. There is a long carry of Color A across the back of the facing, but the facing is turned back and tacked down so it is not necessary to trap the long carries. Follow **Chart A** for stranded knitting.

Rounds 11–162: Miter increases end with Round 10. (Total 401 stitches—369 body stitches, 11 facing stitches on each side of 10 stitch steek) Work as established,

The Star

but without the increases. Change to **Chart B** when required.

Round 163: Arm Openings – Semi Set-In Sleeve as in Model. To accommodate the design, the sleeve is not set in to shoulder edge. (See below for **Optional Drop Shoulder**.) Work steek and facing as established, transfer marker, *start at Point A, knit 88 stitches in pattern and place next 9 stitches on hold on a piece of yarn, place marker. (The stitches on hold will form a *Kangaroo Pouch*, page 17.) With Color A around thumb and Color B around index finger *Cast On: Long Tail* (page 11) a 10 stitch steek, place marker, and knit to Point D.* Repeat between asterisks except end at Point A, transfer marker, work facing and steek.

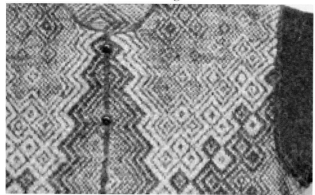

Center Front and Semi Set-in Sleeve

Optional Drop Shoulder: If you prefer a drop shoulder follow **Chart A Round 87**, and knit to Point C, place next stitch on hold. Cast on steeks as described in Round 163. For the following rounds follow **Chart A** in reverse; i.e. Rounds 86, 85 etc., knit in pattern as established, and alternate Rows 1 and 2 of *Steeks: Armhole Chart*, (page 33.)

Rounds 164–183: Knit as established and alternate Rows 1 and 2 of *Steeks: Armhole Chart*. (page 33). (If making a vest, alternate Rows 1 and 2 of *Steeks: Center Front Chart*, page 33.) Decrease at arm openings on **uneven** numbered rounds 10 times; i.e., knit steek and facing, transfer marker, *knit in pattern to 2 stitches prior to arm opening steek, *Decrease: Left*, transfer marker, work steek, transfer marker, *Decrease: Right*.* Repeat between asterisks. Knit to Point A in pattern, transfer marker, work facing and steek. You will have 78 stitches between Point A and armhole steeks and 155 stitches on back between armhole steeks.

Rounds 184–227: (Armhole decreases end on Round 183.) Knit center front steek, transfer marker, work facing, transfer marker, *knit from Point A to E, transfer marker, work armhole steek, transfer marker, knit from Point E to Point D*. Repeat between asterisks but end knit to Point A, transfer marker, work facing, and knit center front steek.

Round 228: Knit around as established. After you reach Point A at center front, bind off facing with Color B and bind off steek with alternate colors.

Round 229: Neck Shaping. With alternate colors bind off steek and with Color B bind off facing. Break yarns. Place 15 stitches on hold on a piece of yarn. With Color A around thumb and Color B around index finger, *Cast On: Long Tail*, 5 steek stitches, place marker. (You have a new center front steek, but you will no longer work a facing.) Start to knit **Chart B** as indicated by dark outline, knit to Point E, transfer marker, work armhole steek, transfer marker, knit from Point E to D. Knit from Point A to E, transfer marker, work armhole steek, transfer marker, knit to 15 stitches of center front steek (indicated on chart by dark outline). Place next 15 stitches on hold on a piece of yarn, place marker. With Color A around thumb and Color B around index finger *Cast On: Long Tail*, 5 steek stitches.

Rounds 230–248: Knit in pattern and decrease 1 stitch on each side of center front steek as indicated by dark outline; i.e. knit steek, transfer marker, *Decrease: Right*, knit to Point E, transfer marker, work armhole steek, transfer marker. Knit from Point E to D and Point A to E, transfer marker, knit armhole steek, transfer marker. Knit from Point E to 2 stitches prior to center front steek, *Decrease: Left*, transfer marker, knit steek.

Round 249: With alternate colors bind off 5 steek stitches, knit in pattern to armhole steek, with alternate colors bind off armhole steek, break yarns. **Slip** Back stitches to same size or smaller needle. (For the pattern to match at shoulders, the back is not knit this round.) With alternate colors bind off second armhole steek, knit in pattern to center front steek, with alternate colors bind off 5 steek stitches.

Steeks: *Slip Stitch Crochet* (page 21) all steeks. Cut center front steek.

Join Shoulders: *Have outsides facing each other and use needle one size larger than stranded knitting needle. Begin at armhole edge and *Bind Off: Three Needle* (page 7) in pattern following Row 249 of **Chart B**.

The Star

Break yarns.* Turn and repeat between asterisks for opposite shoulder. Place center back stitches on hold. Weave in ends.

Sleeve Variations: Decision and possible swatch time. A single strand of the Icelandic lace weight yarn did not have the proper drape to be used in combination with the stranded knit body of this jacket. Therefore, the sleeves were knit with 2 strands and not at the same gauge as the body. If you use a heavier yarn, the sleeves may be knit with a single strand at the same gauge as the stranded knit. (See *Highland Jacket*, page 40.) If knitting with a medium-weight yarn, you may wish to use a single strand, but knit at a smaller gauge to give it more the feel of the stranded knit gauge. Inspect your hem. If you like the feel of that, use the hem for your gauge. If not, knit a swatch to determine the drape and feel you like and thus obtain your gauge.

Measure the depth of your arm opening. Subtract 1/2 or 1 inch from the depth, and multiply that figure by your sleeve stitch gauge. Multiply your answer by 2 for the number of stitches required for your sleeves. If you have an even number, add 1 for the center under-arm stitch. One inch was subtracted from the depth of sleeve for the model. (See *Design: #10. Decide arm opening*, page 122.) Follow sleeve directions below, but insert your number for the stitches required.

Knit Up Sleeves: (Model) Armhole steeks may be cut before or after sleeves stitches are knitted up. Use appropriate stockinette needle and place 9 underarm stitches on hold onto needle. With double strand of Color B, *Knit Up* (page 18) 100 stitches evenly spaced around arm opening. (*Spacing Decreases/Increases Evenly*, page 21) Total 109 stitches. End; knit 4 underarm stitches, and place marker for start of round (center underarm).

Following Rounds: Decrease every **5th round**; i.e., slip marker, knit 2, *Decrease: Left*, knit to 3 stitches before marker, *Decrease: Right*, knit 1. Continue knitting around and decreasing to desired length. For a bloused sleeve, knit an inch or two beyond wrist (as in model). If you reach desired number of stitches for cuff before you reach your desired length, continue to knit around without decreases.

Cuffs: Decision time again. Use 54 stitches for a tight fit or [72] stitches for a loose fit cuff. To aid your decision, mark off the number of stitches along bottom of

jacket and wrap that portion around your wrist. When you decide the number of stitches to knit your cuff, subtract that number from the total number of stitches you now have on your sleeve. Decrease around evenly the number of stitches in your answer.

Cuff Round 1: Use stranded knitting needles and join Color A. Follow **Cuff Chart** from Point A to B, 3 [4] times.

Cuff Rounds 2–25: Follow **Cuff Chart** as established.

Cuff Round 26: Bind Off. *Cast On: Cable* (page 10) 3 stitches for I-cord. *I-Cord. Bind Off* (page 15) around. *Kitchener Stitch: Half-Graft* (page 18) 3 I-cord stitches over cable cast-on stitches.

Knit second sleeve.

I-Cord trim: With Color B, *Cast On: Invisible* (page 11) 3 stitches and work *I-Cord: Applied* (page 14) around the top of cuffs, around the sleeve and body joins, and around the entire jacket making 7 I-cord buttonholes approximately 3-1/2 inches apart on the appropriate front edge of jacket. *Kitchener Stitch: Graft* (page 17) the 3 I-cord stitches to the 3 invisibly cast-on stitches at the end of each application.

Weave in ends, block, sew on buttons. Proudly wear and expect compliments.

Cuff Chart

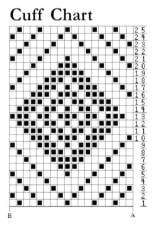

The Star

Chart A

Chart B

Latvian Dreams

DESIGN, E.P.S. AND CHARTS

Design

DESIGN

Shapes were kept simple so the design for book garments feature pattern rather than shape. Elizabeth Zimmermann's Percentage System (E.P.S.) for Drop or Modified Drop-Shoulders (see drawing, page 123) was used as a base for all designs. Therefore, the book does not include schematics.

I am enthralled with the Latvian charts in this chapter, but I doubt if in my lifetime I will be able to knit all of them. Because I would love to see all used, I think every knitter should design something using one or more of the charts. I have been an avid knitter my entire life (at least it seems so), but the enjoyment was enhanced tremendously when I started to design garments. I encourage every knitter to do the same. Since each knitter creates something with their hands, I suspect all knitters have a certain desire to be creative. If you do not feel ready to design a total garment, why not use a different chart for *Don's Vest*, *Circles*, the sleeves of *Joyous Jacket*, etc? I think you will find great joy in a garment that is unique.

Step by Step Process of Design

Following are the steps I used to design garments in the book. Remember I let the design be the driving force and used simple shapes. There are many excellent books available on knitwear design if a more shaped garment is desired.

1. Select one or more charts to use in garment. (The most difficult task, as I want to knit all of them.)

2. Usually yarn and colors are selected after choosing a design, but this process may be reversed. Keep in mind that although the charts are black and white, you are not limited to knitting with two colors.

3. Determine pattern repeat. For horizontal pattern repeat, select a stitch at the bottom of a pattern that is a **central point** of a pattern. (This is not always the bottom right stitch on the chart.) Count across horizontally to where that particular stitch is repeated for **stitch** pattern repeat. From the starting stitch, count up vertically to where that stitch is repeated for **row** pattern repeat.

In some designs (usually where there is an obvious diagonal), the full pattern repeat does not show on the chart. To determine repeat, these charts may be extrapolated either on graph paper or by use of a computer program such as Cochenille's *Stitch Painter*.

4. Determine gauge. With relatively small pattern repeats, select yarn and determine a gauge to give the drape wanted for that garment. (See *Swatches*, page 22.) Multiply gauge by desired circumference. (Desired cir-

cumferences are a personal preference and vary widely between garment styles. My garments average 8 inches larger than my actual bust measurement, but may vary from 6 to 14 inches larger.)

Example: 42 inch circumference multiplied by gauge of 6 stitches/inch equals 252 stitches. This indicates the closest number to attain size with an even 10 stitch repeat would be 250 stitches. However, I would choose to go up to 260 stitches because 260 is evenly divisible by four and a pullover pattern repeat started at the side can be easily centered at center front and back.

To attain desired size when using a large pattern, it is not always possible to have full pattern repeats around. In these circumstances, center pattern at center front and back, and have partial patterns at the sides. The partial repeats may mirror image, or be separated by a design side panel that continues down the underarm. A side panel may always be added as a whimsical touch as in *Circles*, page 64.

With large pattern repeats, where there are two repeats for the entire garment as in *What a Difference a Gauge Makes*, *Highland Jacket*, *Bountiful Harvest*, *Cornfields*, and *The Star*, the number of stitches is established by the design. Wanted circumference is divided into the total number of stitches to determine gauge. A workable gauge may not be possible for all sizes and all patterns.

5. If total number of stitches is not evenly divisible by four, or when working with a large pattern which will not be a complete pattern repeat at sides, center pattern at center front and back. If a side panel is used, add one stitch to both front and back to balance and mirror image. Divide front and back stitches by two. Look at your pattern. If it has a one stitch center, the number of stitches in front and back must be odd. If it has a two stitch center the number of stitches must be even.

Determine number of stitches to center front and back from the side or the end of panel design. Divide by the number of stitches in your pattern repeat. The answer is number of full pattern repeats to side or panel from center, plus a remainder. Count the remainder from left to right in the pattern repeat. This is where to start pattern repeat either at both sides or after working the side panel designs.

6. Cardigan designing is very similar to pullover designs. After determining the total number of stitches in pattern multiples, add one stitch to total so pattern stitches at center front are mirror images. Pattern repeats are started at center front after either the steek stitches or

border design have been knit. At end of round, before the border or center front steek is knit, knit the first stitch of pattern repeat to mirror opposite side. On designs with I-cord buttonholes, use the same number of stitches for fronts and backs of garments. But where button bands overlap, only one button band is counted in the total number of stitches for body measurement.

7. Figure chart design. I usually chart the entire circumference of approximately the lower quarter of a garment. I chart this large area to have an overall view of the proportions of the design as well as to determine sleeve placement. I work only in black and white on charts with color decisions made with yarn.

8. Decide length. I have a relatively accurate idea what my row gauge will be in relationship to the stitch gauge. One color stockinette stitch is usually 1:1.4; i.e., 5 stitches/inch x 1.4 = 7 rows/inch. Garter stitch is 1:2; i.e., 5 stitches/inch x 2 = 10 rows/inch. Stranded knitting is quite square, i.e. close to same number for stitches and rows. The more the design is on a diagonal, the squarer it seems to get, so the result may be slightly more stitches per inch than rows per inch as in *The Star*, page 114. Knit/purl stitch patterns as in *Bountiful Harvest* are close to garter stitch relationship. As the knitting proceeds, I verify my estimated stitch and row gauges and adjust if needed. **If** you knit a swatch and **if** you knit your garment the same as your swatch, you **may** determine exactly the length of your garment.

9. Start knitting. Many designers design the entire garment before starting to knit, but my knitting starts after the lower body is designed. This is one of the things I find exciting about designing. I get great pleasure watching the pattern unfold as I knit and this helps me decide the design for sleeves, shoulder and neck treatment. Cardigans with knit-in-the round mitered corners were started with the hem, but many of my designs are started with invisible (provisional) cast-on and the bottom treatment is decided later. Because I like to knit the hem to the body, when I do cast on a hem I use the same number of stitches as the body, but use a smaller needle.

10. Decide arm opening. As I approach length for arm openings, I make sleeve decisions. Should this garment be a vest, have a drop shoulder, semi-dropped, or sleeve set in to shoulder ? Vest arm openings begin lower than that for a sleeved garment because a vest arm opening should be lower than the bottom of any sleeve worn under the vest. I deviate from E.P.S. for depth of a drop shoulder sleeve of 45 to 50 percent. I use 50% for more fitted garments, 45% for average fit, **but** use 40% when making a

garment oversized in width. The result is always an arm depth of approximately 10 inches.

When wanted length to underarm is reached, stitch(es) are put on hold on a piece of yarn, and steeks are cast on. For a drop shoulder, one to 3 stitches are put on hold. If a side panel is used that will continue down underarm, panel stitches are put on hold. For a sleeve set in to shoulder width, place 8% of total stitches on hold at underarm and decrease at both sides of each armhole. Decrease every other, third or fourth round to number of stitches for desired shoulder width.

When knitting a drop shoulder garment, my sleeves are usually 1/2 to 1 inch narrower than sleeve depth; i.e, for a 10 inch sleeve depth, my actual sleeve depth will be 9-1/2 to 9 inches, or a circumference of 19 to 18 inches. This eliminates the sleeve sticking out at the shoulder join.

To obtain length of sleeve for a drop shoulder, either measure a garment with the desired sleeve length or the recipient from center back at neck to wrist, with arm held out at shoulder height and the elbow bent at a 45 degree angle. Measure project garment from center back to armhole opening, and subtract that from total measurement for sleeve length. Or, for a sleeve set in to the shoulder, measure sleeve length from shoulder to wrist with elbow bent at a 45 degree angle.

11. Shoulder and Neck Opening. I decide on shoulder treatment at the time I design sleeves. Again I may deviate from E.P.S. system if the design dictates and have the neck circumference larger than 40%. I chart the shoulder and neck area and plot neckline decreases usually as the pattern dictates.

DROP OR MODIFIED DROP SHOULDER SWEATER USING E.P.S.

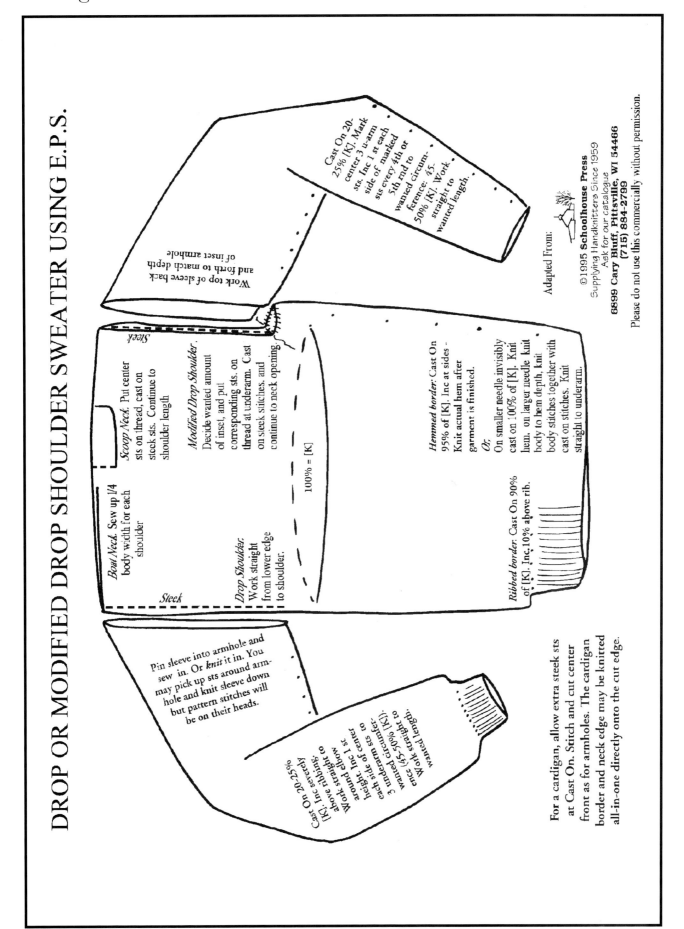

Cast On 20-25% [K]. Mark center 3 u-arm sts. Inc 1 st each side of marked sts every 4th or 5th rnd to wanted circumference: 45-50% [K]. Work straight to wanted length.

Work top of sleeve back and forth to match depth of inset armhole.

Steek

Scoop Neck. Put center sts on thread, cast on steek sts. Continue to shoulder length

Modified Drop Shoulder. Decide wanted amount of inset, and put corresponding sts. on thread at underarm. Cast on steek stitches, and continue to neck opening.

Boat Neck. Sew up 1/4 body width for each shoulder

Drop Shoulder. Work straight from lower edge to shoulder.

Steek

100% = [K]

Hemmed border: Cast On 95% of [K]. Inc at sides - Knit actual hem after garment is finished.

Or:
On smaller needle invisibly cast on 100% of [K]. Knit hem, on larger needle knit body to hem depth, knit body stitches together with cast on stitches. Knit straight to underarm.

Ribbed border: Cast On 90% of [K]. Inc 10% above rib.

Pin sleeve into armhole and sew in. Or *knit* it in. You may pick up sts around armhole and knit sleeve down but pattern stitches will be on their heads.

Cast On 20-25% [K]. Inc severely above ribbing Work straight to elbow around. Inc 1 st height or center to each side of underarm 3 u-arm circumference (45-50% [K]). wanted straight to circumference Work straight to wanted length.

For a cardigan, allow extra steek sts at Cast On. Stitch and cut center front as for armholes. The cardigan border and neck edge may be knitted all-in-one directly onto the cut edge.

Adapted From:

©1995 **Schoolhouse Press**
Supplying Handknitters Since 1959
Ask for our catalogue
**6899 Cary Bluff, Pittsville, WI 54466
(715) 884-2799**

Charts

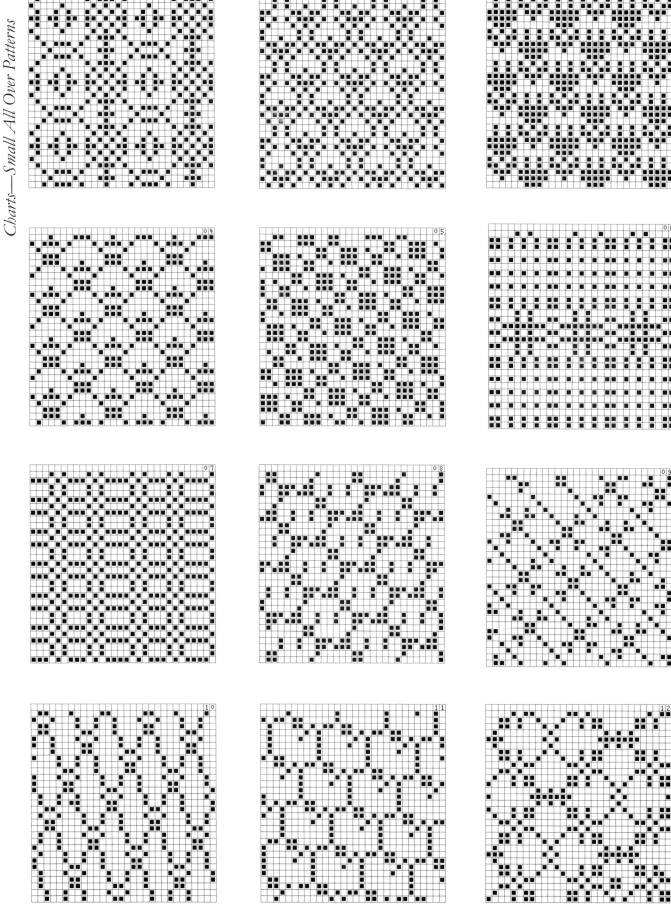

Chart 13

Chart 14

Chart 15

Chart 16

Chart 17

Chart 18

Chart 19

Chart 20

Chart 21

Chart 22

Chart 23

Chart 24

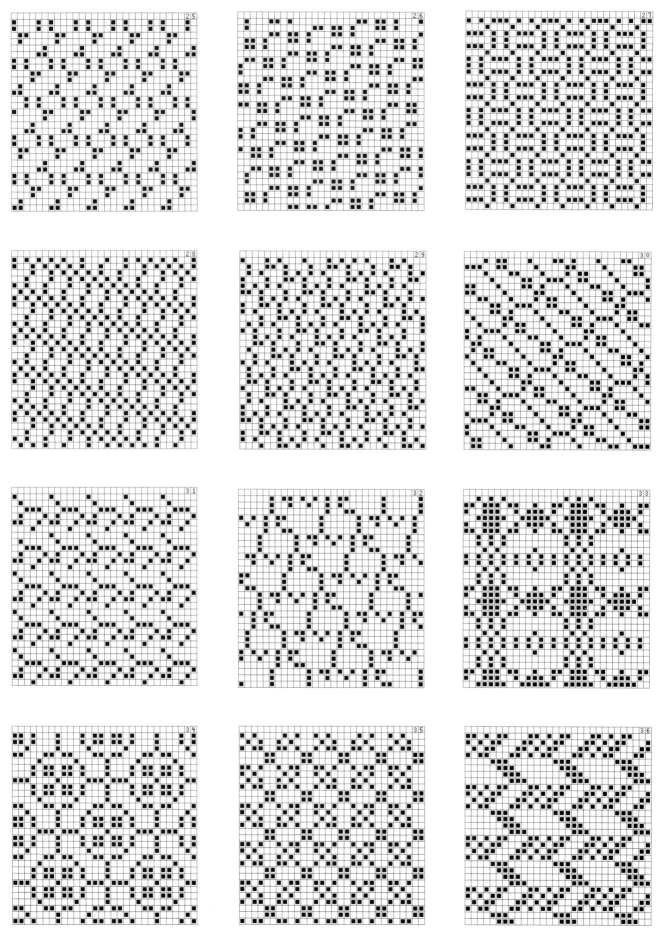

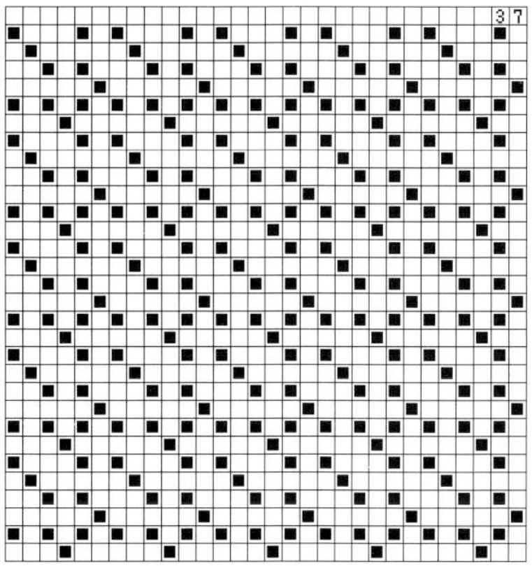
37

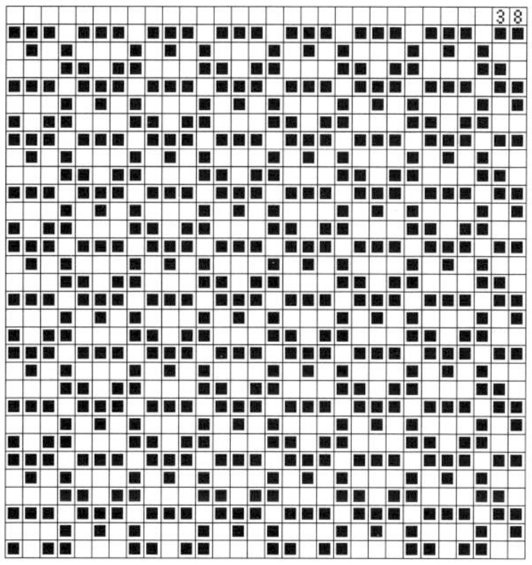
38

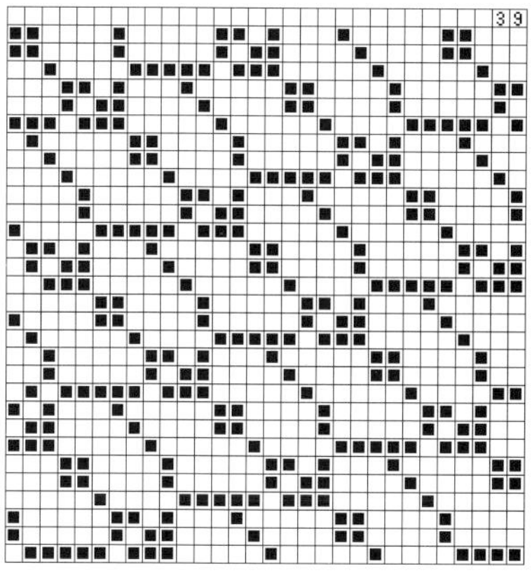
39

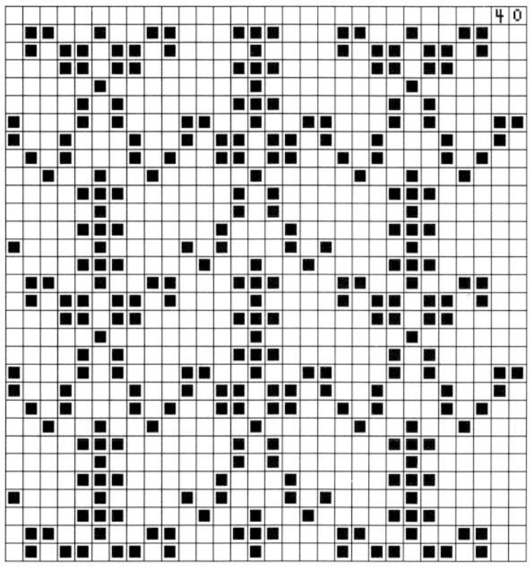
40

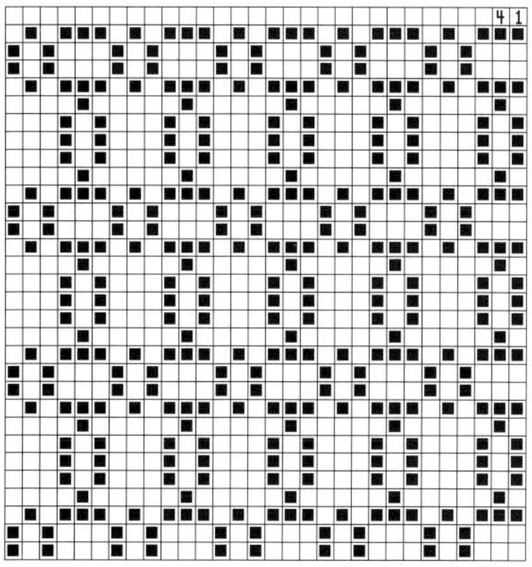
41

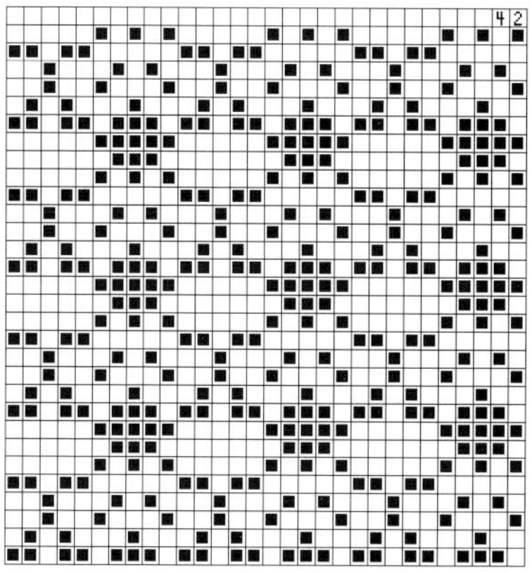
42

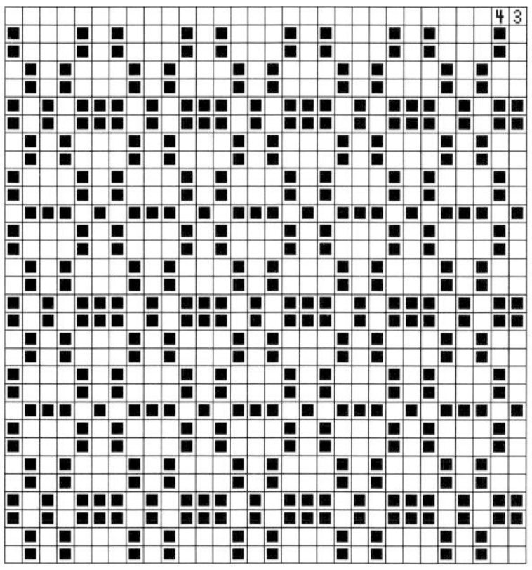
43

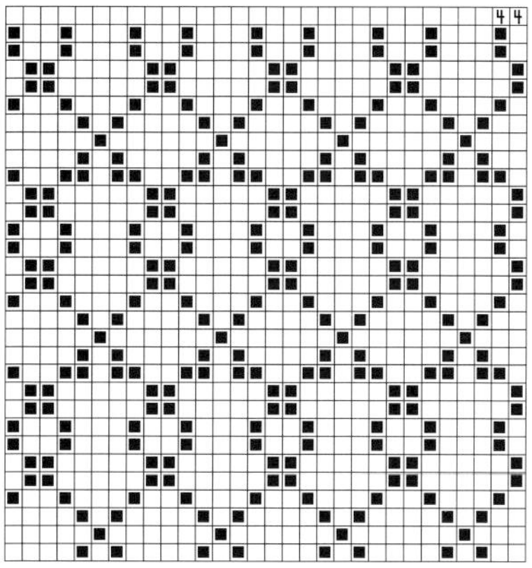
44

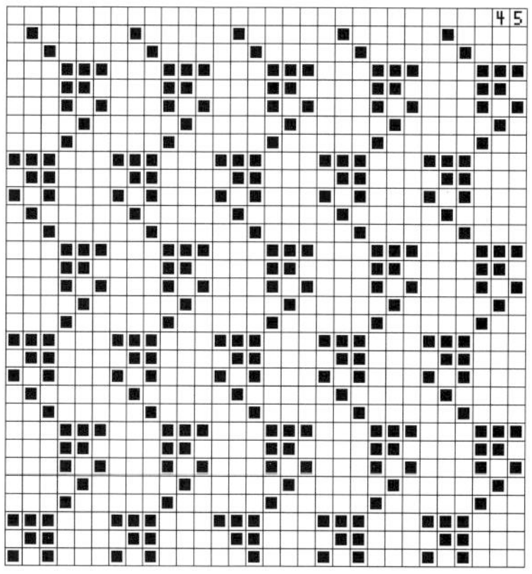
45

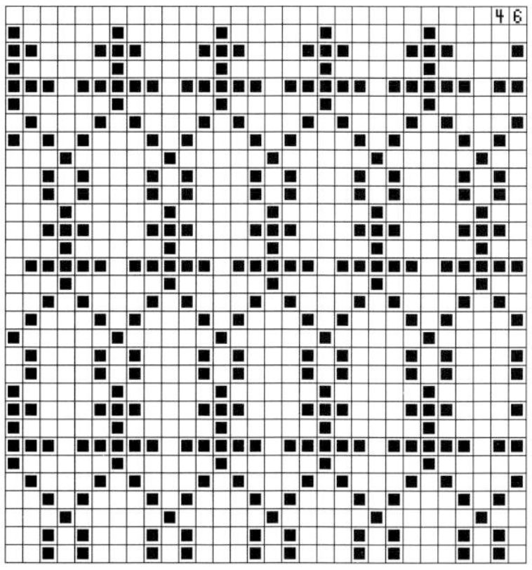
46

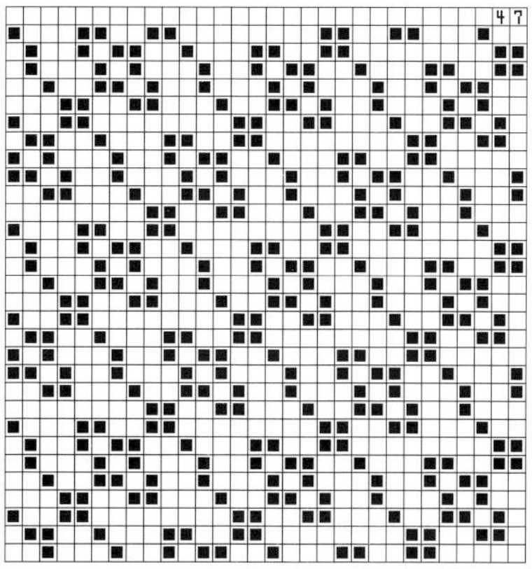
47

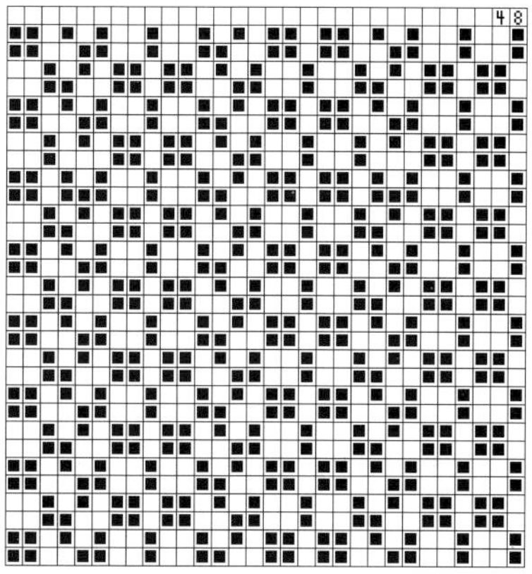
48

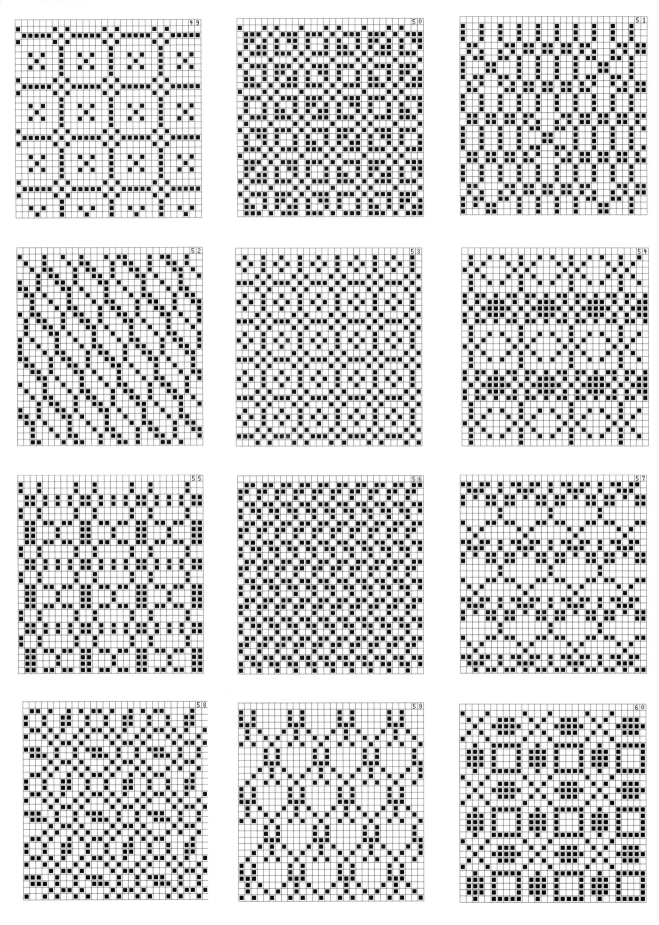

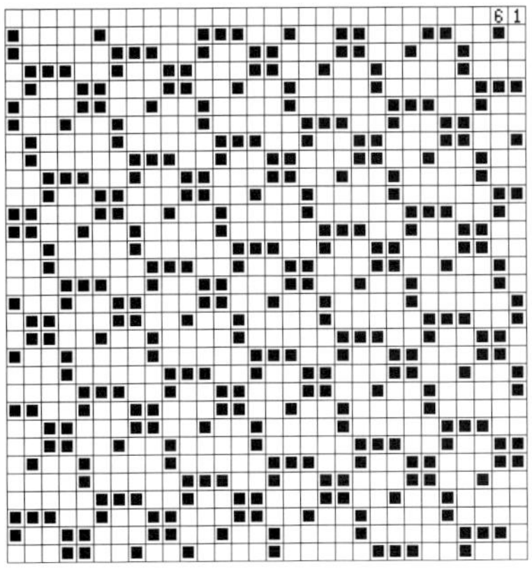
61

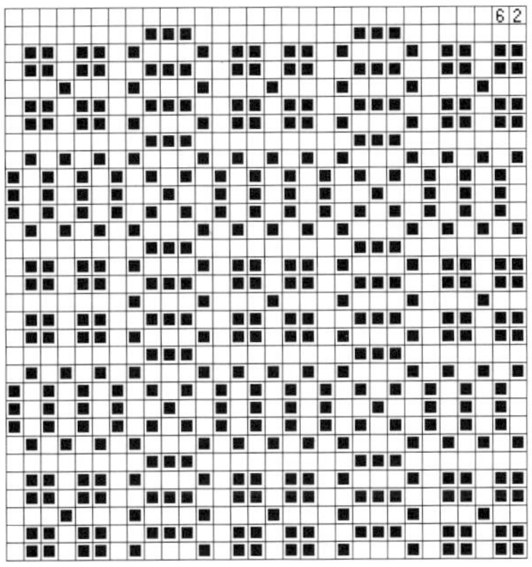
62

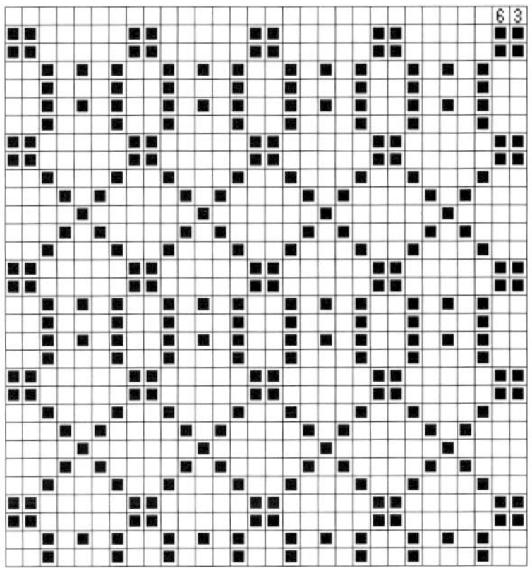
63

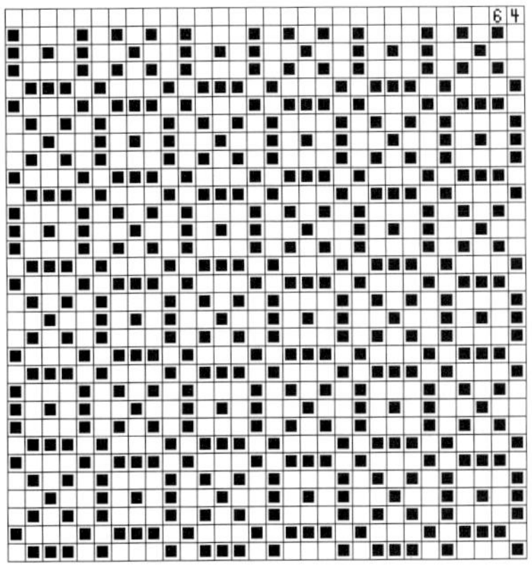
64

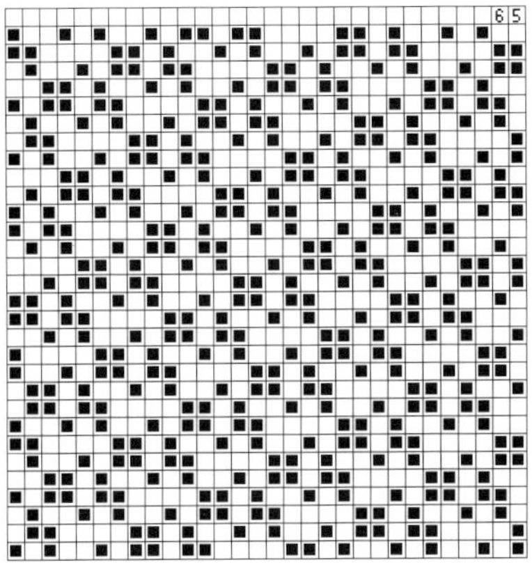
65

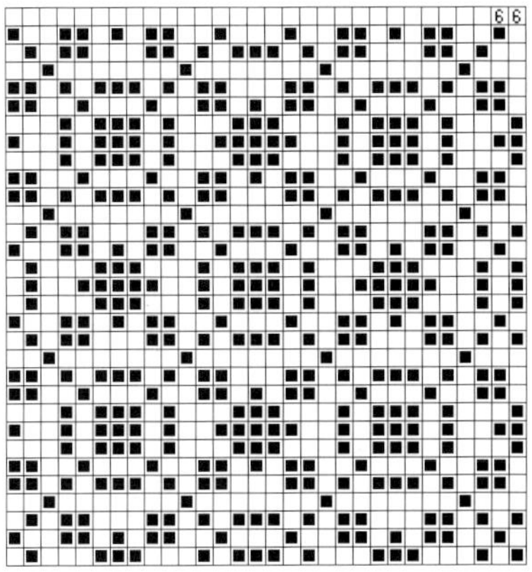
66

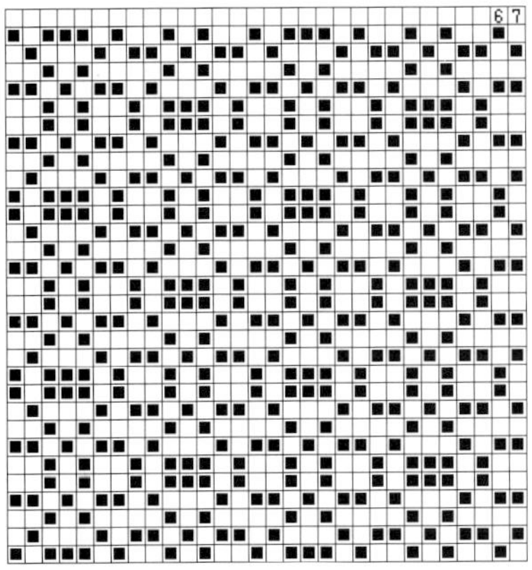
67

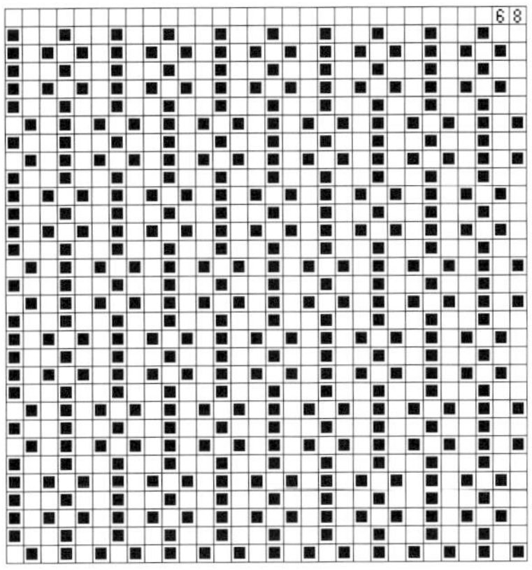
68

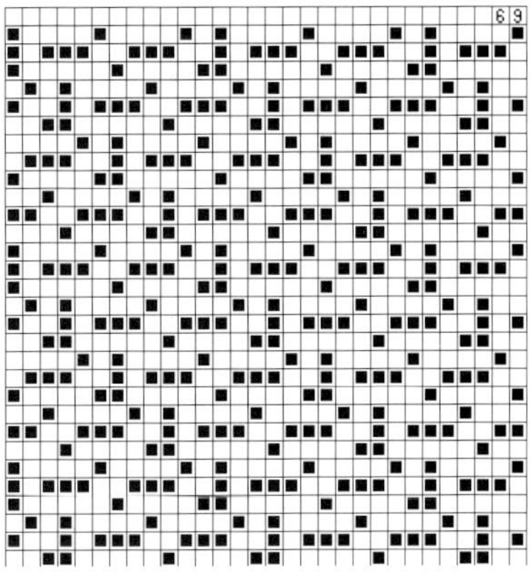
69

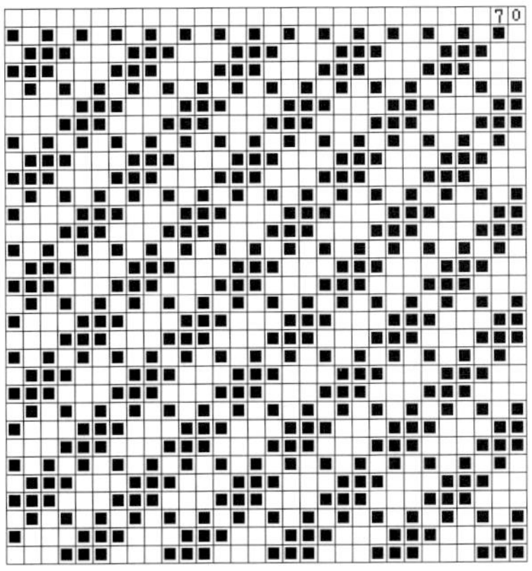
70

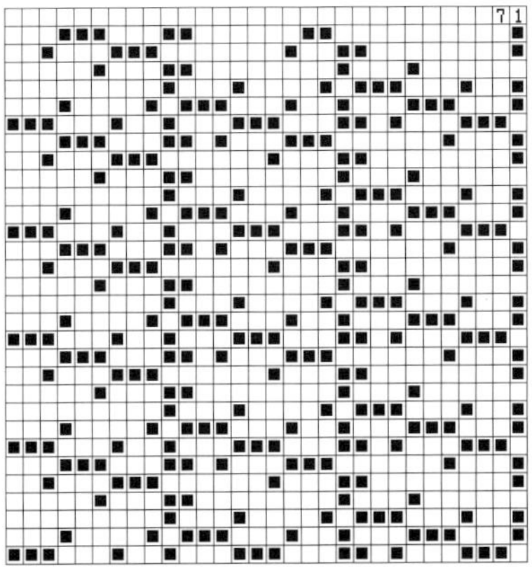
71

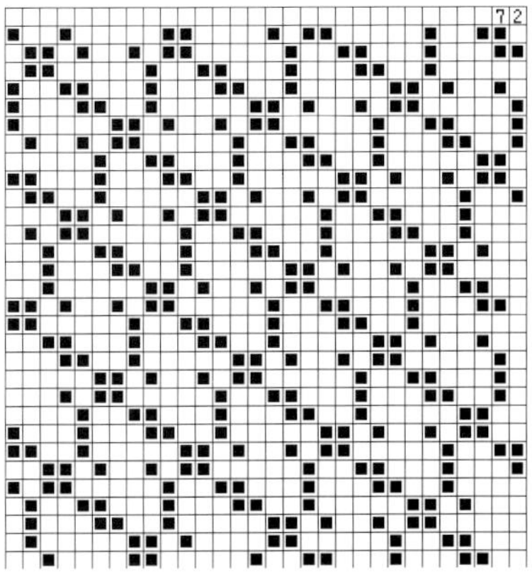
72

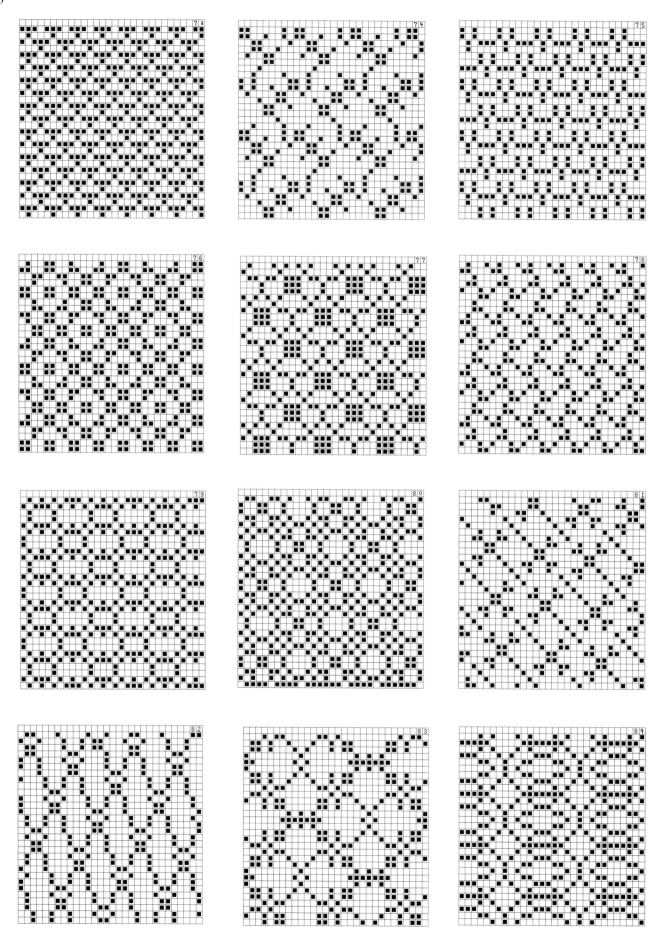

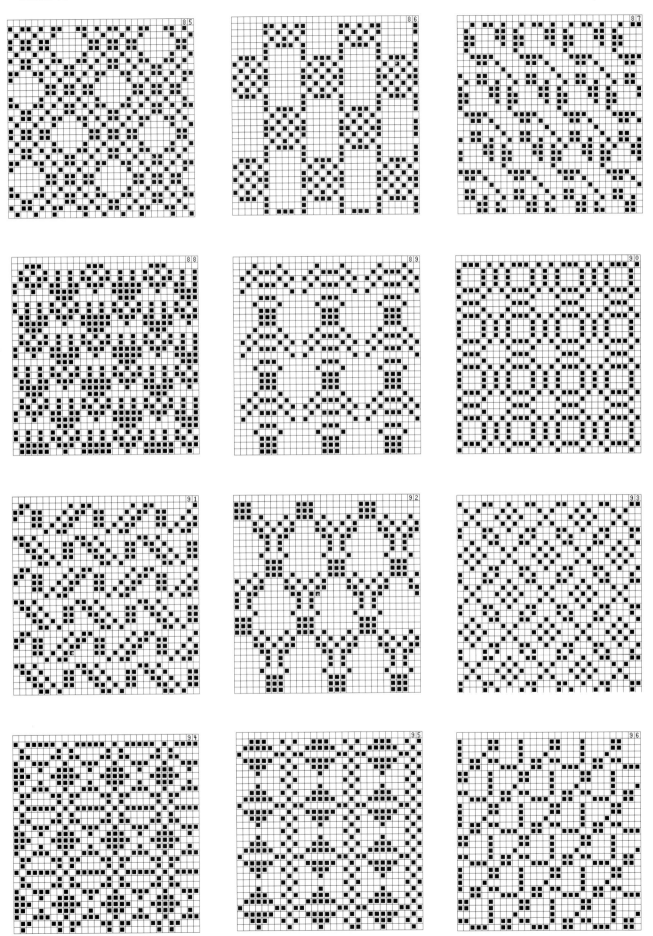

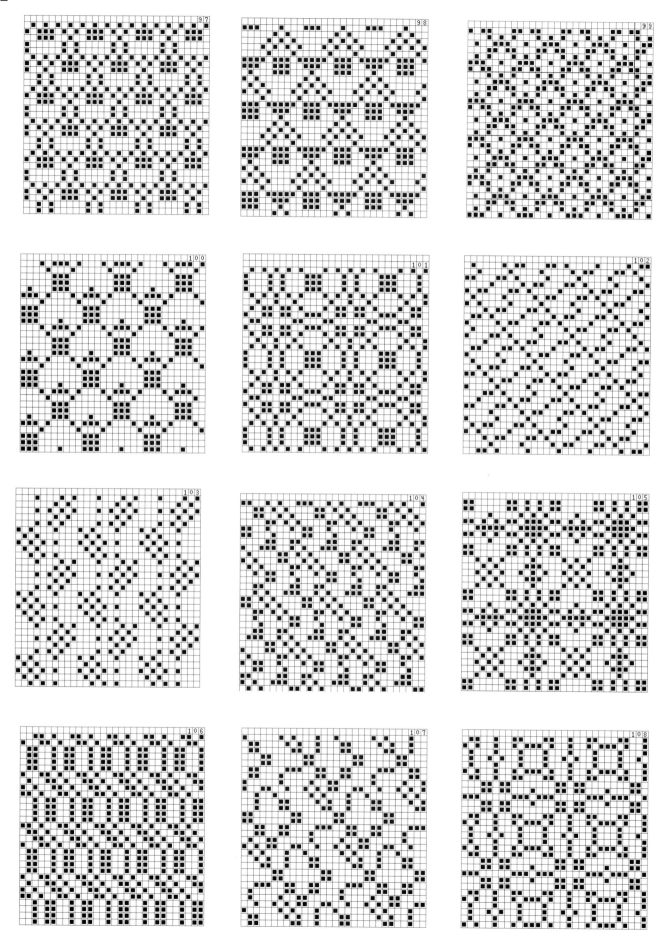

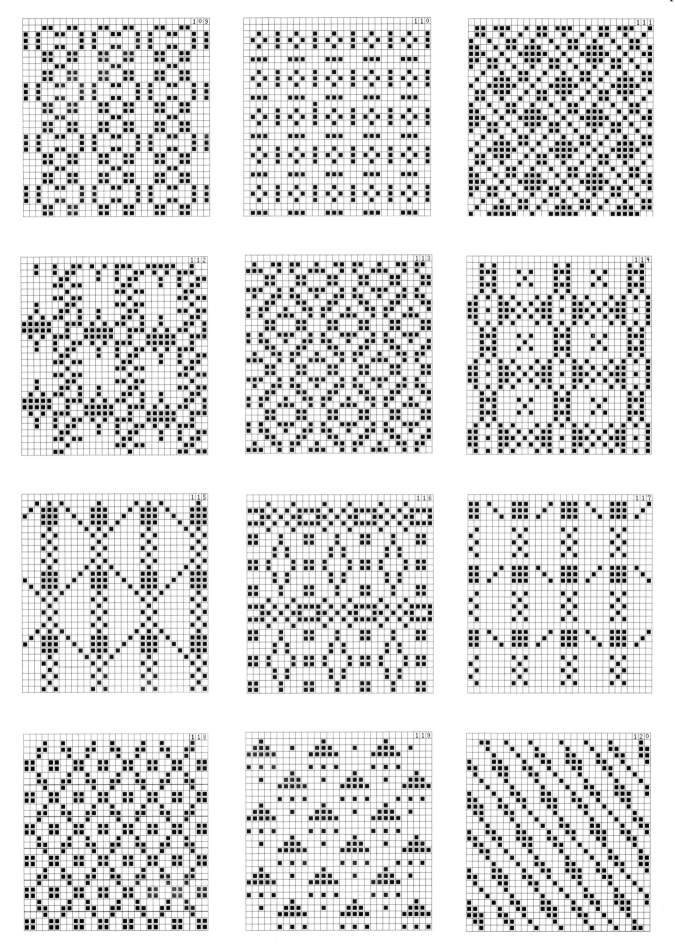

Charts

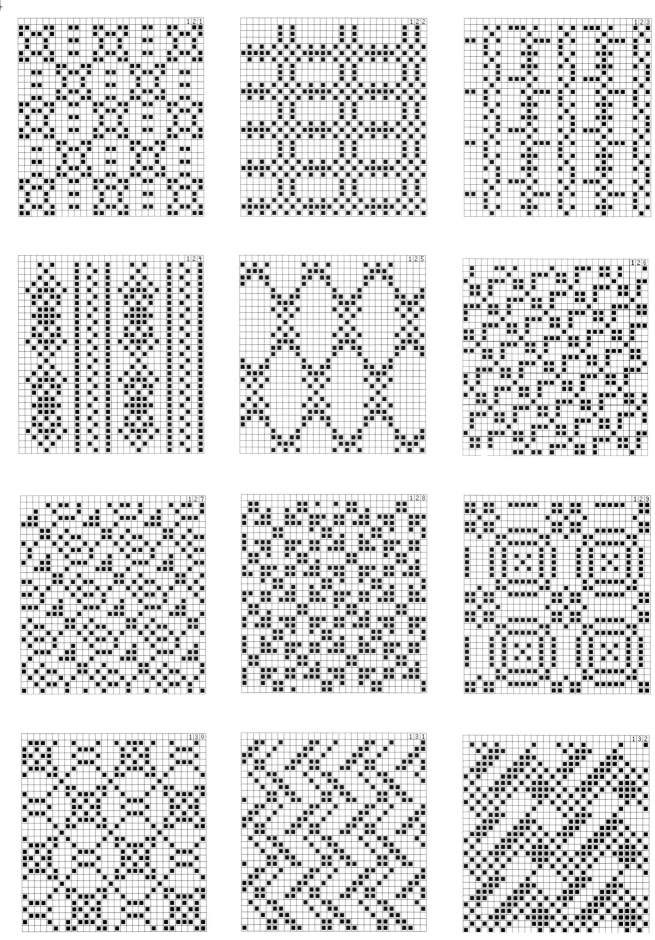

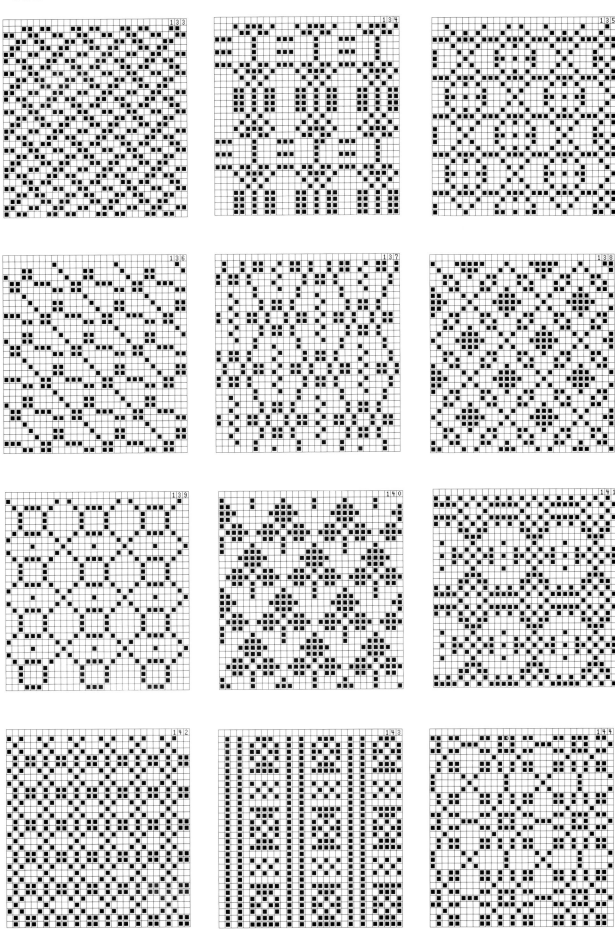

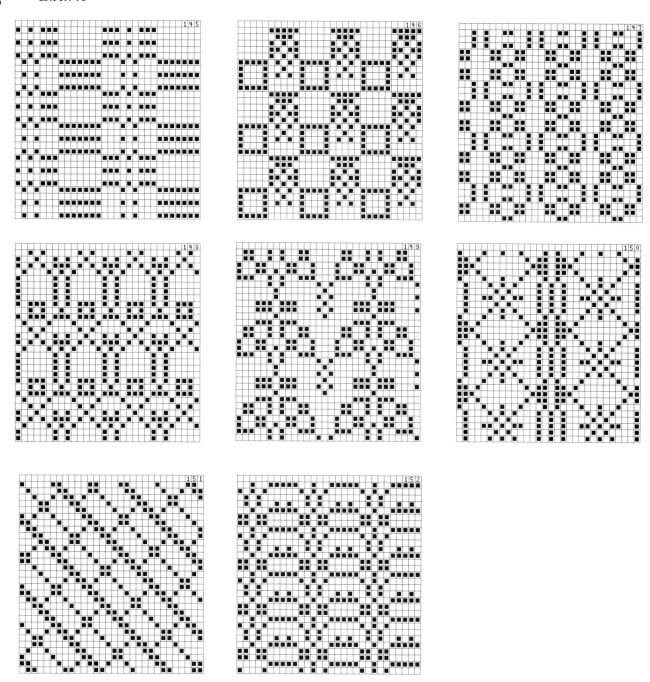

Charts

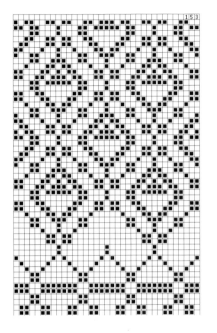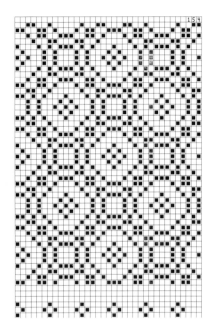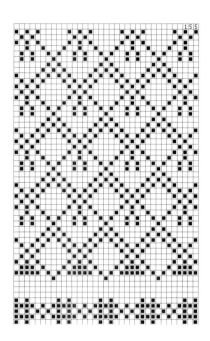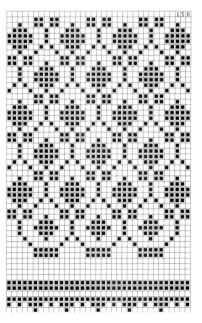

Charts

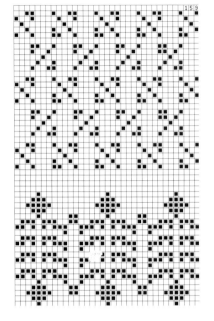

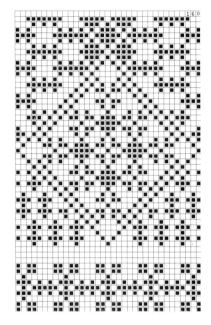

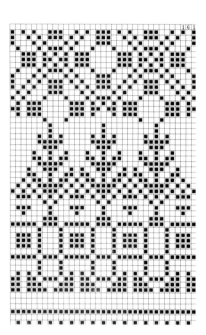

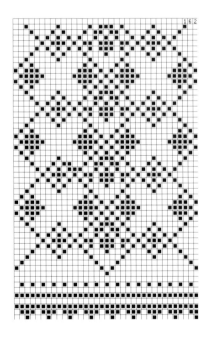

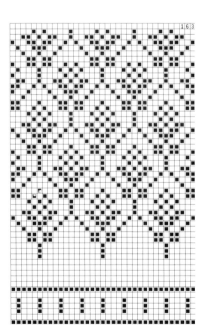

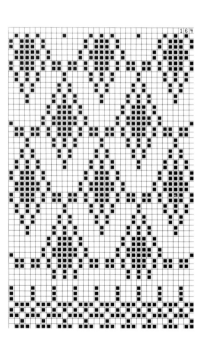

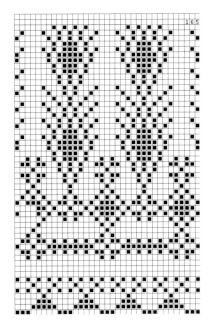

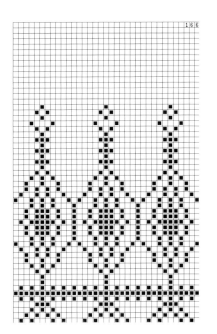

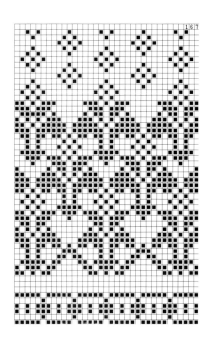

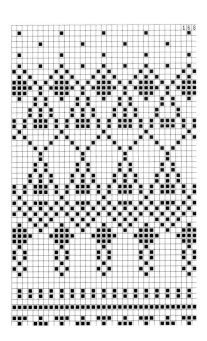

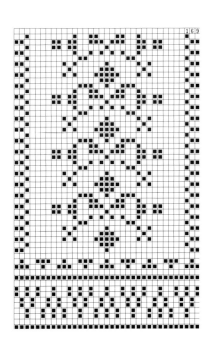

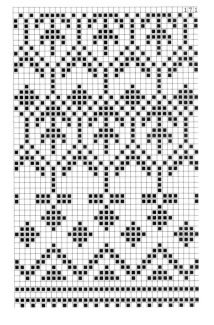

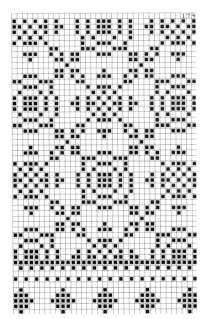
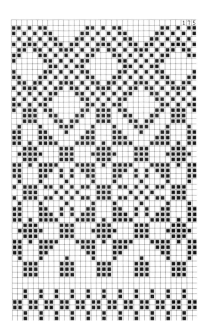
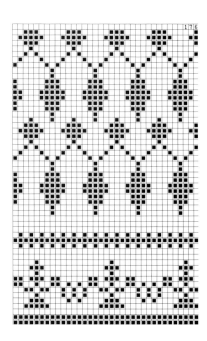

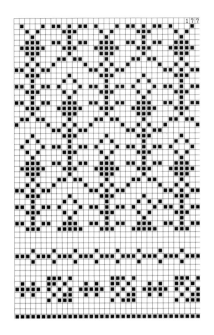

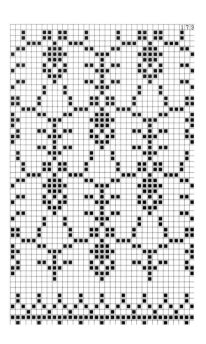

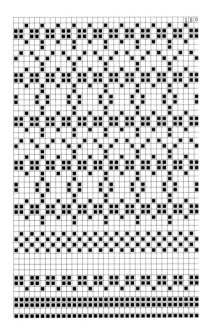

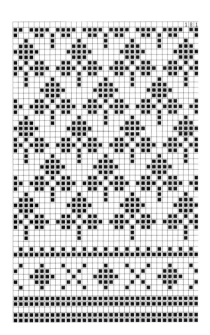

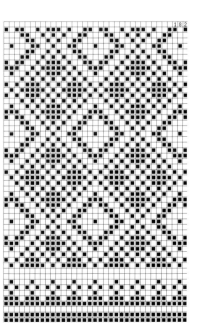

Charts

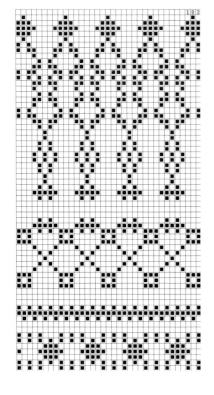

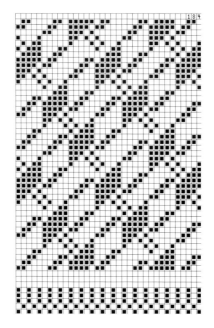

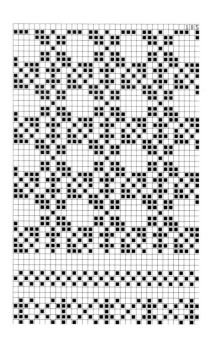

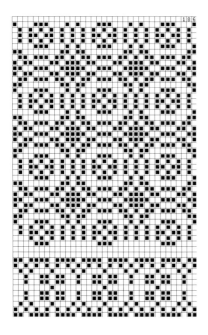

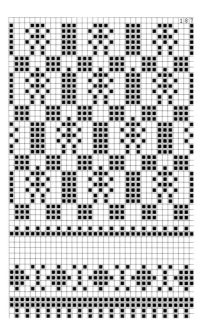

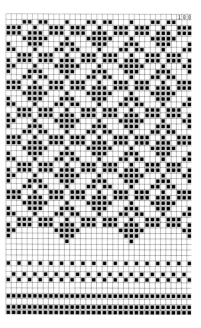

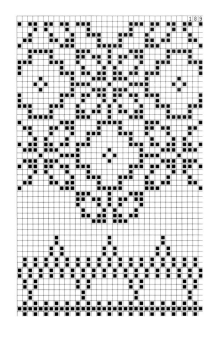

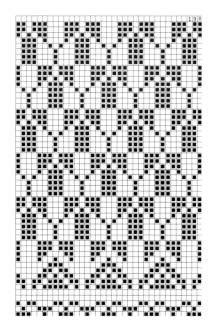

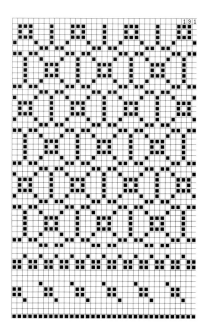

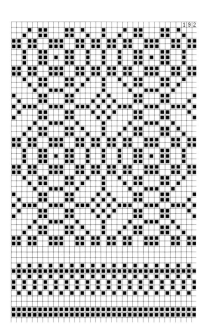

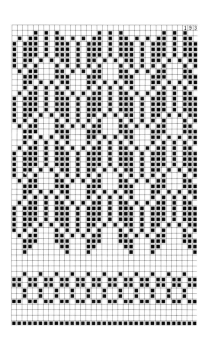

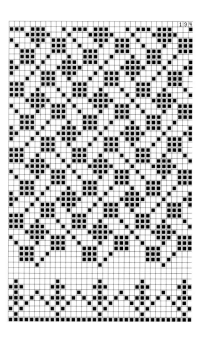

Charts

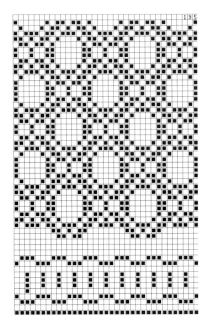

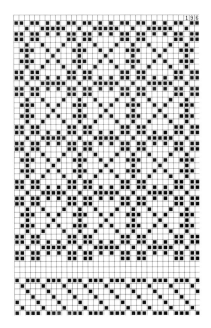

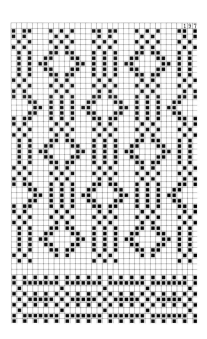

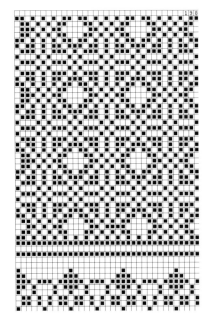

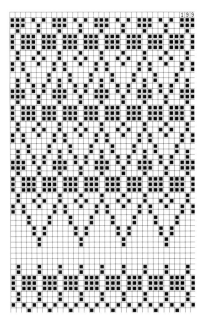

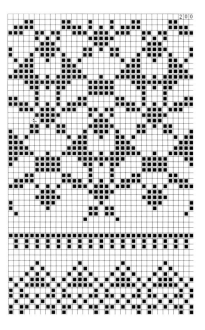

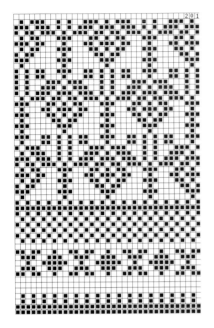

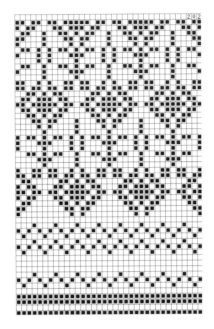

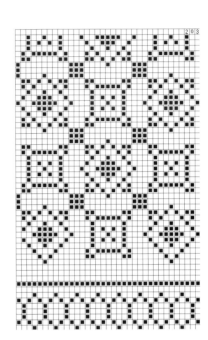

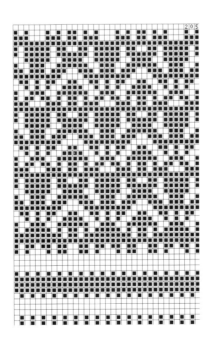

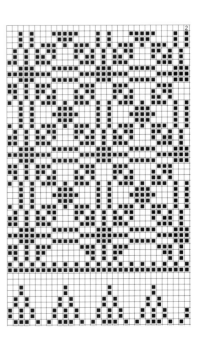

Charts

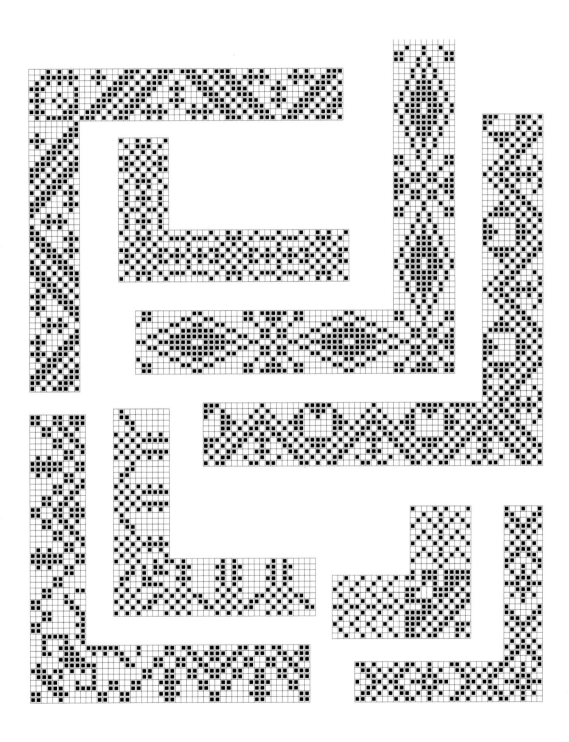

Charts

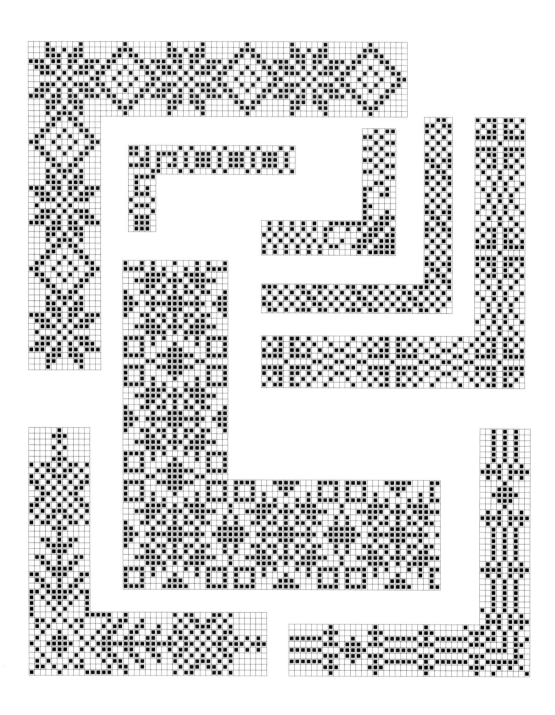

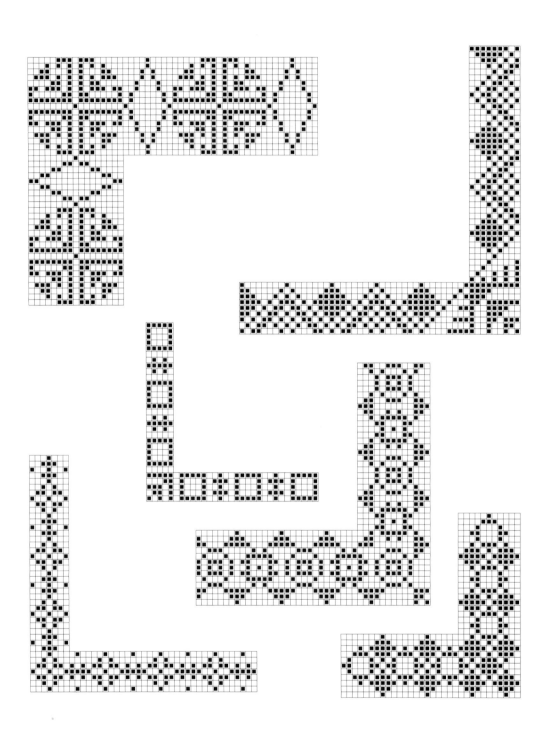

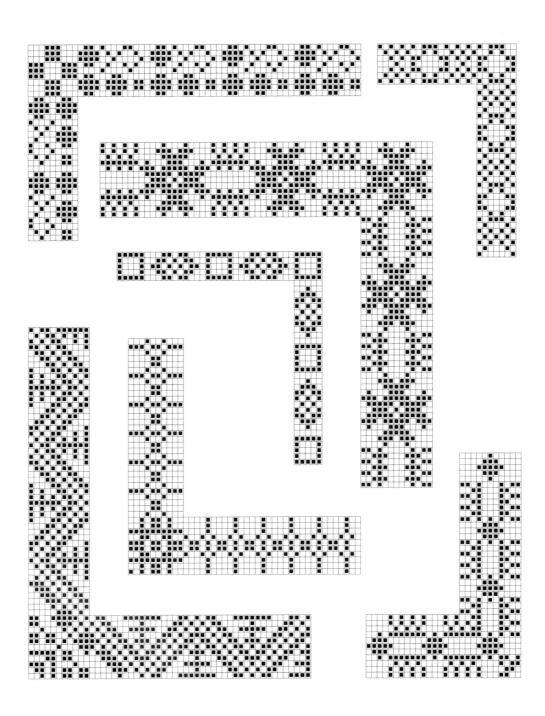

Charts

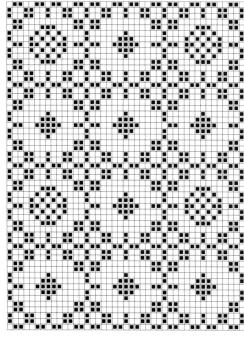

Charts

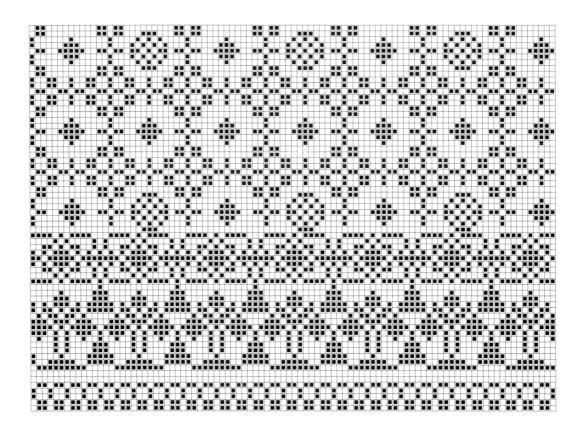

FINAL DIGRESSION AND ACKNOWLEDGEMENTS

Today began dark and dreary, which was apropos as I heard that Elizabeth Zimmermann had died during the night. The sky is now clear except for some scattered clouds, which reflect my mood. There is sadness, but there is also great joy that my path in life met up with Elizabeth's, for knowing her changed my life in many ways. I was inspired by Elizabeth to start to design and without that this book would not be a reality. Meg Swansen, her daughter, has become my mentor and a wonderful friend. Words cannot describe what that means to me.

Through Elizabeth's and Meg's Knitting Camps I gained much of my knitting knowledge. There are too many to thank individually, but I thank all Campers for sharing their knitting knowledge. A special thanks to my late night camp friends and roommates Joan Debolt, Judy Franklin, Becky Skidmore, Ann Swanson and Sally Wall. My expanded knitting life led me to many knitting events throughout the country where I made friends in the world's knitting community who shared their knowledge personally and in workshops. To all, thank you.

Thank You:

Lizbeth Upitis, my technical editor. I appreciate all the work you did on the book, but especially your encouragement and compliments. Working with you brought much joy and laughter, but best of all a closer friendship.

Juli Martin, for stepping in when needed to do the graphic layout and prepare the book to go to press. You were a life saver. (Note Juli is also one of the models.)

Alvis Upitis, whose color photography enhanced this book.

Eleanor Haase at Schoolhouse Press for keeping me supplied with needles and whose lively giggle (and threats) helped me continue on when discouraged because of computer down times, etc.

Knitters, Pattern Checkers, and Friends: Mary Anderson, Mary Jane Kane, Connie Keil (my sister), Betty Kendricks, Karen Kress, Becky Skidmore and Connie Slotten.

Models: Laura and Samantha Endres, Juli Martin, Cully Swansen, and Michelle Wolfe. (The sixth model for Cornfields is me!)

Anu Liivandi, Royal Ontario Museum, Toronto, ON, Canada, who assisted me when I did research at the museum and granted permission to use Royal Ontario Museum photographs and charts in this book.

Last, but by far the most important, I want to thank Don, my husband, whose love and support were truly significant.

The skies have now cleared and we have a beautiful Fall-blue sky. It has been an exceptionally lovely Fall, and I am trying to capture some of the beauty in a multicolored Latvian design sweater. Many a day I spent at the computer while working on the book watching the passing of beautiful Wisconsin seasons. I figure it helped me maintain my "hobby" knitter title as the definition is "a pursuit or interest engaged in for relaxation." Thank you, dear Meg, for allowing me not to have a deadline and to maintain the feel, "C'mon kids, let's put together a show in the garage!" It has been fun.

It is with a touch of sadness and nostalgia that I end this book. My hope is that you enjoyed it and found it an inspiration. My greatest joy would be to see the Latvian designs used for many, many years to come. That would be a legacy.

Brown-Reinsel, Beth. *Knitting Ganseys*. Loveland, CO: Interweave Press, 1993

Bush, Nancy. *Folk Knitting in Estonia*. Loveland, CO: Interweave Press, 1999

Collingwood, Peter. *The Maker's Hand, A Close Look At Textile Structures*. Asheville, NC: Lark Books and Loveland CO: Interweave Press, 1987.

Don, Sarah. *Fair Isle Knitting*. New York, NY: St. Martin's Press, 1979

Evans, Jane A. *A Joy Forever, Latvian Weaving, Traditional and Modified Uses*. St. Paul, MN. Dos Tejedoras Fiber Arts Publications, 1991. (Now owned by Interweave Press, Loveland, CO.)

Gainford, Veronica. *Designs for Knitting Kilt Hose and Knickerbocker Stockings*. Pittsville, WI: Schoolhouse Press, 1995

Gibson-Roberts, Priscilla A. *Knitting In The Old Way*. Loveland, CO: Interweave Press, 1985

——— *Ethnic Socks & Stockings, A compendium of Eastern design and technique*. Sioux Falls, SD: XRX, Inc., 1995

Johansson, Britta and Nilsson, Kersti. *Binge - en hallandsk stricktradition*. Stockholm, Sweden: LTs forlag, 1980 (out of print)

LeCount, Cynthia Gravelle. *Andean Folk Knitting, Traditions and Techniques from Peru and Bolivia*. St. Paul, MN: Dos Tejedoras Fiber Arts Publications, 1990. (Now owned by Interweave Press, Loveland, CO)

Lesina, Irma. *Latviesu Cimdu Raksti*. Lincoln, NE: Text Printed and Binding done at Augstums Printing Service, 1969

Lewis, Susanna E. *Knitting Lace, A Workshop with Patterns and Projects*. Newton, CT: The Tauton Press, 1992

Lind, Vibeke. *Knitting In The Nordic Tradition*. Asheville, NC: Lark Books, 1984

McGregor, Sheila. *The Complete Book of Traditional Fair Isle Knitting*. New York, NY: Charles Scribner's Sons, 1981

Melville, Sally. *Sally Melville Styles*. Sioux Falls, SD: XRX, Inc. 1998

Oelsner, G.H. *A Handbook of Weaves*, 1875 Illustrations. New York, NY: Dover Publications, Inc., 1952

Righetti, Maggie. *Knitting In Plain English*. New York, NY: St. Martin's Press, 1986

Rowley, Elaine, Editor. *Socks-Socks-Socks*. Sioux Falls, SD: XRX, Inc., 1999

Slava, Mirdza. *Latviesu Rakstainie Cimdi*. Riga, Latvia: The Latvian Academy of Sciences History Institute, 1992

Stanley, Montse. *The Knitter's Handbook*. Pleasantville, NY: Reader's Digest, 1993

Starmore, Alice. *Book of Fair Isle Knitting*. Newton, CT: The Tauton Press, 1988

Swansen, Meg. *Handknitting with Meg Swansen*. Pittsville, WI: Schoolhouse Press, 1995

——— *Meg Swansen's Knitting*. Loveland, Colorado: Interweave Press, 1999

Thomas, Mary. *Mary Thomas's Knitting Book*. New York, NY: Dover Publications, Inc., 1972

———*Mary Thomas's Book of Knitting Patterns*. New York, NY: Dover Publications, Inc. 1972

Upitis, Lizbeth. *Latvian Mittens, Traditional Designs and Techniques*. Pittsville, WI: Schoolhouse Press, 1981

Ventaskrasts, Z. *Izsuvumu, Adijumu un Audumu Raksti*. Riga, Latvia: Latvijas Valsts Izdevnieciba, 1959

Vogue Knitting Editors. *Vogue Knitting*. New York, NY: Pantheon Books, 1989

Walker, Barbara G. *Charted Knitting Designs, A Third Treasury of Knitting Patterns*. Pittsville, WI: Schoolhouse Press edition, 1998

———*Knitting from the Top*. Pittsville, WI: Schoolhouse Press printing, 1996

Zilboorg, Anna. *Fancy Feet, Traditional Knitting Patterns of Turkey*. Asheville, NC: Lark Books, 1994

Zimmermann, Elizabeth. *Knitting Without Tears*. New York, NY: Charles Scribner's Sons, 1971

———*Knitter's Almanac*. New York, NY: Dover Publications, 1981

———*Knitting Workshop*. Pittsville, WI: Schoolhouse Press, 1981

——-*Knitting Around*. Pittsville, WI: Schoolhouse Press, 1989